Celebrating the Jewish Year

The Fall Holidays

Celebrating the Jewish Year

The Fall Holidays

Rosh Hashanah ▲ Yom Kippur ▲ Sukkot

Paul Steinberg

Edited by Janet Greenstein Potter

2007 • 5767

JPS is a nonprofit educational association and the oldest and foremost publisher of Judaica in English in North America. The mission of JPS is to enhance Jewish culture by promoting the dissemination of religious and secular works, in the United States and abroad, to all individuals and institutions interested in past and contemporary Jewish life.

The Jewish Publication Society
2100 Arch Street
Philadelphia, PA 19103
www.jewishpub.org

Composition and design by Masters Group Design

Interior artwork by Adam Rhine, with permission from the artist, www.HebrewArt.com

Cover artwork by Adam Rhine, with permission from Sounds True, 413 S. Arthur Avenue, Louisville, CO 80027

Manufactured in the United States of America

07 08 09 10 11 12 13 10 9 8 7 6 5 4 3 2 1

ISBN 13: 978–0-8276–0842–9
ISBN 10: 0–8276–0842-X

Library of Congress Cataloging-in-Publication Data

Steinberg, Paul.
Celebrating the Jewish year / Paul Steinberg; Janet Greenstein Potter, editor. — 1st ed.
v. cm.
Includes bibliographical references and index.
Contents: v. 1. The fall holidays: Rosh Hashanah, Yom Kippur, Sukkot
ISBN 978-0-8276-0842-9 (alk. paper)
1. Fasts and feasts—Judaism. 2. Calendar, Jewish. I. Potter, Janet Greenstein. II. Title.
BM690.S72 2007
296.4'3—dc22
2007010805

Publisher's Note:
With few exceptions, the essays taken from other sources are as they appear in the original.
As a result, there are variations in spelling and language from piece to piece.

For Maureen,
Rina, and Nili

Start small.
Bless one moment for what it brings you.
Say one ancient prayer; link yourself with continuity and eternity.
Fill one silence with your end of the conversation.
No one can do this for you; it belongs to you.

— A High Holiday message, Jewish Theological Seminary

Contents

Acknowledgments xv
Introduction xvii
Framework of This Book 1

Part 1: Heart, Mind, and Celebration

The Spiritual Cycle of the Jewish Holidays 5
Reason, Faith, and Jewish Observance 6

Part 2: Origins of the Jewish Calendar

Seeing the Moon 13
Setting the Calendar 14
A Fix for the Two-Day Fix 15
Naming the Months and the Days 16

Part 3: Rosh Hashanah

The Head of the Year 23
Rosh Hashanah in the Bible 24
The Month of Elul: A Footpath to Mercy 26
Is It Two Days or One Long Day? 29
Food and Other Customs on Rosh Hashanah 30
Pathways Through the Sources 33
- Midrash Rabbah: Presence and Pardon 33
- Jerusalem Talmud: God's Partners 34
- High Holiday Machzor: The Decree 34
- The Zohar: A Shofar's Harmony 35
- Moses ben Jacob of Coucy: Self-Mastery 36
- Or Ha-Chaim: Gentle Justice 37
- Mei Ha-Shilo'ach: The Original Intention 38
- The Rebbe of Strelisk: Heeding Advice 38
- Rav Kook: Sacred Freedom 39
- Arthur Green: Returning to Wholeness 40

Interpretations of Sacred Texts 42
Judgment and Injustice 42
Remembrance and Compassion 44
The Shofar and Prayer from the Heart 46
Significance of the Holiday: Some Modern Perspectives 48
From Obscurity to Prominence 48
by Reuven Hammer

Remembering Creation 50
by Paul Steinberg

A Clarion Call to Fixing the World 53
by Elliot N. Dorff

The Days of Awe and Israel 55
by Miriyam Glazer

The Shofar: A Cry into Eternity 57
by Will Berkovitz
Alternative Meditations 59
Singing Creation into Being 59
by Shlomo Carlebach

Facing the Music : A High Holiday Meditation 59
by Shefa Gold

Hagar and Sarah, Sarah and Hagar 61
by Rosellen Brown

Part 4: Yom Kippur

The Day for Spiritual Second Chances 65
Yom Kippur in the Bible 66
Days of Awe 71
Erev Yom Kippur: The Threshold of Sanctity 72
Yom Kippur and Self-Denial 75
Pathways Through the Sources 77
Mishnah: Between God and Fellow 77
Maimonides: Perfect Repentance 77
Zohar: The High Priest's Intervention 79

Yehudah Ha-Levi: Attending to the Spirit 79
Kitzur Shulchan Arukh: Observance and Practice 80
The Maggid of Mezritch: Discovering Unity 81
The Rebbe of Lizensk: Forgiving God 83
Franz Rosenzweig: To Stand before God 84
Abraham Joshua Heschel: The Unforgivable 85
Erich Fromm: No Judgment Without Love 86
Interpretations of Sacred Texts 88
Festivity and Marriage 88
Sin and Confession 90
Truth versus Mercy 92
Significance of the Holiday: Some Modern Perspectives 94
An Evolution in Rite and Prayer 94
by Cheryl Peretz

Repentance, Confession, and Atonement 97
by Bradley Shavit Artson

Moral Freedom and Responsibility 99
by Elliot N. Dorff

Accepting the Decree 102
by Miriam Burg
Alternative Meditations 105
Elul 105
by Judith Sarah Schmidt

The Ritual of the Scapegoat 107
by Ellen Frankel

Meditation before Yom Kippur for One Who Cannot Fast 107
by Simkha Y. Weintraub

A Carnival at the Gates: Jonah and Laughter on Yom Kippur 108
by Rachel Adler

Part 5: Sukkot

A Merging of Worlds 117
Sukkot in the Bible 118

Symbols of Sukkot 120
The Heavenly Guests 128
The Water Ritual 130
Three "Last" Days 134
Reading Kohelet 138
Pathways Through the Sources 141
Midrash: A New Reckoning 141
Midrash Rabbah: Prolonging the Celebration 143
Rashi on Kohelet: The Joy of Now 143
The Zohar: Hosting the Divine 144
Sefer Ha-Hinnukh: The Power of Four 145
Moses Chaim Luzzatto: Engulfed in Light 146
The Rabbi of Kamionka: The *Etrog's* Glow 147
Samson Raphael Hirsch: Minding What We Share 147
Elie Wiesel: Joy under Adversity 149
Interpretations of Sacred Texts 150
Materialism and Redemption 150
Prayer and the Powers of Rain 152
The Law and the Lesson of Fragility 154
Significance of the Holiday: Some Modern Perspectives 156
History and Tradition Interwoven 156
by Joel Roth

Harvest and New Seed 159
by Arthur Waskow

Open to the Earth and All Humanity 164
by Arthur Waskow

The Season of Our Rejoicing 165
by Miriyam Glazer

Never-ending Joy 168
by Alan Abrams
Alternative Meditations 170
Imagining Zaydeh's Sukkah 170
by Harold M. Schulweis

That Tzaddik's Etrog 172
by S. Y. Agnon

New Rituals for Simchat Torah 175
by Jill Hammer

Part 6: Guidance along the Way

Is It Law or Custom? 181

Exploring Traditional Sources 182

Endnotes 197

Glossary 219

Contributing Authors 235

Index 239

Acknowledgments

This book has undergone several transformations. It began as one thing, and only because of the grace and guidance of Janet Greenstein Potter, the editor, does it arrive in its current form. I am indebted to her undying persistence in pursuit of excellence and her careful reading of the manuscript. If there are any errors, they are indeed my own.

I must also acknowledge all of my teachers who have helped and supported me in my learning from the American Jewish University and its Ziegler School of Rabbinic Studies. The Ziegler School is a unique place of study, one that embodies the essence of both academic integrity and the true spirit of Torah learning. I am especially grateful to two of my rabbis there: Bradley Shavit Artson and Elliot Dorff. Thank you for being my models of *hokhmah, yirat Shamayim,* and *hesed.*

Furthermore, I am thankful to those who generously contributed original pieces for this volume, namely Rabbis Alan Abrams, Bradley Shavit Artson, Will Berkovitz, Miriam Burg, Elliot Dorff, Miriyam Glazer, Reuven Hammer, Cheryl Peretz, Joel Roth, and Arthur Waskow.

Finally and most of all, I thank my wife, Maureen, and our children, Rina and Nili, for your patience and support. You are my greatest teachers of all.

I would also like to extend my gratitude for permission to use material from the following sources:

"Return to Wholeness" In *Seek My Face, Speak My Name: A Contemporary Jewish Theology* by Arthur Green. Lantham, Md.: Rowman & Littlefield Publishing Group, 1997, 173–174.

"Facing the Music: A High Holiday Meditation" by Shefa Gold. Originially published in its entirety in *New Menorah,* the journal of ALEPH: The Alliance for Jewish Renewal, 2001. The full meditation is available at http://www.RabbiShefaGold.com.

"Hagar and Sarah, Sarah and Hagar" by Rossellen Brown and "A Carnival of Gates: Jonah and Laughter on Yom Kippur" by Rachel Adler. In *Beginning Anew: A Woman's Companion to the High Holy Days,* edited by Gail Twersky Reinmer and Judith A. Kates. New York: Simon & Schuster, 1997, 32–34; 325–331.

"The Rabbi of Kamionka: The *Etrog's* Glow," retold by Howard Schwartz. In *Gabriel's Palace: Jewish Mystical Tales* by Howard Schwartz. New York: Oxford University Press, Inc., 1944, 265–266.

"Imaging Zahdeh's Sukkah." In *In God's Mirror,* by Harold M. Schulweis. Jersey City, NJ: KTAV Publishing House, 2003, 260–262.

"The Tzaddik's Etrog." By S.Y. Agnon, translated by Shira Leibowitz and Moshe Kohn. In *S.Y. Agnon, A Book That Was Lost and Other Stories,* edited by Alan Mintz and Anne Golomb Hoffman. New York: Schocken Press, 1996, 184–187.

"New Rituals for Simchat Torah" by Jill Hammer. Originally published on http://www.ritualwell.org. Ritualwell is a project of Kolot: The Center for Jewish Women's and Gender Studies at the Reconstructionist Rabbinical College.

Introduction

Fall and the Holidays of Renewal

The story of human life is the story of rebirth: over a normal lifespan, we die and are reborn thousands of times. We say goodbye to one year as it yields to another; we overcome one obstacle as it evolves into another; we correct one mistake as it produces another. The rotations of life spiral along parallel lines, where we "relive" profound moment after profound moment. On this dual path, each thing connects with another.

So too the pattern of rebirth is manifest in the Jewish experience of the fall season. In the Land of Israel, after the long months of summer heat, the slow death and decay of pastures, and the drying up of the waters, the world endures and is fertile again. Different from the blooming of spring, the fall rebirth—its desert-oasis palms heavy with sweet and sticky dates—hearkens back to the land's biblical identity, "flowing with milk and honey."

The Jewish tradition recognizes this time of year as the rebirth of the world itself. God's creative impulse is rekindled by remembering the earth and humanity. And as God remembers us and freshens the universe with compassion, we remember God. At Rosh Hashanah, Yom Kippur, and Sukkot, we contemplate our part during the past year in upholding our covenantal relationship with our Creator. We look ahead, as well, to the spiritual transformation of the next season and celebrate the hope that it too will be blessed.

Framework of This Book

THE JEWISH TRADITIONS ARE ROOTED IN certain assumptions about the meaning of human existence and the world in which we live. Such assumptions play out in Jewish holiday observance and ideology. The first two parts of this book explore those foundational beliefs, particularly focusing on the relationship between the human spirit, the seasons, and the calendar. Then each of the three holiday sections includes a discussion of the holiday's biblical origins, followed by several explorations of its special ideology and customs. Although synagogue ritual is touched upon, the primary focus of the book is on personal and home customs and their rationales. These are often the clearest expression of the encounter between the spirit and the world.

Another one of the most significant forms of spiritual expression in Judaism is found in the study of texts. As Rabbi Louis Finkelstein of the Jewish Theological Seminary has said, "When I pray I talk to God, but when I study, God talks to me." To help us experience the diversity of viewpoints held and traditions practiced throughout time, each holiday section also includes four groups of writings. In the first group, "Pathways Through the Sources," we look at writings from some of the greatest Jewish thinkers in history, each of which reflects an ideological aspect of the holiday. The richness of these sources invites your own analysis to discover the many treasures each text possesses.

The Jewish tradition teaches that we learn sacred texts on different levels of understanding. Thus in the second group of selections, "Interpretations of Sacred Texts," are passages that I examine at three levels, the first two of which follow traditional patterns of commentary. The first level is *peshat,* the literal, most obvious meaning of the text. The second is *derash,* an interpretation that incorporates explanations of the text given over thousands of years of rabbinic and historical inquiry. The third is "Making It Personal," my own interpretation, which addresses new ways by which we today may identify with this sacred text and apply it to our lives. I hope that by following these three levels of interpretation you will be enabled to grow cognitively along with the development of ideas in the text. If you ease the integration of the text into your personal life, ultimately it may become a part of your self-knowledge. These three levels—two that are traditional and one that is more modern—reflect the ways we converse and build relationships with the voices of the past, and how those voices live on through us.

The third group of selections, "Significance of the Holiday: Some Modern Perspectives," comprises contributions, original to this book, from acclaimed scholars and rabbis of our time. These essays discuss the historical development of the holiday, as well as its theological, ethical, agricultural, and seasonal meanings. Also provided are additional essays on important themes and practices unique to the holiday.

Judaism has always recognized that the truth can only be understood in a multiplicity of voices and manners. The fourth group of selections for each holiday is "Alternative Meditations." These pieces include essays, stories, poems, anecdotes, and rituals that add profound expression to a holiday in a nonclassical, innovative manner. The volume is rounded out in Part 6 with two components: a discussion of the relationship between Jewish law and customs and sketches of many traditional sources and scholars—guideposts on our spiritual journey through the holidays.

PART I

Heart, Mind, and Celebration

The soul that You, my God, have given me is pure. You created it, You formed it, You breathed it into me; You keep my body and soul together. One day You will take my soul from me, to restore it to me in life eternal. So long as this soul is within me I acknowledge You, Adonai my God, my ancestors' God. Master of all creation, Sovereign of all souls.

—Daily blessing for the gift of our soul

The Spiritual Cycle of the Jewish Holidays

WITHIN US ALL IS AN UNQUENCHABLE FIRE that continues to ask questions, that continues to be awestruck by the mysteries of the world and the human spirit. We constantly seek out that which distinctly connects us to this world. Furthermore, we yearn to express the fulfillment and meaning we discover in life's most profound moments, whether it is experiencing the birth of a child or the rising of the sun on a new day. The Jewish holidays, which pervade all the seasons of the year, are fundamental expressions of our spirituality. By reflecting the physical nature of God's world and providing centuries of accumulated symbolic meaning, they create a powerful link in our ever-evolving relationship with the Creator of the universe. When we explore and study the spirit and seasons of the Jewish holidays, we grow in our relationship with God and the world around us.

We all recognize and can define the seasons—tangible, distinct, and inevitable as they are. But what is the "spirit" and what is "spiritual"? What do these terms actually mean to us? Recently, in some Jewish circles, they have become taboo, as words to be used only by those who look to participate in the so-called flightier aspects of Jewish life and religious practice, rather than by those who are committed to "real" religion. This is a tragedy, for Judaism itself is ultimately an expression of the spirit. Each practice and observance, whether it is *tefillah* (prayer), kashrut (dietary laws), or Shabbat (the Sabbath), is an avenue along which we connect to the Divine. To refrain from work on Shabbat or a holiday is not an end in itself, but a means to spiritual betterment. For example, the blessings before and after a meal are important because they connect us to a unique spiritual tradition; but, at the same time, we must remember the purpose of the words. They are meant to direct our minds and hearts toward thoughts about God and to deepen our awareness of the One to whom we give our thanks. The letter of the law is essentially a reflection of the spirit of the law.

Perhaps some definitions would help us understand. Consider the word "spirit." The English is derived from the Latin *spiritus,* the noun derivation of *spirare,* meaning, "to breathe." Interestingly, the same word for "spirit," or vital energy force, in Chinese—*chi*—is also derived from the verb "to breathe." Most pertinent to this book, the

Hebrew word for spirit, or soul, is *neshamah,* meaning breath, from the verb "to breathe" (*linshom*). Thus spirit is connected to energy, the particular force that causes us to breathe—receiving, taking in, and then giving out. By extension, the word spirituality means the cycle of energy that informs our being each time we inhale, reflexively pause, and exhale—exchanging information with the universe. It is the intellectual and the emotional combined, and that which is beyond them both. It is the unscientific and immeasurable, the thoughts between the thoughts and the moments between the moments, the "knowing" before speech and response, and the essence of intuition.

Judaism particularly nourishes the human spirit by acknowledging its brilliance, complexity, and eternal nature. These qualities of the spirit are portrayed in the variety of organic expressions found in the yearly cycle of the holidays. In fact, the Jewish calendar is itself a product of the spirit, as we shall see in part 2 of this volume. It addresses not only the earthly changes in season and time, but also the human experience of season and time. So it is that on the holidays of Sukkot and Tu b'Shevat and during the "counting of the Omer" we become spiritual witnesses to changes in nature. Moreover, the Jewish calendar, with great value, narrates the human saga. We need to remember "what happened and when" for the stories of Hanukkah and Purim, not because we should simply remember dates and places, but because we should reexperience how events changed our relationships with the world and with God.

Throughout the year, by observing each of the holidays, Jews undergo a progressive cycle of significant and inspirational experiences. For example, Rosh Hashanah and Yom Kippur stir deep responses of self-judgment and contemplation; Passover empowers us with freedom and responsibility; and Tisha b'Av moves us to mourn human loss and suffering. Touching upon both intellect and emotion, these are essential annual experiences for spiritual growth and fulfillment. The Jewish year, therefore, is a cycle both of spirit and of season.

Reason, Faith, and Jewish Observance

In our modern world we are witnesses to the clash between faith and reason, Bible and science, and spirituality and psychology. Yet as early as the Middle Ages, great rabbis and scholars, such as Sa'adia Ga'on, Maimonides, and Yehuda Ha-Levi, attempted to bridge these seemingly contradictory approaches to life. They, along with countless other rabbinic giants, follow the approach that Judaism is a religion based upon reason as much as it is one of faithful devotion. The Talmud articulates Judaism's intellectual appeal as it emphasizes that study is equal to all the hundreds of other commandments put together.[1] Many medieval Jewish philosophers, most notably Gersonides and Hasdai Crescas, wrote that the mind, with its power of philosophic inquiry, could serve as an instrument to understand God. Over the past century, our modern rabbinic sages, such as Abraham Joshua Heschel, David Hartman, and Elliot Dorff, have utilized the tools of science and reason to elucidate and expand the spirit of the Jewish tradition.

This approach has certainly been used to attract Jews who participate somewhat peripherally in Jewish practice, especially the ultraliberal and secular streams. In fact most Jews today, whatever their level of religious participation, cannot help but view the world through the lenses of Darwin, Freud, Einstein, and Marx, and understandably so. Those innovative thinkers caused great changes in worldviews, ultimately leading societies to become in some ways more self-aware and to even shift directions. Modern Jews can be helped to reconcile ancient and contemporary beliefs through the words of Maimonides. Rabbi Moses ben Maimon, the single most influential thinker of medieval Judaism, taught in his *Mishneh Torah,* the first written Jewish legal code, that we should aim to "know God" through the faculties of the intellect, not simply through blind faith.[2] He maintained that harmony is to be found between belief and reason and between God and the disciplines of science. The spirit of this claim has led others to write volumes of literature on *ta'ammei ha-mitzvot,* the reasons for the commandments.

This volume also offers some of the traditional explanations for why the customs and practices of the Jewish holidays are what they are. What, however, is one to do if the reasoning seems unreasonable? What if one finds the rationale personally unacceptable, seemingly superstitious, or nearly impossible to believe? Consider these practices and some of their explanations, rarely taught nowadays, yet found within the primary sources of Rabbinic literature, such as the Talmud and the Shulchan Arukh: waving the *lulav* on Sukkot to bring in good weather for the season by "keeping away evil rains and winds";[3] not blowing the shofar on Erev Rosh Hashanah so that Satan (the accuser) will be misled and think the time of judgment has already passed;[4] and avoiding nuts on Rosh Hashanah because the numerical equivalent of their Hebrew letters is also the numerical equivalent for the Hebrew word for "sin."[5] With our modern sensibilities, do we really believe in such things? If the answer for us is no, should we then continue to keep these holiday mitzvot (commandments) and customs?

These are difficult questions, and the talmudic rabbis, thousands of years ago, were quite aware of them. In fact, they questioned the whole concept of sharing the rationale of mitzvot. They feared that knowing the reasons would lead some people to refrain from performing the mitzvot. In particular, they were concerned that a person might mistakenly believe that simply knowing the reason for a mitzvah was just as good as doing it. The Talmud argues, for example, that King Solomon made such a mistake. He was a wise man who knew the rationale behind the mitzvot, and he stumbled in trying to keep them.[6]

The Rabbis' fear, however, did not prevail. Teaching the reasons for the mitzvot is simply a part of Jewish education. From the moment Jews were introduced to Greek philosophy in the first centuries of the Common Era, reason and logic were integrated into Jewish thought. Yet, as one sees in parts of this book, many of the reasons that still exist for customs are quite archaic, and a concern remains that Jews will refrain from performing mitzvot or continuing customs because they seem antiquated from a modern perspective.

Even when the reason for a particular mitzvah or custom seems primitive and untenable, we should not abruptly abandon the practice. At the same time, according to many people, neither should we abandon our reason and intellect; and some customs and mitzvot should be stopped or changed in accord with new insights. They maintain that this is what Judaism has always done: each generation brings forth its own judges and decisions.[7] Nevertheless, our first reaction to mitzvot and customs that seemingly defy reason should be to turn our thinking in multiple directions to gain alternative perspectives.

A good way to gain perspective is to consider the emotions. The world has recently become more aware of "emotional" intelligence as opposed to strict cognitive intelligence. That is to say, there is a wholeness to the human experience and a "knowing" that is beyond reason. There may very well be a benefit or a kind of knowledge that can be gained from nonrational customs and mitzvot. This view is what the Christian theologian Soren Kierkegaard offered to the world in the 19th century with his newfound concept of existentialism, as well as what Jewish theologian Abraham Joshua Heschel poetically contended in the 20th century with his philosophy of antiphilosophy. The religious experience is not intended to prove a point, but rather to answer a question and to quench a burning emotional curiosity. Thus we need to honestly ask ourselves what the effect of performing the mitzvah or custom is, despite its ancient rationale. Only through this question will we be able to arrive at the truth—the real truth that lies at the essence of existence, beyond both intellect and emotion.

For those who do not regularly participate in Jewish ritual life, it is difficult to understand through reason alone why people choose to perform certain mitzvot and customs, such as parading the *lulav* around the synagogue and beating the willows against the ground during Hoshanah Rabbah (the seventh day of Sukkot). Learning about all these practices can help us to accept them, but nothing replaces doing them. Informed by the sacred covenant between God and Israel, the sages of old preached a spiritual benefit from performing what may seem primitive to us. Rabbis of today argue that there are several advantages garnered from Jewish practice. One is a communal benefit to making oneself a part of the social and historical context of like-minded Jews. Another is a personal benefit from the feeling of belonging not only to the Jewish people, but also to something that is much larger than oneself. Finally, the process of doing rituals like these, through their penetration into the symbolic language of the subconscious, helps people to open themselves in positive ways to aspects of both personal and communal life that they otherwise would not have.

Judaism presents a holistic approach to spirituality wherein the intellectual, emotional, and physical aspects of a person interact. There are clearly times when one or even all of those elements are challenged, especially when we wonder why we should observe certain practices and customs or why we should believe what is being espoused. Such questioning can be understood as a good thing and consistent with Jewish living. Jews are meant to live an entire life of study and learning. Without intellectual challenges, doing so would be dull and thus difficult. When confronted with conflicts of faith and reason, we should humbly take every possibility seriously, by using all of our God-given faculties to consider them.

The Jewish holidays and their observances are the principal elements that incorporate the holistic Jewish approach. In totality, they tie us to history, the earth, the Jewish people, and God—the most sacred features of the Jewish experience. It is true that fully celebrating these holidays throughout the cycle of seasons can be challenging in the modern world with our modern minds, and especially so in the Diaspora. But challenges are a part of healthy spirituality, and embracing the Jewish seasonal and holiday cycle means embracing all of the sacred bonds that make up the spirit.

PART 2

Origins of the Jewish Calendar

It is a land which the LORD your God looks after, on which the LORD your God always keeps His eye, from year's beginning to year's end.

—Deut. 11:12

Seeing the Moon

THE JEWISH CALENDAR, one of the most complex pieces of Jewish life, provides great insight into the history, practices, and holidays of the Jewish people. Its development goes from the dawn of time, when the ancients first observed, and even memorized, the yearly patterns of the stars, planets, sun, and moon, all the way to today, when we foresee and manage our entire year on handheld, digital screens. As we shall see, the calendar highlights not only how the Jewish tradition is intimately grounded in the patterns of the natural world, but also how those patterns inform the nature of Jewish spirituality.

Early in their history, the Hebrews lived a nomadic life. They knew the location of the most fertile lands to feed and water their flocks, and they knew the patterns of sunlight and rainfall that dictated which seasons were best for moving the animals. When these nomads settled permanently in ancient Israel, life transitioned to an agricultural one, in which people also used the clues of nature and the seasons to plan their work—so they would know when to sow, harvest, and store each crop.[1] They also needed to coordinate planning for community and religious events. For all of these things, our ancestors used the moon and its phases as markers. The cycles of time during which the moon travels around the earth and renews its visible form became the months. In fact, the Hebrew word for month, *hodesh,* is derived from the word *hadash* or "new," which refers to the ever-renewing lunar cycle for marking time.

Particularly for their holy days, the Jews had to set a standard calculation for the moment at which a given month begins. Before 586 B.C.E., in the time of the First Temple, the king or the High Priest *(Kohen Gadol)* was probably responsible for announcing the new month to the community. We know that in the time of the Second Temple, the Jewish supreme court and legislative body, "the Sanhedrin," was charged with with that responsibility. The Talmud describes in detail the process used by the Sanhedrin for taking the evidence of eyewitnesses to determine if the new moon had appeared. Once satisfied, the Sanhedrin sounded the shofar to proclaim the new month to the community. For Jewish communities outside the Land of Israel, such as Babylonia, which also relied upon the Sanhedrin's proclamation, a series of mountaintop bonfires were lit as signals to transmit the news.[2] For Jews in even more distant lands, such as Persia, Rome, and Egypt, messengers from the Sanhedrin brought them the times and dates of the new months and holy days.

Setting the Calendar

This system for announcing the new months was never flawless. Signals and messages were often confused or lost, making it impossible for some communities to know exactly when the new month or holiday actually arrived. And unfriendly non-Jewish neighbors certainly increased communication difficulties.[3] To ensure correct observance, distant Jewish communities began to observe two days of the new-month celebration, called Rosh Hodesh, and of the pilgrimage festivals, Passover, Shavuot, and Sukkot, thus establishing a pattern of two-day holidays.[4] After the Romans destroyed the Second Temple and home of the Sanhedrin (the supreme court and legislative body of ancient Israel) in 70 C.E., the signal-and-message system became even more challenging, as Jews had dispersed all over Asia, Europe, and North Africa. By the 4th century, a fixed Jewish calendar had been created. It was defined by Hillel II,[5] a Jewish communal and religious authority (not to be confused with the famous sage Hillel the Elder), and the Sanhedrin, of which he was the president. This assembly continued to meet for several hundred years beyond the destruction of the Temple.[6]

Fixing the Jewish calendar had not been an easy task. A principal objective was to systemize the blending of the lunar calendar with another kind of calendar, one based on the sun. Two issues in particular had to be addressed. In the first, the challenge was the difference between the length of a solar year and a lunar year. For the sun to fulfill its yearly cycle, once again reaching the same point in the sky takes 365 days, 12 hours, and 49 minutes—a solar year. For the moon to complete one cycle around the earth takes 29 days, 12 hours, and 44 minutes, which, when multiplied by 12, makes a lunar year of 354 days, 8 hours, and 49 minutes.[7] That means the lunar year is about 11 days shorter than the solar year. Were this difference to be unaccounted for, our holidays would slip back year after year, and, for example, at the end 10 years, Yom Kippur would fall in mid-June. Some religions follow the lunar calendar only, and their holidays shift seasons from one year to the next. Jews wished to follow a lunar cycle, yet maintain the same season for each holiday, which requires a solar perspective. The second issue was finding a way to resolve the number of days between the start of one month and the next. Measured in days, it takes 29-and-a-half days to go through all of the moon's phases and reach the new moon. A solution was required, because a month cannot start in the middle of the day.

To formally reconcile the discrepancy betweeen the solar year and the lunar year, Hillel II and the Sanhedrin established a pattern for inserting a *shanah me'uberet* (literally, "pregnant year") of 13 months on a set basis. In the past, such leap years had been designated randomly at the discretion of the king or High Priest; the only requirement of their scheme was that Passover fall in the spring. On the fixed Jewish calendar, a month is added in seven out of every nineteen years, specifically to the third, sixth, eighth, eleventh, fourteenth, seventeenth, and nineteenth years. Each of these years receives an extra month of Adar, called Adar II *(Adar Sheini).*[8]

To resolve the other issue—the number of days in each month—Hillel II taught a simple, easily learned formula that calculates the length for every month, with some months *malei* ("full"), having 30 days, and some *chaser* ("deficient"), having 29 days. Before the fixing of the calendar, people knew the mathematical calculations that could predict the new moon; but physical observations were also necessary, and these could be obstructed by natural occurrences, such as a cloudy sky. The fixed calendar provided, and still provides, a system that negates the necessity for visual testimony; the actual new moon in the sky and the notation of Rosh Hodesh on the calendar will always coincide.

A Fix for the Two-Day Fix?

A controversy exists over an issue that has its origin in the time before the calendar was fixed. It concerns the second holy day celebrated in the Diaspora for the holidays of Rosh Hashanah (which always falls on Rosh Hodesh);[9] Sukkot, Passover, and Shavuot (the three pilgrimage holidays); and Rosh Hodesh (in months preceded by a 30-day month).[10] The Hebrew phrase for this day is *yom tov sheini shel galuyot,* the second day of the festival celebrated outside the Land of Israel. With the fixing of the calendar in the 4th century and the ease of communication in modern times, some people argue that there is no longer a need to observe the second day. In fact, some contend that prolonged celebration and extended ritual, such as two Passover-seder nights, actually detract from the intended joyous spirit of the holiday. Thus most Reform and a small minority of Conservative Jews do not observe the second day of the *hag* (festival) for the three pilgrimage festivals or for Rosh Hodesh. Nor do they do so for the so-called second day of Rosh Hashanah.[11] In Israel, because communication of the new moons was not a problem in the ancient land itself, the Jews who lived there long ago and those who live there now have never observed the second day of these occasions. The seeming exception is Rosh Hashanah; but this two-day holiday is really considered to be one long day (*see* part 3 of this volume).[12]

Naming the Months and the Days

The Gregorian calendar, the standard secular calendar in use today, was established in 1582 and named for Pope Gregory XIII. It is a modified version of the Julian calendar fixed by Julius Caesar in 45 B.C.E. (five centuries before the fixing of the Jewish calendar). The names of the months tell an interesting story and underscore the differences between the current secular and Jewish calendars. Each Gregorian month is named after a god, a Roman ruler, or the month's numerical placement in the year. Before Julius Caesar's reformation of an even earlier Roman calendar, the first month of the year was March, marking the beginning of spring.[13] We still see the remnants of the original calendar in the names of September, October, November, and December, which are the ninth through twelfth months, not the seventh through tenth as their names suggest.

The names of the week also provide an interesting historical picture. Their origins are debated, but most likely the names used by many cultures arise from a combination of two prominent sky features that were of much importance to ancient peoples: the seven visible heavenly bodies (sun, moon, Mars, Mercury, Jupiter, Venus, and Saturn) and the monthly cycle of the moon (which can be calculated in quarters). The English names for the days of the week remind us of the planets, as well as of the Roman and Nordic pagan deities. The pagans had many gods, among them heavenly bodies; the Jews had only one God. The Hebrew days of the week are thus named according to the seven-day process of Creation. Since the last day, the day of rest, is Shabbat, Jews begin their week with a day called simply *yom rishon* (literally, "first day"), known in English by its pagan name—Sunday. It is interesting that the Romance languages, such as Spanish, French, and Italian, use Christian names for their "day of the LORD" (Domingo, Dimanche, Domenica) rather than the pagan "Sunday," because of discomfort the Catholic Church has with any pagan associations.

Names of Days

ENGLISH	FRENCH	PLANET OR DEITY	HEBREW
Sunday (Sun Day)	Dimanche	Sun	*Yom Rishon* (First Day)
Monday (Moon Day)	Lundi	Moon	*Yom Sheini* (Second Day)
Tuesday (Tiu's Day)	Mardi	Mars; same as Nordic god Tiu	*Yom Shlishi* (Third Day)
Wednesday (Woden's Day)	Mercredi	Mercury; same as Nordic god Woden-Odin	*Yom Revi'i* (Fourth Day)
Thursday (Thor's Day)	Jeudi	Jupiter, derived from Roman god Jove; same as Nordic god Thor	*Yom Chamishi* (Fifth Day)
Friday (Freya's Day)	Vendredi	Venus; same as Nordic god Freya	*Yom Shishi* (Sixth Day)
Saturday (Saturn's Day)	Samedi	Saturn	*Shabbat* (Sabbath)

The Months and the Holidays

SECULAR MONTHS	NAMESAKES	ORIGINS OF SECULAR MONTHS
January	Janus	Roman god of doors and gates, beginnings and endings; opens the year and starts the consul election period
February	Februus	Roman god of purification; month of sacrifices and purification
March	Mars	Roman god of war; start of the year for soldiers, because no fighting occurred in winter; once the first month of the year
April	from the Latin *Aprilis*, meaning "to open"; or from the Etruscan god Apru, corresponding to Aphrodite (goddess of love)	Possibly refers to the opening of leaves, flowers, and light during spring days; or to the opening of men's hearts
May	the Greek god Maia, who is identified with the Roman god Bona Dea	Gods of fertility, Maia and Bona Dea (connection of spring to fertility)
June	Juno	The wife of Jupiter; the queen of all gods and the patroness of marriage
July	Julius Caesar	Roman military and political leader who reorganized the calendar; a day was added posthumously to July in his honor
August	Caesar Augustus	Roman emperor honored for era of peace and prosperity; grandnephew of Julius Caesar.
September	from Latin *septimus*	Originally the seventh *(septimus)* month
October	from Latin *octomus*	Originally the eighth *(octomus)* month
November	from Latin *nonus*	Originally the ninth *(nonus)* month
December	from Latin *decimus*	Originally the tenth *(decimus)* month

HEBREW MONTHS*	ORIGINS OF HEBREW MONTHS**	JEWISH HOLIDAYS	ZODIAC SIGNS***
Tevet (Dec.–Jan.)	from Tebetu, meaning "to dip or to sink," possibly referring to the mud from the rain of the season	no holidays in Tevet	Capricorn *Gedi*
Shevat (Jan.–Feb.)	from Shabatu, related to the meaning of "beating or striking"	Tu b'Shevat	Aquarius *Deli*
Adar (Feb.–Mar.)	from Adaru; meaning is uncertain, possibly "to worry"	Purim	Pisces *Dagim*
Nisan; called *Aviv* in Bible (Mar.– Apr.)	from Nisanu, meaning "first produce"	Passover Yom Ha-Shoah	Aris *Taleh*
Iyar; called *Ziv* in Bible (Apr.–May)	from Ayaru, meaning "light and brightness of blossoming flowers" (related to Hebrew word *or*)	Yom Ha-Zikaron Yom Ha-Atzmaut Lag ba-Omer	Taurus *Shor*
Sivan (May–June)	from Simanu, meaning "to mark or appoint" (related to Hebrew word *sim*)	Shavuot	Gemini *Te'umim*
Tammuz (June–July)	from Du'uzu, named for Dumuzi, the Sumerian god of fertility	no holidays in Tammuz	Cancer *Sartan*
Av (July–Aug.)	from Abu; meaning is uncertain, possibly related to "father"	Tisha b'Av Tu b'Av	Leo *Aryeh*
Elul (Aug.–Sept.)	from Ululu, meaning "to become pure"	no holidays in Elul	Virgo *Betulah*
Tishrei; called *Ethanim* in Bible (Sept.–Oct.)	from Tashritu, meaning "beginning"	Rosh Hashanah Yom Kippur Sukkot: Hoshanah Rabbah, Shemini Atzeret, Simchat Torah	Libra *Moznayim*
Heshvan or Marheshvan; called *Bul* in Bible (Oct.–Nov.)	from Warhu Shamnu or Arakh Samna, meaning "eighth month"	no holidays in Heshvan	Scorpio *Akrav*
Kislev (Nov.–Dec.)	from Kislimu; meaning is uncertain	Hanukkah	Sagittarius *Keshet*

* Hebrew months do not correspond directly to secular months. The overlapping secular months are in parentheses.

** Hebrew names of the months are derived from the months of the pre-Babylonian, Akkadian-Sumerian civilization and language.

*** The Zodiac has played a significant role in Jewish life for thousands of years. It was a prominent artistic feature of Jewish homes, and even synagogues, from the 4th to 6th centuries. The Hebrew names of the signs are in italics.

PART 3

Rosh Hashanah

The LORD *looks down from heaven; He sees all mankind.*
From His dwelling-place He gazes on all the inhabitants
of the earth—He who fashions the hearts of them all,
who discerns all their doings.

—Psalms 33:13–15

The Head of the Year

AS THE RABBINIC SAGES TEACH US, throughout the year there are truly four new years.[1] One falls upon the first day of the spring month of Nisan. It commemorates the day when the princes of the Jewish tribes brought offerings for the dedication of the Tabernacle (the portable sanctuary the Israelites used in the wilderness). Another is the new year of the trees, Tu b'Shevat (which usually falls in February), on the 15th of the winter month of Shevat. A third new year, falling in late summer, signifies the annual renewal of tithing of cattle, on the1st of Elul. The fourth is Rosh Hashanah (literally, "the head of the year"). Arriving in early autumn, on the 1st of Tishrei, this new year is the most familiar of the four—when many Jews spend time in synagogue, spiritually awaken to the cry of the shofar, and then go home to dip apples and challah in honey for a sweet year. Rosh Hashanah is when the seasons of the earth are renewed and is understood by some to be the birthday of the universe.[2] Most importantly, however, Rosh Hashanah is also known as *Yom ha-Din*—The Day of Judgment—as the Talmud says, "for all who take part in the world, each evaluated and counted like sheep passing through the gate of their shepherd."[3]

As the Year Turns

This [Nisan] marks the beginning of our redemption, not the beginning of the year, which starts with Tishrei; "The Feast of Ingathering" [Sukkot, one of the fall holidays] is "at the turn of the year."[4] Nisan is the beginning of the months "for you"[5] [your national freedom] not for the year.[6]

—Nachmanides[7]

Certainly, having four new years can be be confusing. For example, in the biblical Book of Exodus, we are told that the counting of months is to begin with Nisan,[8] and the Bible continues to use this method of counting months all the way through the Book of Esther.[9] Even today, the spring month of Nisan, in which Passover falls, is technically month number one on the Hebrew calendar, although not the start of what we now traditionally call the New Year. A measure of clarification occurred in the 1st to 3rd centuries C.E., when the oral laws of the Jewish people were redacted as the Mishnah. During this process, the Rabbis debated which of the four new years should stand out as the momentous birthday of the universe—the official Rosh Hashanah.[10] Why did they now need to ponder such a question? The Second Temple in Jerusalem had been destroyed in 70 C.E. and the Jews exiled from the Land of

Israel. They were living dispersed in other nations, among pagans, whose tempting and influential religions celebrated various sorts of new years, typically either in spring or fall. Perhaps the Rabbis saw a reason to make distinctions about and apply greater specificity to the practice and understanding of our observances, because the Jewish nation was no longer physically together. They elevated Rosh Hashanah—associated with the birth of the universe and the renewal of the soul—to its status as the official "Head of the Year."

Observing the Meaning

The Book of Jubilees *(Sefer Ha-Yovlim)* is an ancient Jewish text written in the 2nd century B.C.E. that reworks material found in the biblical books of Genesis and Exodus. One of its passages captures the essence of Rosh Hashanah in the depiction of a prayerful Abram (the given name of the Patriarch Abraham) before he ventures from his home on this deeply moving holiday:

"Abram sat up during the night on the first of the seventh month, so that he might observe the stars from evening until daybreak so that he might see what the nature of the year would be with respect to rain. And he was sitting alone and making observations; and a word came into his heart, saying, 'All of the signs of the stars and the signs of the sun and the moon are all in the hand of the LORD. Why am I seeking?'"

—Jubilees 12:16–17[12]

Today Rosh Hashanah stands as a poignant moment in the Jewish experience. Jews are to take account of their lives for the year to come—a *cheshbon nefesh* (literally, "accounting of the soul")—and begin to make the adjustments in their attitudes and behavior that will help them become better human beings. Awe-inspiring themes such as judgment, self-assessment, meditation, renewal, and *teshuvah* (returning to one's spiritual core) permeate the Jewish psyche from Rosh Hashanah through the next 10 days, until the end of Yom Kippur. It is clearly in this spirit that many early sages referred to these 10 days as *Aseret Yemei Teshuvah,* the Ten Days of Repentance.[11] In the 14th century, Rabbi Jacob Moelin, known by the Hebrew acronym Maharil (for "Our teacher, the Rabbi, Israel Levi"), coined the phrase *Yamim Noraim,* the Days of Awe, as they are still known today.

Rosh Hashanah in the Bible

Considering the magnitude of Rosh Hashanah in the spiritual cycle of the Jewish people, one might suspect that it would warrant frequent mention in the Bible. On the contrary, Rosh Hashanah is scarcely mentioned and it is not even referred to by a specific name. The first and fundamental source for Rosh Hashanah is in Leviticus.

The LORD spoke to Moses, saying: Speak to the Israelite people thus: In the seventh month, on the first day of the month, you shall observe complete rest, a sacred occasion commemorated with loud blasts. You shall not work at your occupations; and you shall bring an offering by fire to the LORD.
—Lev. 23:23-25[13]

Rosh Hashanah was not designated as the official "Head of the Year," as we know it today, until talmudic times. In Leviticus, the then-nameless day is identified only by its placement at the start of the seventh month, Tishrei. (We starting counting months on the Hebrew calendar with Nisan, the spring month in which Passover falls.) It is referred to as a sacred day marked with "loud blasts." This brief description, with which we are now so familiar, is the one that the medieval rabbi and philosopher Maimonides[14] later codified as the source for sounding the shofar.[15] Not until the biblical Book of Nehemiah, which was written in the period after the Jews returned from the Babylonian exile (6th century B.C.E.), do we find a lengthier and more magisterial account of this profound holiday (Neh. 7:72b–8.13). We see the gravity, significance, and greatness of this day, as we experience the community gathering for the first time in its entirety to listen to and participate in the sage Ezra's recital of the sacred words of Torah (Five Books of Moses).

When the seventh month arrived—the Israelites being [settled] in their towns—the entire people assembled as one man in the square before the Water Gate, and they asked Ezra the scribe to bring the scroll of the Teaching of Moses with which the LORD had charged Israel. On the first day of the seventh

Ishmael and Isaac

On Rosh Hashanah, the portions read from the Torah are from Genesis. One is the compelling story of the birth of Abraham's son Ishmael and his expulsion from home along with his mother, Hagar (an Egyptian slave). The other is the story of the near-sacrifice of Isaac by his father, Abraham, in an incident called the *Akedah,* which means "the Binding of Isaac." As the editors of *Etz Hayim: A Torah Commentary* observe, these stories are very appropriate for Rosh Hashanah because they epitomize the humanity of Judaism.[16] Judaism is a tradition that emphasizes the struggles of real people with real-life complications, such as those that occur between siblings or between parents and children. Rosh Hashanah is the holiday that provides the space to wrestle with such complexities and to reawaken to the imperfections and humility that accompany the human experience.

month, Ezra the priest brought the Teaching before the congregation, men and women and all who could listen with understanding. He read from it, facing the square before the Water Gate, from the first light until midday, to the men and the women and those who could understand; the ears of all the people were given to the scroll of the Teaching.
—Neh. 8:1–3

The Month of Elul: A Footpath to Mercy

Because there is so much at stake spiritually during Rosh Hashanah, we make preparations beginning a full month earlier. At Rosh Hodesh Elul, or the start of the new month of Elul, we begin to stir with anticipation for this day of spiritual renewal. We set out our spiritual provisions by readying our minds for prayer and our hearts for forgiveness and by doing whatever we can to attain God's compassion and mercy when the day of judgment arrives.

The most prominent feature of the month of Elul is the sounding of the shofar each morning, except on Shabbat.[17] Three primary reasons are given for this practice. The first one is to confuse Satan[18] about the date for Rosh Hashanah, so that he will not be able to affect God's judgment of people with his accusations against them.[19] The second one pertains to a Rabbinic legend, which says that Moses' ascent to receive the second tablets on the 1st of Elul was accompanied by blasts of the shofar. Therefore, the shofar reminds us of the story of the Golden Calf and that we must always be aware of our potential for sinning.[20] The third one has as its source the famous phrase heard at many weddings from the Song of Songs (6:3) *Ani ledodi v'dodi li,* meaning "I am my beloved's and my beloved is mine." The first letters *(aleph.lamed.vav.lamed)* of each Hebrew word form an acrostic for the word Elul. From this hint, we gather that the period extending from the beginning of Elul through Yom Kippur (a total of 40 days) is a time ripe to become beloved by God. The shofar alerts us to that loving relationship.[21]

Another important practice during Elul is the recitation of *Selichot* (literally, "forgivenesses"), which are penitential prayers and poems added to the daily morning prayers. This custom is based on a legend portraying King David as troubled over how the Israelites will be able to truly atone for their transgressions. God responds by advising him that the people should confess their sins by saying poems and prayers of penitence.[22]

Sephardim (the Jews of Spain, Portugal, the Mediterranean basin, North Africa, and the Middle East, and their descendants) recite *Selichot* for the entire month of Elul until Yom Kippur (except on Shabbat), early every morning. That 40-day span of time parallels the period that Moses spent on Mount Sinai. However, Ashkenazim (the Jews of Eastern Europe and their descendants) follow a different tradition. They begin saying *Selichot* closer to the start of the holiday. Depending on the pattern of the calendar, recitation of *Selichot* begins either just after the Shabbat that precedes Rosh Hashanah or exactly a week earlier. (Because a minimum four days of saying *Selichot* is required, if Rosh Hashanah begins on a Tuesday or Wednesday, the saying of *Selichot* must be moved forward.[23]) Either way, the preferred hour for the first recitation in Ashkenazic tradition comes on Saturday night, *motzei Shabbat* (the "exit" of the Sabbath), rather than Sunday morning. Sundown is the actual start of the Jewish "day," and we honor a tradition by beginning at the earliest possible opportunity. In this case, however, Ashkenazim wait until midnight to say the first *Selichot* because of a desire to extend the beauty of Shabbat until the last minute.

A 19th-century Russian rabbi Yechiel Michel Ha-Levi Epstein, compiler of the *Arukh Ha-Shulchan,* offers a beautiful reason for the Ashkenazic *motzei Shabbat* tradition, a reason that he bases on the order of Creation. Human beings were created on the sixth day, or Erev (the day before) Shabbat. The first full day of life for human beings was Shabbat, a time when things remain still. It is therefore appropriate that when Shabbat "leaves" on Saturday night, human beings express one of their primary purposes in life, which is to offer *Selichot,* passionate pleas of devotion to the Master of the Universe.[24]

Four-day Minimum

The part of the Ashkenazic tradition that requires a minimum four days of *Selichot* is based upon the laws about sacrifices during biblical times. The laws required isolating the perfect sacrificial animal from contact with other animals for four days to preserve it from becoming blemished. Consequently, we say *Selichot* for at least four days to symbolically offer ourselves as a sacrifice. We meticulously engage in prayer and self-examination to rid ourselves of any spiritual defilement that might impede our pure commitment to God on the Day of Judgment.[25]

The day before Rosh Hashanah, referred to as Erev Rosh Hashanah (as is the evening that actually begins the holiday), also holds special significance and has its own special customs. In preparation for this sacred holiday the *Selichot* are more extensive and the shofar is not sounded.[26] As mentioned in part I of this volume, the omission of the shofar is meant to deceive Satan, by making him believe that Rosh Hashanah has already ended.[27] In addition, the *parochet* (curtain that covers the Torah scrolls), the cover to the reading table, and the dressing of the Torah itself are often changed to white, to represent the motifs of purity and atonement. Other customs include visiting the graves of relatives and loved ones, contributing something significant to charitable causes, and sending greeting cards.

On Erev Rosh Hashanah, some people choose to perform a ritual of introspection and spiritual mediation called *hatarat nedarim,* the "annulling of vows." The ritual covers only vows made to themselves or to God (not ones made to another person) and only to a particular kind of vow. In *hatarat nedarim* an individual asks to be released from vows that may have been said in a heated moment, but were not truly of the heart, and from casual statements that may have been worded as vows, but were not intended as such. This ritual is part of Judaism's system for giving people second chances; but of course not every vow can or will be annulled.

In this case, a person who wishes to be released from vows makes a declaration in the presence of three others whom he has asked to serve as a *beit din* (literally, "house of judgment")—a legal court according to Jewish law.[28] After the first is told that he or she is absolved of those vows, another takes a turn asking for absolution while the remaining three serve as the *beit din,* and so on with the group. Whether or not one uses the traditional formula found in some prayer books, it is important to practice *hatarat nedarim* with people who can be open and honest, as well as thoughtful, in their responses.

Rosh Hashanah Greetings

During the month of Elul and on Rosh Hashanah itself, Jews have a custom of wishing each other well with the expression *le-shanah tovah tikatevu* (often shortened to *shanah tovah*), meaning "may God inscribe you [in the Book of Life] for a good year." This expression refers to the talmudic teaching that God opens three books on Rosh Hashanah in which to inscribe each person's fate for the coming year. The wicked are immediately inscribed and sealed for death—understood as spiritual, not necessarily physical, death; the righteous are immediately inscribed and sealed for life; and those who are *beinoni* (literally, "intermediate")—or inbetween wicked and righteous—are inscribed but not sealed. The *beinoni* linger in this state, striving to assure a good outcome, until Yom Kippur when their fate will be finally determined.[29] Since most of us assume that we are in the category of *beinoni* during the days after Rosh Hashanah and before Yom Kippur, some people change the greeting during that period to *gemar chatimah tovah,* which essentially means "a good finishing seal [in the Book of Life]." Others say *le-shana tovah tikatevu v'tichatemu* for "good year, may you be written and sealed."

Is It Two Days or One Long Day?

To understand the length of the Rosh Hashanah holiday, we must first look at three other days and ask a question that has been discussed extensively for many years. If the pilgrimage festivals of Sukkot, Passover, and Shavuot are one day each, why do many of us celebrate them for two days? The answer reaches back to the history of the Jewish calendar. As explained in part 2 of this volume, the sages in Jerusalem were responsible for marking the times to observe Rosh Hodesh (each new month), festivals, and other celebrations. Every month, for a starting point, they learned when the month began by using a system of witnesses who routinely identified the phases of the moon. After listening to the witnesses' accounts, the sages would then declare the start of that month. From that announcement, people could count forward to the day when a given holiday in that month would start. This system was adequate for those living in Israel, where the news spread easily, but getting immediate news to Jews in foreign lands via messengers was difficult. For many reasons, the messenger system was not always reliable; subsequently the people living outside of Israel, in the Diaspora, began to keep each of these holidays for two days. The extra day was insurance that they would celebrate at the correct time, even if the news was late or garbled.[30] Today, people who have returned to live in the Land of Israel follow the one-day pattern of observance for some of the new-month celebrations and for all of the pilgrimage festivals. Most Jews who remain in the Diaspora (except those in the Reform movement) continue to follow the ancient two-day pattern.

Rosh Hashanah, while not a pilgrimage festival, has the singular characteristic of being a holy day that falls at the start of a new month (the month of Tishrei). One might expect Jews in Israel to follow the one-day tradition described above. Such is not the case. There seems to have been a time when Rosh Hashanah was kept for only one day, but in the Middle Ages the rabbis set it back to two days, claiming that it was intended to be a two-day holiday everywhere and for all time.[31] They taught that it should not be thought of as two days, but as one long day, a *yoma arikhta.* Most people sanctify both days with the special blessing of *Shehecheyanu,* which acknowledges the arrival of another year to celebrate a new time in the life of all gathered. Because of a doubt about whether we should say this blessing two days in a row, some authorities have suggested eating a new fruit or wearing a new garment (events that people often mark with a prayer) on the second night to provide reason for another *Shehecheyanu* blessing of thanksgiving.[32]

Food and Other Customs on Rosh Hashanah

Learning about customs often begins with learning about food, and Rosh Hashanah has several food customs that express the different attitudes, hopes, feelings, and fears that surround the holiday. Although many of these customs represent hope, the symbols used can also convey a sense of anxiety over the magnitude of the holiday—an anxiety that Jews have experienced throughout history.

The centerpiece of the festival table is the challah (plural, *challot*), the oval or rectangular loaf of braided bread that is traditionally eaten on almost every Jewish holiday and on Shabbat. Rosh Hashanah *challot* are customarily baked in symbolic shapes. The most familiar one is round, which symbolizes the cyclical nature of the year and the never-ending eternity of life. A more unusual design is a challah in the shape of a bird, hearkening to the biblical passage from Isaiah (31:5), "Like the birds that fly, even so will the LORD of Hosts shield Jerusalem. . . ." A challah baked in the shape of a ladder signifies the awesome gravity of the holiday: one is judged and may potentially ascend to life, success, and wealth—or fall to death, failure, and poverty.[33]

On Shabbat, after saying *Ha-Motzi* (the blessing recited over bread before a meal is eaten), we dip the challah in salt to create a parallel between the salted sacrifices on the Temple altar and the food on our own table. In contrast, for Rosh Hashanah, and for the Shabbats between Rosh Hashanah and Sukkot, we dip the challah in honey. Then we say a second prayer—one said before eating fruit from trees—and we dip apples in honey.[34] These customs, along with avoiding bitter and sour foods, symbolize hope for a sweet and good year to come.

Other food customs, practiced less often today, include eating the head of a ram or of a fish with the saying, "May this year bring the status of the head (i.e., positive and good) as opposed to the tail."[35] The ram head also reinforces the Rosh Hashanah Torah reading, which tells of a ram being sacrificed instead of Isaac.[36] The fish head, however, is a controversial food on Rosh Hashanah. For example, some people deliberately eat it as a symbol of our prayer to increase in numbers just as fish proliferate.[37] On the other hand, Iraqi Jews traditionally stay away from fish on Rosh Hashanah because the Hebrew word for fish, *dag,* is extremely close to the word for worry, *da'agah.*[38] Other people avoid nuts because of the negative association between the Hebrew word for nut, *egoz,* and the word for sin, *het.* These two words share the same *gematria,* the total numerical value of their letters, determined from an ancient system in which each Hebrew word was assigned a number.[39]

Many fruits and vegetables are important on Rosh Hashanah, and different explanations exist for why apples in particular are so special during this holiday. One is that they have beautiful qualities and give sustenance, and we wish for both sustenance and beauty for the new year. Another is that the shape of apples also resembles the shape of the accumulated heaps of ashes from the sacrifices. We learn in the Torah reading for Rosh Hashanah that Isaac was not turned to ashes as a sacrifice.[40] We pray that we too will survive and carry on in the coming year.[41] Other fruits and vegetables are customarily eaten because of symbolic word associations or because of their *gematria*—in this case for the good—such as peas (abundance), dates (end of misfortune), and pomegranates (mitzvot—the good and worthy accomplishments with which our year should be filled).

With all of that delicious food, we might be inclined to nap a bit; but it is customary not to sleep during the day of Rosh Hashanah. First, the day is meant to be dedicated to meditation, introspection, and facing the self. Sleeping is quite the opposite of such things. Second, a medieval teaching says that a person cannot be condemned to death when he or she is not present at the trial. According to this teaching, when a person is asleep, the soul ascends to heaven and appears before the heavenly court. There, Satan can make his case against the soul, leaving it more liable for penalty. So it's best to just stay awake and keep the soul on earth for the day of the trial.[42]

TASHLIKH

The custom of *Tashlikh* (literally, "casting away" or "throwing") is a distinctive aspect of Rosh Hashanah for many people. This custom is not mentioned in the Bible, nor is it mentioned in Rabbinic literature until the work of Maharil, who lived in 14th-century Germany and who codified the customs maintained by Jews at home and in the synagogue.[43] Apparently, the custom is based upon verses in the Book of Micah (7:18–19) that refer to the attributes of God and are thus central to the Days of Awe. These verses actually use the word *tashlikh* when stating about God, "He will cover up our iniquities, you will hurl *(tashlikh)* all our sins into the depths of the sea." Therefore, during the afternoon of the first day of Rosh Hashanah (the second if the first day is Shabbat), we go to a flowing, natural body of water, ideally containing fish, to recite prayers and psalms and to symbolically remove our sins and transgressions by shaking out our pockets.

There are three primary associations with *Tashlikh* all of which describe the emotional and spiritual nature of the holiday. One is made by Maharil, using a midrashic legend (a Rabbinic exposition of the literal meaning of the Bible through homilies, legends, and legal interpretations) of the Rosh Hashanah Torah reading.[44] The legend tells of Abraham on his way to follow God's command to sacrifice Isaac. While traveling, Satan tries to prevent Abraham from going forward by setting up a great body of water as a barrier. Undeterred, Abraham plunges forth and when the water is about to rise above his head, he cries to God, "Deliver me, O God, for the waters have reached my neck. . . ." (Ps. 69:2). God then rescues him for his great faith and devotion. The ceremony of *Tashlikh* inspires us to dedicate ourselves to God in the faith of Abraham.

The second association with *Tashlikh* is the presence of fish in bodies of water. The lives of fish represent our own great anxiety about the weight of this Day of Judgment. Fish swim quickly, change direction almost instantaneously, and head potentially into nets. Thus they symbolize the uncertainty and changing nature of our lives.[45]

Finally, another understanding of this custom, emphasized by modern rabbis and teachers, incorporates the cleansing attributes of water, as water can symbolically purify and cleanse our souls. Today, some people throw bread crumbs for their sins in addition to the medieval custom of shaking out the corners of their garments, because the crumbs will either be consumed by fish or dissolved in the water.

Rosh Hashanah
Pathways Through the Sources

Midrash Rabbah

Presence and Pardon

Midrash is a powerful form of Rabbinic literature that weaves theology and practice together in poetic style. The following midrash explains many of the most significant aspects of Rosh Hashanah, including its connection to the beginning of the universe and its role as a day for individual and national judgment. It gives us insight into the relationship between humankind and God by exploring God's intention for our creation and God's mercy for us. This text deserves particular study, because in many ways it serves as a frame within which to view all Rosh Hashanah texts.

> It was taught in the name of Rabbi Eliezer: "The world was created on the twenty-fifth of Elul." The view of Rav agrees with the teaching of Rabbi Eliezer. For we have learned in the Shofar Benediction [of the *Zikhronot* "Remembrance" passages in the additional service on Rosh Hashanah] composed by Rav: "This day, on which was the beginning of work, is a memorial of the first day, for it is a statute for Israel, a decree of the God of Jacob. Thereon also sentence is pronounced upon countries, which of them is destined to the sword and which to peace, which to famine and which to plenty; and each separate creature is visited thereon, and recorded for life or for death." Thus, you are left to conclude that on New Year's Day [the sixth day from the twenty-fifth of Elul], in the first hour the idea of creating man entered His mind, in the second He took counsel with the ministering angels, in the third He assembled Adam's dust, in the fourth He kneaded it, in the fifth He shaped him, in the sixth He made him into a lifeless body, in the seventh He breathed a soul into him, in the eighth he brought him into the Garden of Eden, in the ninth he was commanded [against eating the fruit of the tree of knowledge of good and evil], in the tenth he transgressed, in the eleventh he was judged, in the twelfth he was pardoned. "This," said the Holy One, blessed be He, to Adam, "will be a sign to your children. As you stood in judgment before Me on this day and will come out from My presence with a free pardon, so will your children in the future stand in judgment before Me on this day and will come out from My presence with a free pardon." When will that be? *In the seventh month, on the first day of the month* (Lev. 23:24).[46]
>
> —Midrash, *Leviticus Rabbah* 29:1

Jerusalem Talmud

God's Partners

The Talmud, the most significant collection of laws, stories, and thought in all Rabbinic literature, appears in two versions: the Jerusalem Talmud (5th century) and the Babylonian Talmud (circa 6th century). This somewhat humorous text shows the covenantal partnership between God and the Jewish people.[47] The text portrays a relationship in which—even during the most awe-inspiring and humbling days and moments of the Jewish year—we are still unique, covenantal partners with God. We acknowledge God's right to judge, while simultaneously maintaining our own dignity and worth by acknowledging God's need for us.

> Hurnah said: "What nation is like this nation? It is the custom among men that if the ruler says, 'The trial is today,' and the accused say, 'The trial shall be tomorrow'—to whom do you listen? Surely to the ruler. With regard to God, however, this is not the case. If the [human] court declares, 'Today is Rosh Hashanah,' God says to the ministering angels, 'Set up the [heavenly] court, let the defense attorneys arise, let the prosecuting attorneys arise, because my children have declared that today is Rosh Hashanah.' If the [human] court deliberates and decides to postpone it to the next day, God says to the ministering angels: 'Remove the [heavenly] court, let the prosecuting attorneys leave, because My children decided to postpone it to tomorrow.'"
>
> —J. Talmud, *Rosh Hashanah* 1:3

High Holiday Machzor

The Decree

Of the better-known pieces in the High Holiday *machzor* (prayer book), the section called the *U-netaneh Tokef* ("Let us proclaim the holiness of this day.") is the most popular. The third paragraph of the *U-netaneh Tokef,* generally introduced with a dramatic chanting of the first line, is possibly the most haunting of all. It challenges us to consider what we believe about God and life and to categorize our possible destinies, including heartbreaking ones. The last sentence of encouragement, however, is given special emphasis: we have the power to change the severity of our destinies through pious acts of repentance, prayer, and righteousness.

On Rosh Hashanah the decree is written; on *Yom Tzom Kippur,* the Fast Day of Atonement, it is sealed. How many will pass away and how many will be born; who will live and who will die; who will reach the measure of his days and who will not reach it; who will die by fire and who by water; who by sword and who by wild animal; who by hunger and who by thirst; who by earthquake and who by disease; who by strangling and who by stoning; who will be tranquil and who will be disturbed; who will be at ease and who will be afflicted; who will become poor and who will become rich; who will be lowered into darkness and who will rise to be exalted.

U-teshuvah, u-tefilah, u-tzedakah ma'avirin et ro'a ha-gezeirah.
But repentance, and prayer, and acts of righteousness avert the evil [variously translated as "severity"] of the decree.[48]

—Part of the Rosh Hashanah *Musaf* (additional) service

The Zohar

A Shofar's Harmony

Rosh Hashanah is a time of judgment, a time when people pass before God's heavenly court, with Satan as the skilled prosecutor (or accuser). This judgment is not based solely on strict justice, for strict justice only accounts for the crime, not the culprit. True judgment, which comes only from God, includes judging the soul, not merely the actions, of the culprit; and true, rather than strict, justice includes mercy and compassion. Humans are not able nor expected to achieve God's level of true justice. Furthermore, Kabbalah (the Jewish mystical tradition) and the Zohar (the sacred book of Kabbalah) teach that perfect harmony is a blend of *din* (justice) and *hesed* (lovingkindness). According to the Zohar, when God judges, the world is harmonized with the "voice of Jacob" and "compassion prevails."[49]

Come and see: Similarly, on Rosh Hashanah—when judgment looms over the world—[Satan] stands poised to accuse. So Israel must arouse with a shofar, arousing a sound blended of fire, water, and air, becoming one, trumpeting that sound from the shofar. The sound ascends to the site of the Throne of Judgment, impinges on it and ascends. As soon as this sound arrives from below, the voice of Jacob is attuned above, and the blessed Holy One is aroused to compassion. For just as Israel arouses below a single sound blended of fire, water, and air, issuing as one from the shofar, so too above is a shofar aroused, and that sound blended of fire, water, and air harmonizes—one issuing below, one above; so the world harmonizes, compassion prevails. Then the accuser is confounded. Whereas he expects to accuse the world and prevail in judgment, once he sees compassion aroused, he becomes confounded, his strength is sapped, unable to do anything. So the blessed Holy One judges the world compassionately. For if you say that judgment is eliminated, not so! Rather, compassion joins judgment, and the world is judged compassionately.[50]

—Zohar, *Va-yera* 1:114a–b

Moses ben Jacob of Coucy

Self-Mastery

Rosh Hashanah is a time of self-reflection, a day to ask ourselves—really ask ourselves—what is it that drives our attitude and behavior? What is it that we really want for ourselves out of life? Are we acting in a way that makes progress toward our vision of a good life, or are we actually acting in a way that inhibits us from progressing? Rosh Hashanah is a day to take back control and to master those things that may have been mastering us.

Moses ben Jacob of Coucy, a distinguished rabbi who lived in 13th-century France, wrote Tosafot (medieval commentaries on the Talmud) and was an authority on *halakhah* (Jewish law).

It is because man is half angel, half brute, that his inner life witnesses such bitter war between such unlike natures. The brute in him clamors for sensual joy and things in which there is only vanity; but the angel resists and strives to make him know that meat, drink, and sleep are but means whereby the body may be made ready for the study of truths and the doing of the will of God. Not until the very hour of death can it be certain or known to what measure the victory has been won. He, who is but a novice in the love of God, will do well to say audibly each day, as he rises: "This day I will be a faithful servant of the Almighty. I will be on my guard against wrath, falsehood, hatred, and quarrelsomeness, and will forgive those who wound me." For who forgives is forgiven in his turn; hard-heartedness and a temper that will not make up quarrels are a heavy burden of sin, and unworthy of an Israelite.[51]

—Moses of Coucy

Or Ha-Chaim

Gentle Justice

An unavoidable part of the Rosh Hashanah spiritual experience is wrestling with what may be the greatest philosophic dilemma of all time—is there true justice in life? For if there is true justice, why do the good frequently suffer and the evil often go unpunished? Judaism insists that there is indeed justice and that God is the great judge. But still—when a hurricane wreaks disaster, or a murderer goes free, or a child dies—we ask in anguish: where is this true justice to be found? The Jewish tradition offers many different and compelling answers. This teaching is by one of the great Sephardic kabbalists, Chaim ben Attar, born in Morocco in 1696. (Later he moved to Italy, then Israel.) Like many scholars, he is traditionally referred to not by his birth name, but by his best-known work—in his case, *Or Ha-Chaim.* His words offer an answer that comforts us and yet, simultaneously, stirs up a healthy level of anxiety on this Day of Judgment.

> There are two ways in which the Creator evaluates His creations. One way is that God judges and weighs people's acts in the most precise and accurate manner. He overlooks no error, forgives no sin.... This is known as *Din,* the Divine Attribute of Strict Justice. When Scripture refers to God as *Elohim,* it refers to *Din.* Our sages teach us that God saw that the world could not survive were He to exact Strict Justice, for by their nature mortals are prone to sin. Therefore God introduced a second Divine Attribute and blended it with the first: *Rachamim,* the Divine Attribute of Mercy, and, when Scripture uses the [inexpressible] name, it refers to this attribute. When God deals with his creations with this attribute, he is not so precise or unforgiving.
>
> In heaven above, the Divine Attribute of Strict Justice prevails when God deals with the celestial forces and the ministering angels. True, these celestial beings are not subject to seduction by an Evil Impulse. Yet they are given to error because they sometimes deviate slightly from the precise Divine Truth they are expected to follow. Thus, what the [Divine] Attribute of Mercy accomplishes is this: Instead of administering punishment instantly, God waits. Instead of administering the powerful punishment all at once, God divides the pain into small parts and deals out the suffering little by little. But in the end the demands of the [Divine] Attribute of Strict Justice is executed precisely and completely, albeit in a gentle manner.[52]
>
> —Or Ha-Chaim

Mei Ha-Shilo'ach

The Original Intention

Hasidic rabbi Mordechai Yosef Leiner of Izbitza lived in Poland during the first half of the 19th century and was known by the name of his most famous work, *Mei Ha-Shilo'ach* (The Living Waters). Judaism teaches that Rosh Hashanah is the beginning of all the beginnings of the universe, and Mei Ha-Shilo'ach comments that the manner in which something begins is of the most extreme importance. Beginnings do not merely happen; they happen with a force of intention, a spiritual undercurrent. Mei Ha-Shilo'ach says that this spiritual undercurrent carries onward, ultimately defining the destiny of what was begun. With poetic detail, he explains that the original intention and spiritual undercurrent of the beginning of the universe is *hesed* (lovingkindness), one of God's attributes that was impressed upon us for eternity.

> It is written in the Holy Zohar (*Vayechi,* 226b), "it is taught that it is the beginning of the year of the king." Everything is included in the beginning of the intention. If at the outset of something one turns to the blessed God, thus all the resulting adventures will be included in the initial intention.... For this is the principle that everything goes after the first intention. And this is the matter with "mitzvot need intention," meaning that even after the intention, when a man starts the action of the mitzvah, the light dresses itself in the forms of actions, and the light becomes hidden. But for this, it needs intention, so that everything goes after the intention, and this is in the realm of man. And so it is with the blessed God, as it were. For in truth, the beginning of the intention of the creation was as it is written (Ps. 89:3), *Ki amarti olam chesed yibaneh*—"For I said that I will found the world on lovingkindness."[53]
>
> —Mei Ha-Shilo'ach

The Rebbe[54] of Strelisk

Heeding Advice

Rosh Hashanah embodies the essence of spirituality. It teaches us about the virtue of acceptance and emphasizes that none of us are in control of our own births or deaths. In addition, when we achieve greatness, it is mostly because of blessings that are out of our control, such as the timing of events and the kindness of others. Thus, we do not have the right to judge others or circumstances that are beyond our control; rather we are only to stay true to what we do and to have faith that God's justice will prevail.

Mordechai ben David of Strelisker ("The Strelisker") was a learned rabbi in 19th-century Romania and a disciple of the Maggid of Mezritch.

> The Strelisker explained thus the three lines in the Rosh Hashanah hymn: *His secret is uprightness; His advice is faith; His deeds are truth.*[55] "Because the uprightness and justice of God are oftentimes hidden from us, it is His advice that we have faith that His deeds are always truth."[56]

Rav[57] *Kook*

Sacred Freedom

During the *Yamim Noraim* (Days of Awe), most Jews will spend many hours in synagogue reading in the *machzor* about sin and repentance. We know that on Rosh Hashanah we are to repent and begin to atone for our sins, but what does that experience look like and feel like?

Rav Kook (Abraham Isaac Kook) was born in Latvia in the mid-19th century. As an adult, he migrated to the Land of Israel, where in 1921 he became the first chief rabbi of Palestine. Deeply influenced by the mystical and psychological interpretations of Judaism, he illustrates here the psychological and emotional process of repentance, which he describes poignantly as a course that results in great gratitude and joy.

> There is repentance corresponding to a specific sin as well as to many sins. Man places his sin "before his face" and is caught in the snare of his sin. His soul climbs and ascends till he is completely freed of bondage to sin; he senses within himself the sacred freedom, so pleasant to his weary soul, and is progressively cured. And the radiant lights of the sun of mercy, transcendental mercy, cast their rays upon him and he becomes joyful, he becomes filled with inner pleasure and delight, though simultaneously enduring a broken heart as well as a humbled and contrite soul—for he senses within himself that this very feeling, appropriate to him according to his present state, increases his spiritual pleasure and aids him toward true perfection. He constantly senses that he is coming ever closer to the source of life, to the Living God from Whom he was but a short while ago so remote. His yearning soul

remembers with a joyful heart its inner affliction and anguish and it is overwhelmed with feelings of thankfulness; with praise and song it lifts its voice.[58]

—Abraham Isaac Kook

Arthur Green

Returning to Wholeness

Rosh Hashanah is a holiday of such great magnitude that it is difficult to summarize the meaning. Arthur Green, a recognized authority on Jewish spirituality and Jewish thought, has managed to highlight many of the most significant aspects of the holiday in not only a poetic manner, but also in just a few paragraphs. The aspects of Rosh Hashanah he emphasizes are the eternal optimism and hopefulness inherent in Judaism, the intimate partnership between God and the Jewish people, the value of humility, and, most importantly, the purpose of *teshuvah,* which is to bring about more righteous behavior.

This is the message of our "days of awe." There is a possibility of return, of coming home. The original harmony—be it that of parent and child, or of a young and improperly balanced marriage—may have ended in pain and separation. But there is a way to come back. With real human participation in the terms of reunion, the way home remains open, and the prospects for longevity of relationship—if they are to be judged by Jewish history—are more than good. In this lies the eternal optimism of Jewish faith. It is expressed for us in the verse, "As You have borne this people from Egypt up to here," which introduces the 13 qualities of mercy. However far we think we have to go in life, however distant we feel from the goal, we need only recall where we were when we started. Our faith in the One has brought us from Egyptian bondage to the place where we are now. Surely that same faith, if it has brought us all this distance, can carry us the rest of the way as well!

This dream of restored wholeness is sounded out dramatically by the shofar blasts, the central symbolic expression of the *teshuvah* season.... [It] cries out a hundred times on Rosh Hashanah: "I was whole, I was broken, even smashed to bits, but I shall be whole again!"

But our restoration of wholeness is not to be achieved by prayer alone.... [The] liturgy only brings us to the edge of the Jordan, but never takes us into the promised land. For this we need to add the *deed* to our holy thoughts and words. *Teshuvah* and *tefillah* ("prayer") need *tzedakah* ("righteous doing") in order to be effective. We restore the world (and God's name) to wholeness only by doing. In fact, our entire contemplative effort has been pointed toward realization in the realm of action. We are the bearers of compassion in this God-filled universe; so too are we the "limbs of the *Shekhinah*," the ones who can make real in this world our vision of wholeness. Redemption is brought about only by deed.[59]

—Arthur Green

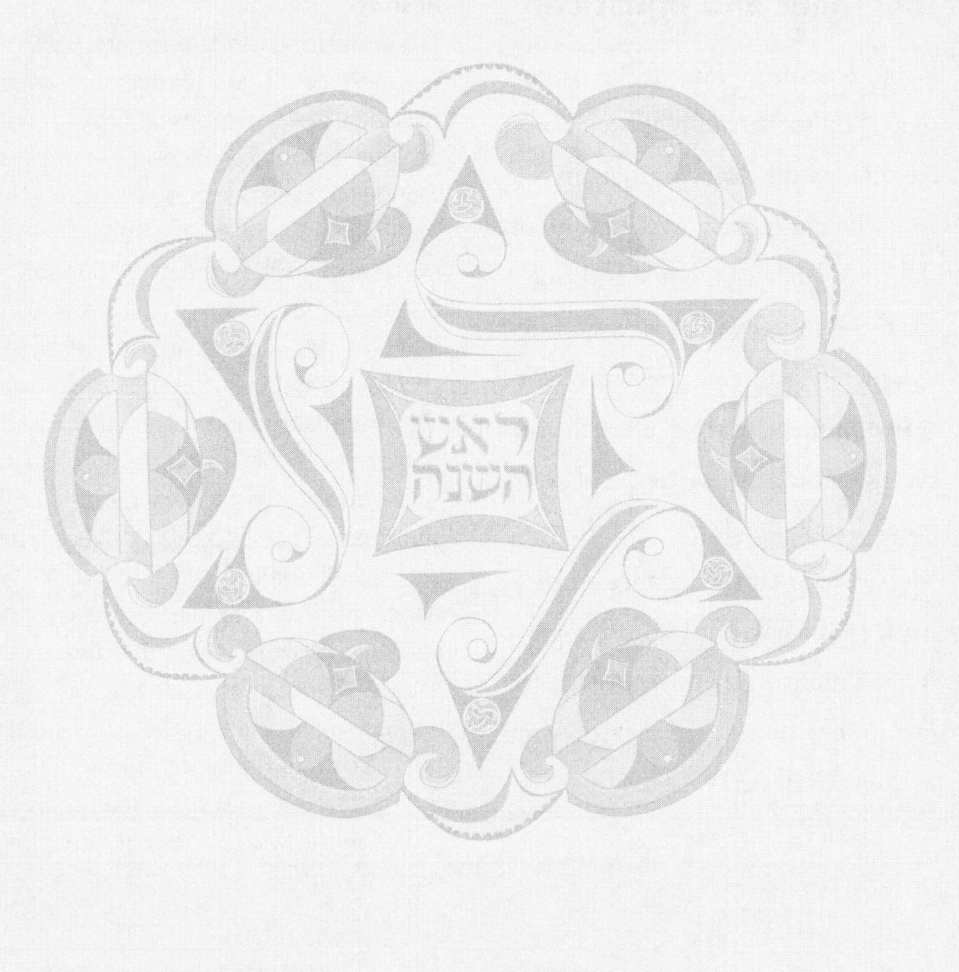

Rosh Hashanah

Interpretations of Sacred Texts

The texts we study in these pages are from the Talmud, the central and most important body of Rabbinic literature. Encompassing the work of seven generations of scholars, the Talmud serves as the primary source for all later codes of Jewish law. It was written in a mixture of Hebrew and Aramaic (the spoken vernacular of Babylonian Jews). Each page of the actual Talmud contains a central text surrounded by numerous commentaries and discussions. In a similar, but far less complex, fashion, each of the translated passages presented here is accompanied by multiple levels of study.

Peshat: simple, literal meaning • ***Derash:*** historical, Rabbinic inquiry
Making It Personal: contemporary analysis and application

Judgment and Injustice

Rabbi Kruspedai said in the name of Rabbi Yochanan:* "Three books are opened on Rosh Hashanah: one is of the completely wicked, one of the completely righteous, and one for those inbetween (*beinonim*). The completely righteous are written and sealed immediately for life, the completely wicked are written and sealed immediately for death, and the *beinonim* hang in the balance from Rosh Hashanah until Yom Kippur. If they merit it, they are written for life; if they do not merit it, they are written for death."

—B. Talmud, *Rosh Hashanah* 16b

Peshat

This well-known and important Rabbinic teaching on Rosh Hashanah evokes two significant responses. One is self-analysis and introspection, where we wonder in which group we belong. As the Talmud elsewhere recommends (*Kiddushin* 40b), most of us view ourselves as *beinonim,* which means that we are faced with the dreadful and overwhelming prospect of each act potentially tipping the balance in or out of our favor. The second response is a doubt in the validity of the statement. That is to say, if it were true, we would expect the wicked to be either punished or die in the coming year. We know, however, that this is not usually the case. In fact, not only the wicked suffer or die in the coming year, but also the righteous. Nonetheless, this statement maintains that there is justice in the world and that God does mete it out.

Derash

Some of the classic talmudic commentators ask an interesting question: why would the Talmud describe justice in this way when we all know that good happens to the wicked and bad to the righteous? In answering, some have redefined the terms of the Talmud, making it hard to be deemed wicked and easier to be called righteous—by having done even one good deed in a lifetime or by tipping the balance between good and bad with just one more good deed.[87] One of the more interesting explanations is found in the Tosafot.[88] These commentaries claim that when the Talmud says "life" and "death," it is not referring to life and death in this world as we know it. Consequently, although our merits are measured in life, only upon leaving this world does God determine whether we will go directly to a good place in *olam ha-ba* (literally, "the world to come") or go first to purge our sins in *Geihinnom* (a temporary place of suffering; the Jewish concept of a hell).

Making It Personal

We live in a world of injustices: people work hard and with good intentions, yet cannot make a living; people, even babies, are murdered just because of their religion, color, gender, or ethnicity; and uncontrollable events, such as natural disasters, bring death and devastation. Jews are certainly very aware of injustice, as it colors our history. Judaism itself was born out of slaves who escaped from Egypt; it was born from the aliens, the disadvantaged, and the destitute (Exod. 22:20, 23:9). The religion acknowledges that people do not necessarily choose to be in a difficult or precarious situation and that much of life is out of their control.

Despite the injustices seen in both the righteous and the wicked, Judaism continues to assert that there is justice and there is a Judge. If not, there would be nothing ultimately meaningful in what we do, a situation that is contradictory to what every emotion and every cell in our bodies tell us—"we care."

We do not merely follow the commandments not to steal or murder because there could be legal sanctions; the statement to "love your fellow as yourself" (Lev. 19:18) does not resonate simply because it is in the Torah. These beliefs touch us because they are affirmations embedded within the structure of the entire universe, including our own spiritual make-up. Judaism provides different understandings as to why evil happens, but just as it says "Don't murder," it unequivocally declares that justice exists.

---

* Rabbi Yochanan (circa 250–290 C.E.) was one of the leading sages of the Jerusalem Talmud and head of the academy in Tiberias. Rabbi Kruspedai is a lesser-known talmudic personality of whom little is known. Some of the Rabbis in the Talmud are mentioned hundreds of times, and we are able to learn a considerable amount about them, whereas others are mentioned only a handful of times. It is quite common in the Talmud for Rabbis to cite the name of the source of their teaching, which lends it more credence.

THE THREE LEVELS
Peshat: simple, literal meaning
Derash: historical, Rabbinic inquiry
Making It Personal:
contemporary analysis and application

Remembrance and Compassion

Rabbi Eliezer* says: "The world was created in Tishrei.... On Rosh Hashanah, Sarah, Rachel, and Hannah were remembered. On Rosh Hashanah, Joseph left prison. On Rosh Hashanah, slavery ended for our forefathers in Egypt."

—B. Talmud, Rosh Hashanah 10b–11a

Peshat

Rabbi Eliezer is posing the argument against his talmudic counterpart Rabbi Joshua. He argues that the world was created in the month of Tishrei. Rabbi Joshua claims that the world was created in Nisan because the Torah says that Nisan is the first month (Exod. 12:2). Rabbi Eliezer is using the historical events of the Torah as proofs for his argument, thus associating the beginning of the world with significant beginnings of the Jewish people. With support from later commentators and the Jerusalem Talmud (*Rosh Hashanah* 8a), the tradition ultimately sides with Rabbi Eliezer.

Rabbi Nissim ben Reuven, "The Ran," a medieval talmudic expert born in Barcelona, notes that when rabbis Eliezer and Joshua are speaking of Creation, they are speaking of the sixth day.[60] Why is the sixth day the epicenter of Creation? Because the sixth day marks the most important act of Creation—the day humans were created. Thus, for the sages, humankind began on the 1st of Tishrei.

Derash

The Day of Remembrance, one of the several names for Rosh Hashanah, signifies that God remembers, visits, and observes us on Rosh Hashanah. This interpretation is clear according to the Talmud, which mentions some very important moments in the Torah when God remembered and visited our ancestors. In particular, it refers to the barrenness of three women: Sarah (whose story, it so happens, is in the Rosh Hashanah Torah reading), Rachel, and Hannah (whose story is in the Rosh Hashanah haftarah).

When the Talmud is discussing Sarah, Rachel, and Hannah, it is referring to the inability of each woman to conceive a child. It says that Rosh Hashanah was the day on which God observed each of their situations and enabled each to conceive.[61] This claim is based on the use of two words for "remember"—*pakad* (literally, "took note of") and *zachar*—that appear in these encounters in the Bible. In Genesis (21:1–2), it says that God remembered Sarah—*pakad et Sarah*—and she conceived and bore a son (Isaac). Later in Genesis (30:22–23), it says God remembered Rachel—*va-yizkor elohim et Rachel*—and she too became pregnant with a son (Joseph). Hannah is remembered by God in two places in the Bible (I Samuel 1:19–20; 2:21), using, in sequence, both words for remember. In the first reference she then bore a son (Samuel), and in the second, she bore three more sons and two daughters.

Finally, although the Talmud does not specifically address this idea, the significance of the same verb of remembrance, *zachar,* also applies to the story of Joseph and to the story of the Israelite slaves in Egypt. It is used repeatedly in chapter 40 of Genesis.[62] Joseph asks his cell mate, the chief cupbearer, to remember him when he is pardoned by Pharaoh. When the cupbearer does remember him, Joseph is freed from prison to become the Pharaoh's vizier, thus forever changing Jewish history. In the time of Moses, when the Jews, as Egyptian slaves, cried out to God, God remembered the covenant with Abraham, Isaac, and Jacob. In that remembrance, God was swayed to take notice of the Israelites (Exod. 2:24) and eventually free them.

Making It Personal

One of the aspects of Judaism that distinguishes it from Christianity and other religions is the Jewish conception of God as invisible and, ultimately, indescribable. This view evokes a particular anxiety and doubt at times, especially at times of suffering. Because we cannot picture God nor know where God is exactly, some people wonder if God is there at all. In fact, the Torah reading for the second day of Rosh Hashanah, which tells the painful story of Abraham nearly sacrificing his son, strikes at such core challenges of faith.

That being said, Judaism still deeply affirms God's presence in the realm of the invisible and indescribable. The Torah, the sages of the Talmud, and the liturgy repeatedly tell us that God remembers. From this perspective, Judaism is teaching us two piercing lessons. The first lesson is that we are never alone; the invisibility of God is the illusion. If we doubt what we see with our eyes, then it is imperative to search our hearts; because it is in our hearts that we discover what we truly care about. We come to realize that the heart is the place where God dwells. The second lesson is that just as God remembers and takes notice, so too should we remember and take notice. Human beings are God's most special and unique creation. We must remember this about ourselves and each other—especially remembering those who are the most invisible in our society, such as the poor, the less able, and the ill; because God is certainly found within them.[63]

---

* Rabbi Eliezer ben Hurkanus of 2nd–3rd century is one of the most quoted sages in the Talmud. He is often quoted along with his contemporary Rabbi Joshua ben Chananyah, mentioned in the *peshat* commentary. Both were students of Rabbi Yochanan ben Zakkai who established Yavneh as the Rabbinic center after the destruction of the Second Temple in 70 CE. They often have opposing opinions.

THE THREE LEVELS
Peshat: simple, literal meaning
Derash: historical, Rabbinic inquiry
Making It Personal:
contemporary analysis and application

The Shofar and Prayer from the Heart

[The Mishnah states.]* The length of the *teruah* [note of the shofar blowing] is like three *yevavot* [generally understood as "whimpers"].

[The Gemara notes a contradiction.] But it was also taught: The length of the *teruah* is like three broken segments (each longer than a whimper), *shevarim.*

[The Gemara answers.]** Abaye said: "In this matter the two certainly disagree.... [The latter] teacher holds that *[teruah]* is like one long sigh, and the other teacher [from the Mishnah] holds that *teruah* is like a series of short piercing cries."

—B. Talmud, *Rosh Hashanah* 33b

Peshat

The shofar is a central symbol for the Jewish people. A large measure of its centrality lies in its use on Rosh Hashanah and Yom Kippur. This piece of Talmud assumes the two most significant reasons why the shofar is blown. First, the Torah commands it (Num. 29:1 and Lev. 25:9); and second, the shofar blowing patently connects our prayer experience to the Rosh Hashanah Torah reading, which tells of Abraham's test of faith. He was willing to sacrifice his own son, until God sent a ram to be used instead.

The end of the text suggests that the actual sound of the shofar, rather than being whimpers, should be similar to the sound of human moans, sighs, and shrieks.

Derash

Rabbis and sages have suggested that people who hear the shofar with proper intent and concentration gain a tremendous spiritual uplift. Of course, the shofar is meant to be sounded during prayer—it is, in fact, a part of prayer. In this context, the great teachers of Judaism have created layers of meaning connected with hearing the shofar as prayer. Most notable among these philosophers are the medieval rabbis Sa'adia Ga'on (born Sa'adia ben Joseph) and Maimonides.

In his 10 reasons why the Torah commands the Jews to blow the shofar, Sa'adia says the seventh reason is to make the listener feel fearful and humbled.[64] Anyone who has been present at the moment when the shofar breaks through silence, understands just how raw and unsettling it sounds. The shofar is not like a trumpet, nor a clarinet, rather its sound awakens something visceral within us. As Maimonides says, "[The] blowing of the ram's horn … is an allusion, as if to say 'Awake, O you sleepers … search your deeds … remember your Creator.'"[65]

Making It Personal

Jewish prayer has two components: *keva,* which is fixed form and liturgy, and *kavanah,* which is focus, feeling, and concentration. The most important component of these two aspects of Jewish prayer originates with the story of Hannah in the Rosh Hashanah haftarah (I Samuel 1). In that story, Hannah represents the desired paradigm because even when she prays to God with her lips moving but a voice we cannot hear, her prayer is of the heart. In other words, what is in the heart is the most important aspect of prayer; the *keva* simply serves as a facilitator for the heart.

The Hasidim understand this notion well, as they are famous for their singing, especially the wordless songs and prayers, *nigunim.* The great 19th-century Hasidic commentary *Sefat Emet* (Language of Truth), makes a beautiful association between wordless prayer and the shofar. It teaches that the shofar's sound expresses the innate emotions embedded deep in every Jewish heart. Furthermore, by hearing the shofar, we can access these emotions, reaching down to our very core, uniting us with God.[66]

---

* The Mishnah is the first compilation of the Oral Law, relayed by word of mouth from generation to generation. It was written down after the destruction of the Second Temple, when the Jews were exiled to live among other nations. Most scholars attribute its compilation to Rabbi Yehudah Ha-Nasi (Rabbi Judah the Patriarch, who lived in Judea under control of the Roman Empire); and they date its final editing to circa 200 C.E. The Gemara is the discussion of and commentary on the laws of the Mishnah by the Rabbinic sages of the 2nd through 5th centuries C.E., who are known as *amoraim* (literally, "explainers"), in contrast to the *tannaim* (literally, "teachers"), who are quoted in the Mishnah. The Talmud often begins its comments by repeating a statement from the Mishnah. The Gemara then either elaborates or discusses problems noted in that statement. In this case, the Gemara notes an inherent contradiction, namely that the sound of the *teruah* note of the shofar is described similarly to the *shevarim* note.

** The Gemara resolves the noted contradiction with a clarifying remark from Abaye, the 3rd–4th century Babylonian sage. Abaye limits the description of the sound of the *teruah* note, distinguishing it from the *shevarim.*

Rosh Hashanah

Significance of the Holiday: Some Modern Perspectives

From Obscurity to Prominence

by Reuven Hammer

It is paradoxical that the holiday that has become of such prime importance in the Jewish religious year, Rosh Hashanah, is nowhere mentioned by name in the Torah. As a matter of fact that name occurs only once in the entire Bible, and there it refers to the 10th of Tishrei—Yom Kippur (Ezek. 40:1)! Instead we are given the date—"the seventh month, the first day of the month," the instruction that this is a "sacred occasion" upon which "you shall not work at your occupations," when we are to bring "an offering by fire" and are to "commemorate it with loud blasts" (*see* Lev. 23:24–25 and Num. 29:1–2). It is not a pilgrim festival when Israelites are to visit the Temple, nor does it commemorate any historical event in the life of the people Israel. Thus we have a sacred day with no name and seemingly no purpose.

One clue to this mystery is the fact that unlike the festivals of Pesach and Sukkot, it is not held upon the full moon, but upon the new moon. We know that every new moon was a holy day in ancient Israel, probably celebrated with even greater sanctity than is Rosh Hodesh today. Since seven is a sacred number in Judaism and since the seventh month is also the beginning of the second half of the tally of months, it seems reasonable that it would be commemorated in a special way and become holier than the other new moons.

The sounding of the horn on that day is another clue as to the origins of the festival. In several psalms we have the combination of the sounding of the horn and the proclamation of God as the sovereign ruler of the world. For example, "With trumpets and the blast of the horn raise a shout before the LORD, the King" (Ps. 98:6). *See also* Psalms 95:1,2 and 100:1 where the *teruah*—the sound of the shofar—is mentioned. This has led many scholars to speculate that in ancient Israel this day was a popular celebration of God's completion of the Creation and assumption of the celestial throne and that Psalms 95 to 100 (known as "coronation psalms") were written for that occasion. If so, this would be a parallel to ancient new year festivals of other Near Eastern religions, commemorating the ascension of the chief god to the throne, having overthrown all rival deities, an assertion also accompanied by the sounding of horns, as coronations of sovereigns are to this day. The fact that this is not mentioned in the Torah could be attributed to a fear of calling attention to the pagan origins of the ritual. In any case, this meaning was certainly ascribed to Rosh Hashanah in Rabbinic times.

During the period of the Second Temple, we know that Rosh Hashanah was still observed as a sacred occasion (*see* Neh. 8:1–3). But if the writings of Philo of Alexandria (1st century B.C.E.) are to be believed, it was not yet known as Rosh Hashanah. He calls it the great "Trumpet Feast" and connects it with the sounding of the horn at Mount Sinai at the time of Revelation (Special Laws 2:188–192).

At some time either prior to the destruction of the Temple in 70 C.E. or thereafter, major changes were made in the celebration of the 1st of Tishrei and the name Rosh Hashanah (literally, "Head of the Year") was applied to that day. These changes are referred to in the Mishnah (edited circa 200 C.E.) and other Rabbinic literature. Several dates for "new years"—i.e., times for beginning the counting of cycles of the year—were instituted and the 1st of Tishrei was considered "the beginning of the year for years." (Mishnah, *Rosh Hashanah* 1:1). More importantly, times were designated for God's judgment on various things, and that date, now commonly called Rosh Hashanah, was the time for the judgment of human beings "when all human beings pass before Him as troops." (Mishnah, *Rosh Hashanah* 1:2).

The Rabbis also established the basic outline of the liturgy for that day, determining three basic themes: sovereignty, remembrance, and *shofarot*. The first has its roots in the ancient idea of God completing the work of Creation and reigning over the world. The second alludes to God's assessment of the worthiness of individuals to be "remembered" by God in that He will fulfill His promises to them and reward them. The third is a reference to the sounding of the horn and in Rabbinic times was specifically connected to the story of the Binding of Isaac, when a ram was caught in the thicket by its horns (Gen. 22:13) and subsequently sacrificed in place of Isaac. The rabbis retold this story and had God tell Abraham that if his children would sound the ram's horn on Rosh Hashanah, God would remember His word to Abraham at the Binding of Isaac and forgive their transgressions.

At the same time, a connection was made between Rosh Hashanah and Yom Kippur, something that had not existed during biblical times. Since Yom Kippur was a time for confession and atonement for sins, this theme was extended backward to Rosh

Hashanah so that, in the words of the Tosefta [a collection of teachings by the Rabbinic sages] (circa 300 C.E.), "All are judged on Rosh Hashanah and the verdict is issued on Yom Kippur" (Tosefta, *Rosh Hashanah* 1:13). Thus the entity known as the *Yamim Noraim*—the "Days of Awe" and the "Ten Days of Repentance" came into existence.

Through these developments the obscure holy day of the first day of the seventh month developed into the beginning of the holiest season of the Jewish year, a truly religious holiday, in the fullest sense of the term, that deals with the deepest and most human themes of any of our holy days—the nature of human beings, the meaning of sin and transgression, the attainment of forgiveness, the very meaning and significance of human life and our existence on this planet. It is a celebration in which we recognize the role of God in the world, but in which we concentrate not upon any event in God's "life" (such a thing is impossible in Judaism) but in the interaction between God and human beings—all human beings. As such it is both a day for celebration—a true holiday—and also a day for introspection and contemplation leading to a renewal of life—a true holy day.

Remembering Creation

by Paul Steinberg

> You remember the act of Creation and are mindful of all that was formed from the beginning. All that is concealed is revealed before You, as well as the multitude of secrets from the beginning of time.... All is revealed and known to You, LORD our God, the One who foresees and gazes to the end of all generations. For You appointed this time of memorial when every spirit and soul shall be visited; to remember Your work of Creation and the vast and infinite creatures. From the beginning, before all, You made it known and revealed that this is the day of the beginning of Your works, a memorial to the first day.
>
> —From the Rosh Hashanah liturgy, *Musaf* service,
> introduction to the *Zikhronot* verses[69]

Some words are untranslatable. Or rather, some words, although the same in surface meaning, do not carry the same root and etymology. Thus they present a different connotation when spoken or heard. Take the example of the English word "universe." From the Latin roots *unus*, meaning "one," and *versum*, meaning "turn," the word "universe" means something like "that which turns into one" or "that which turns into whole."

Now consider the Hebrew word for universe, *olam*. It comes from the root *alam*, which means "to conceal." *Olam* then means something akin to "that which conceals." Therefore, with the very word for universe—our concept of "all there is"—Judaism evokes mystery and awe, suggesting a hidden reality beyond all that appears to be. Rosh Hashanah is the day, the "time of memorial" as the *machzor* puts it, for us to consider the act of Creation and that which is concealed.

On Rosh Hashanah, the birthday celebration of the world, we are called back to the foundations of time and space, in order to rediscover that there is an *Adon Olam*, a Master of the World or Hidden Master, planning and unfolding all Creation. Judaism as a whole, in its purest form, is a celebration of Creation, a joyous affirmation of the universe, with Rosh Hashanah playing the most pivotal role. On this birthday, we draw the Holy One out and, together, recount our beginning—for each New Year we are to sense God both in physical presence and in thought, as the psalmist sings, "When I behold Your heavens, the work of Your fingers ... O LORD, our LORD, how majestic is Your name throughout the earth!" (Ps. 8:4,10).

What exactly do we find when we recount our beginning? What is it that we celebrate about the beginning of all beginnings? Surely we rejoice in life and all it offers; certainly we delight in nature and the oneness of the universe, as the English denotes. On Rosh Hashanah, however, we are summoned to witness the complexity of this oneness, that it is a universe of splendor, grandeur, and awesomeness—it is God's universe. We are to look beyond the galaxy, the Earth, the seas, evolving biological life, and everything that is measurable by scientific method and affirm that there is One who was there before all existed, a LORD who was, who is, and who always will be. As a loving bride and groom might renew their vows on their wedding anniversary, to recall how and why they are united forever, so God and the people Israel remember on Rosh Hashanah the true basis of their covenantal foundation. We awaken our memory with the shofar blast and peel back the garments of the universe that simultaneously clothe and reflect God's foundational light.[70]

Consequently, Rosh Hashanah is also known as the Day of Remembrance (Yom ha-Zikaron). And, even though it is a day to rewind time, by its end we are to be inspired to look forward and "sing to the LORD a new song" (Ps. 96:1). After all, remembering is the primary Jewish action—we are never to forget. Remembering and hearkening back to our beginnings reinvigorates us with a new life, a new time, and a new song.

As the late Israeli scholar Yeshayahu Leibowitz points out, we learn of the greatest principle of Jewish faith when the Torah itself remembers the beginning—the moment when God created the heavens and the earth:

> The world is not God—as opposed to any other outlook which exists in human culture: as opposed to paganism, whose gods belong to the world and are to be found in the world; as opposed to Christianity, which at first blush received from Judaism the concept of a transcendent God, but immediately attired it in human form which existed in the world; and as opposed to atheism for which the world is the totality of being, or, in other words, that it is God.... Rather [Judaism asserts that] God is prime, and the world (including man in it) is subordinate.
>
> —*Accepting the Yoke of Heaven,* 14–15

This great principle of Jewish faith adds something new to the significance of Rosh Hashanah. By remembering our existential beginning and recognizing that "God is prime," we are to accept our subordination to God. Moreover, subordination brings duty and dedication. Our duty is to better ourselves through self-evaluation and judgment—a judgment that can only come down from the vantage point of God, judge of the universe. Therefore, Rosh Hashanah is known by yet another name, the Day of Judgment (Yom ha-Din).

Because we are part of God's universe, of God's foundational light—with each of us a thread woven into the garments of creation—we are obligated to contribute and dedicate ourselves to God's loving will. On Rosh Hashanah, we question whether we have fulfilled this obligation. Yet we remain hopeful that we will prove to be acceptable in the eyes of our parent, because we know that our contemplation leads to comfort, balance, sweetness, and renewed life.

On Rosh Hashanah, known too as the Day of the Sounding (Yom Teruah), we are awakened to the mysterious timelessness of the universe and our souls. Such an awakening brings great faith and inspiration, but none of us can remember the foundational relationship between ourselves and our Creator without acknowledging that we can do better.

A Clarion Call to Fixing the World

by Elliot N. Dorff

Rosh Hashanah—the beginning of the year. What difference does it make that one day falls into a year with a different number than the previous day? Is that not just a matter of an arbitrary convention that we human beings have devised to count time?

In some ways it is. It would be one thing if either the American secular New Year (January 1) or the Jewish new year (Tishrei 1) fell at a time when something was changing in nature—the solstice or equinox, for example—but neither one of them falls on such a date. So the significance of each of these new years is simply that the American and Jewish societies have decided to count time in that way.

This, however, neglects the fact that both the American and Jewish societies have invested meaning into these events. For Americans, New Year represents, for most people, not only the time when people have to remember to write the new number in their correspondence and on their checks, but also when the new tax year begins. It is also, in American culture, a time in which we celebrate having made it to the new year with parties, football games, and a national holiday, and Americans typically make resolutions about how they are going to change things in the year to come. It all has a bit of a frivolous air to it—except for taxes!—but it also is decidedly upbeat as Americans, in a style typical of us as a people, optimistically look forward to a better year to come. As such, the rites of January 1st have become a permanent part of American culture, rites that it would be strange for an American completely to ignore.

The Jewish tradition has invested even more meaning into its new year. This day, according to the liturgy, marks the beginning of Creation: "Today the world was born *(ha-yom harat olam).*" It is therefore nothing less than a celebration of life itself, marked by the eating of something new (or at least something that one has not eaten for awhile), buying new clothes for the occasion, and, as in the American case, a holiday—actually, a holy day—during which one is not supposed to work but rather gather with family and friends both at home and in the synagogue.

But that is as far as the analogy between the American and the Jewish new years goes, for there is a world of difference between a holiday and a holy day. As Rabbi Sidney Greenberg put it in a reading he created for Rosh Hashanah:

> On holidays we run away from duties. On holy days we face up to them. On holidays we let ourselves go. On holy days we try to bring ourselves under control. On holidays we try to empty our minds. On holy days we attempt to replenish our spirits. On holidays we reach out for the things we want. On holy days we reach up for the things we need.
>
> Holidays bring a change of scene. Holy days bring a change of heart.

Rosh Hashanah is certainly joyous; new clothes, new foods, *Kiddush* over wine, and time with family and friends are all markers of the fact that it is indeed a *yom tov* (literally, "a good day"). But unlike all the other biblical festivals throughout the year, Rosh Hashanah has a special designation: it is Yom ha-Zikaron, the Day of Remembrance. On it we are supposed to remember what we have done in the past year, and we believe that God does as well. That remembrance is not just for the sake of nostalgia; it is rather for the sake of taking account of what we have done—the good, the bad, and the morally neutral; the effective, the ineffective, and the practically neutral—as part of our charting our course for the year to come. If this Rosh Hashanah resembles a process of strategic planning, we need to take account of what has been in order to make it possible for us to improve what will be.

Unlike a process of strategic planning, though, Rosh Hashanah is not solely for our own benefit, to be done if and only if we want to engage in such reflective thought or think it will help us achieve our personal or corporate goals in some way. In fact, the kind of personal and communal accounting and planning that Rosh Hashanah demands of us is probably what few, if any, of us would choose on our own—certainly not with this degree of intensity and in this public, communal way. But we have no choice in the matter because God calls us to do this each and every year. That is the message of the central blessings of the *Musaf* prayer on Rosh Hashanah, *Malkhuyot, Zikhronot,* and *Shofarot. Malkhuyot,* the verses pronouncing God as sovereign, inform us that this process of personal and communal reflection on the past and planning for the future is a demand from on high, one that we cannot ignore or avoid. *Zikhronot,* the verses reminding us that God pays attention to us and remembers what we have done, tell us that we cannot cover up what we have done or pretend that it does not matter; on the contrary, life itself matters, and as individuals, families, and communities we have to hold ourselves accountable for what we have done and what we will do in the year to come. Finally, *Shofarot,* the verses recalling the times when the blasts of the shofar were heard, use those blasts to wake us up to the challenge of making things better in our own personal lives, in the life of the Jewish community, and for all of humanity.

Thus very much unlike January 1st, Rosh Hashanah has a message of responsibility for what we have done and what we must now do. It is a loud clarion call to engage in *tikkun olam,* fixing the world—the world of our own individual lives, the world of our family, the world of the Jewish community, the world of humanity as a whole, the physical world (the environment), and, ultimately, the world of our relationships with God. And the fixing that we must attend to affects every part of our lives and demands many different things of us, including deepening our own spiritual lives, strengthening our relationships with the members of our family and friends, enriching the Jewish character of our lives, providing a real safety net for those in need, inventing new ways to prevent and cure disease and to give access to health care to those who currently do not have it, improving interfaith relations, and so on and so on. The very impossibility of achieving all these goals requires that we mark Rosh Hashanah each year in the synagogue and in our homes to reinvigorate our commitment to do what we can in this central Jewish agenda to make this a better world.

May both the joy of the new beginnings marked by Rosh Hashanah and the responsibility it proclaims to fix all of those worlds of which we are a part be our blessings for the new year. That is what we mean when we say to each other not just "Happy New Year," but "*Shanah tovah,*" "May you have a *good* new year."

The Days of Awe and Israel

by Miriyam Glazer

> For the land you are entering to inherit is not like the land of Egypt from which you have come, where, after sowing your seed, you irrigated it…, like a vegetable garden.… The land is a land of hills and valleys, watered by the rains of heaven … the eyes of the LORD your God are upon it from the year's beginning to the year's end.… If you heed My commands … to love the LORD your God and to worship God with all your heart and with all your being, I will give the rain of your land in its season, early rains and late, and you shall gather in your grain and your wine and your oil … you shall eat and be sated.
>
> —Deut. 11:10–14

> The world was created in Tishrei.
>
> —B. Talmud, *Rosh Hashanah* 10b

From Egypt, whose agricultural plenty was due to the great irrigation canals of the Nile Delta, the ancient Israelites traveled through the desert of Sinai into a land with a much more complex ecosystem. Despite its "streams, springs, and underground waters" (Deut. 8:7), *Eretz Yisra'el* was in biblical times just what it is today: a land of "hills and valleys" whose fertility was utterly dependent upon the "rains of heaven" pouring down "in its season." No wonder, then, that a talmudic sage taught that "a day of rain is as great as the day on which heaven and earth were created"; another, that "a day of rain is as momentous as the ingathering of the exiles" (B. Talmud, *Ta'anit* 7b, 8b). Without "rain in its season" the land would suffer drought, crops fail, and the people perish.

But "rain does not fall unless the sins of Israel have been forgiven," the sages also teach (B. Talmud, *Ta'anit* 7b). In midsummer, just around the time of the festival of Tu b'Av (15th of Av), as the sun's strength begins to weaken, dew and moisture so increase that, from that day on, in ancient Israel, no wood for the temple altar could be cut. At the same time, all over the country, white squill flowers burst out in blossom, and the olives begin to fill with oil. The very air is filled with promise.

The month of Av, then Elul, then the fall begins with the month of Tishrei. An ancient farmer's calendar, unearthed at Tel Gezer, tells us that just about now there are two months of harvesting followed by two months of planting. For the coming of fall heralds the new agricultural year, when the world itself, like the land and its produce, was not only first created, but is continually created anew. "How do we know that the world was created in Tishrei?" asks Rabbi Eliezer. Because, he answers, "And God said: 'Let the land be covered with vegetation ... [and] fruit trees.' Which month is it in which the land is filled with vegetation and the tree is laden with fruits? You must say, this is Tishrei. And that period was the rainy season, and rains fell and plants came forth, as it is stated, 'and a mist arose from the earth'" (B. Talmud, *Rosh Hashanah* 11a). The aggadic tradition intensifies the sense of fertility associated with this time by teaching that it was in Tishrei that the Patriarchs were born, and the time it was decreed that both Sarah and Hannah would bear children.

But each year, as Tishrei arrives, the "Day of the Sounding of the Shofar," the farmers and the people who depended upon them couldn't help but feel filigrees of trepidation. For the crops, the whole food supply depends upon rain. Will God send rain this coming season? Will the nation of Israel be worthy of rain? Thus the sages worry: just as rain falls for the sake of those who are "trustworthy in business," so *lashon ha-ra,* speaking evilly of another; or being brazen, or stealing, or neglecting

Torah study, cause rain to be withheld. Nor is a person's prayer accepted "unless he puts his heart in his hands" (B. Talmud, *Ta'anit* 7b, 8a). Thus, too, the prayer of the High Priest on Yom Kippur: "May it be your will ... that this year be a year when prices are low, a year of plenty ... a year of rain ... and that your people Israel may not need one another's help ... and that they do not rise to rule over one another" (J. Talmud, *Yoma* 5).

For the ancient Israelites, so for us today. In our day, environmentalists and meteorologists have made us well aware of the intricate relationship between how we live our lives and the state of the earth we live on—whether we are rapacious in our treatment of the land, or whether we act as stewards of the Holy One on this good earth. Rosh Hashanah and Yom Kippur—the time when those white squill flowers begin to fade, and the olives of midsummer begin to be harvested, is the time our tradition gives us to make our full account.

The Shofar: A Cry into Eternity

by Will Berkovitz

The shofar is the mortar binding the High Holy Days together. In a tradition known for its intellectual history no other ritual stirs such a visceral response as the primordial wail of the shofar. According to the Midrash, the blowing of the shofar has its roots with the Binding of Isaac, when God told Abraham that it would be the sound of the ram's horn that will stir God's compassion toward the Jewish people on Rosh Hashanah.

The ram that served as Isaac's substitute in the story retold every Rosh Hashanah is said to have been created during twilight on the sixth day of Creation and plays a central role in the history of the Jewish people. According to the sage Rabbi Chanina ben Dosa, its ash was the foundation for the altar within the temple hall; its sinews provided the 10 strings for David's harp; and each of its two horns were made into a shofar. During the birth of the Jewish people on Mount Sinai, God blew the left horn, and at the end of days God will blow the right and larger horn in order to usher in the Messiah (*Pirke de-Rebbe Eliezer* 31). The epic story of the Jewish people is held in place by the tension of these two events—one resounding from our past and the other calling out to us from our future.

Rosh Hashanah is a remembrance of God's coronation at the beginning of Creation, and it is the shofar that declares God's enthronement. It is at once a time of joy and trepidation. Reuven Hammer offers that the shofar "conjures feelings of ancient times and sacred beginnings, and one's place in the universe and one's relationship to the past, to Judaism, and to God."

Perhaps this is the reason we are not obligated to blow the shofar but we are commanded to hear it. Hearing the shofar helps us orient ourselves on the map of eternity. This may be the reason the sages make clear no casual listening will do. It is a hearing that requires attention, a hearing that demands action and response. It is an alarm clock for the soul set to start sounding a month before the High Holy Days, every morning during the month of Elul (except Shabbat and Erev Rosh Hashanah) and concluding after *Ne'ilah* when the gates of heaven close on Yom Kippur.

According to Maimonides, the shofar declares, "Wake up from your slumber and examine your deeds, return and remember your Creator." The cry of the shofar carries within it the realization that God is both sovereign and judge. We are being stirred to attention and a *cheshbon nefesh,* an accounting of the soul. The shofar asks us to examine the ways we have lived in the past year, questioning: Have we been awake to the suffering around us or indifferent toward it? Have we striven to be our highest selves or caved in to pettiness?

Hearing the voice of the shofar is a challenge to look within our souls. It is a call to godliness, to redouble our efforts toward humility, justice, and mercy and recall that the Day of Judgment has arrived.

The actual sound of the shofar has three distinct voices, known as *teki'ot.* Like an echo that returns in the caller's voice, the shofar asks a different question to everyone who hears it and requires a different response. At once, it resounds as a fierce ancient battle cry and as the mournful sobbing of a broken soul. The voice of the shofar is impossible to ignore. It resonates in the deepest, eternal parts of the soul—accusing, demanding, questioning, imploring.

The first call known as *tekiah* is a sharp unbroken wail that ends abruptly. The second is *shevarim,* a staccato series of three broken blasts that when combined equal the duration of one *tekiah.* And the final cry is called *teruah* a quick succession of nine notes ringing out like an alarm. The sound of *teruah* is equated with shattering. And according to the Zohar it is this shattering that is at the essence of returning to God's path. The shattering call of *teruah* is the core of *teshuvah.*

The pattern of the blasts is: *tekiah—shevarim teruah—tekiah; tekiah—shevarim—tekiah; tekiah—teruah—tekiah.* As if to punctuate the shofar service and the hopeful theme of redemption, the final *tekiah* is lengthened into a bold heroic blast. Known as the *tekiah gedolah,* great blast, it recalls the verse from Isaiah, "And on that day a great ram's horn shall be sounded" (27:13).

Calling out from a dusty mountaintop across the millennia, the shofar reaches out to us, elevating us to the peak of Sinai. There, it offers us a glimpse of our ideal self, not as individuals locked in a moment of history, but as the Jewish people standing with God above eternity—a nation of priests and priestesses. A Holy people.

Rosh Hashanah Alternative Meditations

Singing Creation into Being

by Shlomo Carlebach[71]

When God created the world God said, "Let there be light. Let there be fishes. Let there be people."

Do you think when God was saying this God spoke in a harsh voice?

... The truth is God didn't even say it. God sang it. God sang the whole creation into being.

Reb Nachman says, whenever you talk without singing, you are disconnecting yourself from the creation of the world.

Facing the Music: A High Holyday Meditation

by Shefa Gold[72]

This is the time to know our own song, to allow the echoes of our thoughts, words, and actions of this past year to ripple through us, awakening knowledge and power for the song that is yet to be born.

In "facing the music," I hear the hesitant strains of my own broken dreams. I wince at the dissonance between intention and deed, between ecstatic ideal and sober reality. I listen carefully to tone and timber. Where have I been half-hearted in my loving? I listen for harmony and counterpoint. Where have I created discord with my argument or complaint? And I notice pitch. How carefully have I listened? As I follow the line of my own melody, I ask, "Where is this leading me?"

This song of my life makes a deep groove, and the record will play over and over and over again. The mind weaves an endless loop. repeating mistakes, like bad jingles or notes that fall forever flat without lilt or vigor.

Yet on these High Holy Days we are given a reprieve from the oppression of habit. We are give the chance to "annul the severity of the judgment," which means to stop the song, to hear its complex rhythms and beauty, and to begin to sing again, altering the pattern of this song so that its melody will birth a new singer.

And how is this miracle accomplished? We are given a score consisting of three components. Tefilah, Teshuvah and Tzedakah [Prayer, Return/Repentance, and Righteousness/Return] are the essential instruments necessary for the re-creation of the song, which is the flow of life, ...

This is the time when "[t]he great Shofar is sounded,"... bringing each of these instruments to life. "[a]nd a still small voice is heard,"... calling forth new life, hope, promise and vision ....

The time has come to face the music. At Mount Sinai we heard the lightning and saw the thunder. Facing the music is like seeing the thunder. It is stepping back from the narrowness of normal sense perception that merely sees sights and hears sounds. Revelation happens beyond the confines of "normal" mind, which tries to figure it out and make sense ... and may the music we find coming through us in the year ahead be an inspiration for all.

Hagar and Sarah, Sarah and Hagar

by Rosellen Brown[73]

> Everyone, real or imagined, deserves the open destiny of life.
>
> —*A Conversation with My Father,* Grace Paley

Now Sarai, Abram's wife, bore him no children; and she had a handmaid, an Egyptian, whose name was Hagar. And Sarai said unto Abram: "Behold now, the LORD hath restrained me from bearing; go in, I pray thee, unto my handmaid; it may be that I shall be built up through her." And Abram hearkened to the voice of Sarai. And Sarai, Abram's wife, took Hagar the Egyptian, her handmaid, after Abram had dwelt 10 years in the land of Canaan, and gave her to Abram her husband to be his wife. And he went in unto Hagar, and she conceived; and when she saw that she had conceived, her mistress was overcome with sorrow admixed with joy, for her husband's house was thereby strengthened without her.

Now Sarai would not make free with her pain, but Hagar came before her and said: "How is it with you? Was it not your wish that your house and your husband's house wax with my waxing?" And Sarai wept that her handmaid should supplant her in the eyes of her husband and become the mother of generations by the hand of the Lord. But Hagar embraced her mistress and swore loyalty to her house, saying: "You also shall be as a mother to this child."

And the angel of the Lord, seeing that Hagar dealt kindly with her mistress, said unto her, "I will greatly multiply thy seed that it shall be numbered for multitude." And the angel of the Lord said unto her: "Behold thou art with child, and shalt bear a son; and thou shalt call his name Ishmael. And he shall be a gentle deer of a man; his hand shall be joined in friendship with every man, and every man's with his; and he shall dwell in the heart of all his brethren." And Hagar invited the empty hand of her mistress to lie upon the round of her flesh, and she labored to bring forth the son of Abram.

And Abram, now Abraham by the grace of the Lord, was ninety years old and nine, when he was circumcised in the flesh of his foreskin. And Ishmael his son was thirteen years old, when he was circumcised in the flesh of his foreskin. And all the men of his house, those born in the house, and those bought with money of a foreigner, were circumcised with him.

And the Lord remembered Sarai, now Sarah, and she conceived, and bore Abraham a son in his old age. And Abraham was a hundred years old, when his son Isaac was born unto him. And Sarah said: "God hath made laughter for me; everyone that heareth will laugh on account of me." And she said, "Who would have said unto Abraham, that Sarah should give children suck? For I have borne him a son in his old age." And the child grew, and was weaned. And Abraham made a great feast on the day that Isaac was weaned. And Sarah saw the son of Hagar the Egyptian, who she had borne unto Abraham with Sarah's blessing, making sport. Wherefore she upbraided Hagar that she did naught to make him heed. And Hagar said once more, as she had said at the time of his birth: "Let him do no thing that is grievous in thy sight. Thou also shalt be as a mother to this child. Go thou and reprove him, and he shall pay heed to thee as to a mother." So Sarah spoke words to Ishmael as if he were of her own making, now speaking hard words, now gentle. And in his trust Ishmael became as the Lord had promised, a man who loved goodness and hated injustice.

And they were supple as he-goats running and sporting together, Isaac and Ishmael. And if one called for help, the other heeded his cry. When this one pulled on his bow, the other held the arrows. Whosoever found favor in the sight of one was loved by both. And it came to pass that a stranger, seeing Isaac, asked after Ishmael, for he was tall and strong, wellfavored of face. The stranger said: "Is this Egyptian not a slave for sale to another man's house? Behold, here is a sack of shekels for his purchase." And Isaac refused him, saying: "Go thou and buy some other soul. This is my brother."

Now Hagar and Sarah had seen the love of Isaac and Ishmael and together they rejoiced, but Abraham favored Isaac, who was the seed of Sarah's fathers and her fathers' fathers. But Sarah rebuked him, saying: "There shall be no peace in our house if thou dividest thy love as a loaf of bread, in unequal portions. Forasmuch as God hath opened our wombs together to thee, neither son shalt thou put above the other. Flesh is flesh and blood blood, and the sinew that binds us one to one is nothing but the breath of life."

And all their days their sons were not divided, but as if under covenant they shared their portion and lived as brothers who stood before but a single mother. And each in time was father to a multitude that lived in harmony according to their wishes, Ishmael and Isaac, the sons of Abraham borne by two stars in the firmament who, in this prayer to what might have been, held them close and loved them equally.

PART 4

Yom Kippur

Is such the fast that I desire, a day for men to starve their bodies?. . .
No, this is the fast I desire: To unlock the fetters of wickedness, and untie the cords of the yoke, To let the oppressed go free; to break off every yoke. It is to share your bread with the hungry, and to take the wretched poor into your home; When you see the naked, to clothe him, and not to ignore your own kin. Then shall your light burst through like the dawn and your healing spring up quickly.

—Isaiah 58:5–8; Yom Kippur haftarah

The Day for Spiritual Second Chances

IN MANY WAYS, Judaism can be described as a religion of distinctions. We distinguish between such things as kosher and *tref* (nonkosher) and between the holiness of Shabbat and the mundaneness of the workweek. After all, the Torah itself begins with a division—the act of Creation that separates lightness from darkness and heaven from earth. Yet, we are told, despite these opposites and distinctions, everything comes from God and God is one. Certainly one of the greatest antitheses, the most difficult to reconcile, is the distinction between good and evil. Is it possible that good and evil can come together as one? Judaism answers this question resoundingly: it is possible, but only on one day and in one way—Yom Kippur.

Although the Torah describes Yom Kippur as a *Shabbat Shabbaton,*[1] ("the Sabbath of Sabbaths"), this does not mean it is the ultimate day of rest. Rather, the description emphasizes the absolute holiness of the day. Yom Kippur and the process of self-renewal require special rituals, customs, and intentions. Most of these—such as fasting, wearing all white, beating the breast, and hearing the stirring melodies of the prayers—are not experienced on any other day. Through these interconnected observances, we find that the meaning of Yom Kippur rests in its role as the last of the *Yamim Noraim* (Days of Awe) and in its ultimate purpose: to clean our spiritual slates and to purge and renew our souls, just as our bodies are being purged by the fast.

The following true story of Franz Rosenzweig (1886–1929), a major Jewish philosopher born in late 19th-century Germany, speaks to the essence and possibilities of Yom Kippur.[1] After wrestling with the meaning of religion, this German philosopher was convinced that Judaism had become nothing but a relic of the past. Rosenzweig therefore decided to convert to Christianity, but to do so like the early Christians—through Judaism and not as a pagan. Thus, as preparation, he would attend one last Yom Kippur service and then make his conversion immediately afterward. Before leaving for the synagogue, Rosenzweig walked dramatically down the stairs of his home, Christian Bible in hand, and said, "Mother, here is everything, here is the truth. There is only one way, Jesus."[2] During that Yom Kippur service, however, something happened to Rosenzweig. He experienced himself standing as an individual before God; he again found life and exhilaration within himself and within his Judaism and reversed his decision to convert, eventually becoming one of the most influential Jewish philosophers of all time.

Thus, the sages tell us, Yom Kippur, the Day of Atonement (or "At-one-ment," as some people have termed it) is a day built into the structure of the universe, wherein we have the opportunity to turn the evil inside of us to good.[3] Through the apology and the self-scrutiny that are necessary for change, we experience Yom Kippur as the great spiritual equalizer.[4] It is the most holy of holy days because it signifies the true definition of what it is to be human, which is to be flawed and imperfect. Therefore, Judaism provides this one extraordinary day: a day to face the self, to return and become whole again. Yom Kippur is a day for second chances, and we all need second chances.

Yom Kippur in the Bible

Mention of Yom Kippur, or *Yom Ha-Kippurim* as it is referred to in the Bible, is found primarily in the Book of Leviticus, the book most concerned with ritual and priestly duties.[5] The reason may be that Yom Kippur is centered on special ritual and on the participation of the *Kohanim,* the Priests who practiced until the time of the destruction of the Second Temple in 70 C.E. Besides the type of sacrifice, which is noted in Numbers[6] rather than Leviticus, there are four basic elements in the biblical Yom Kippur. First, it is a day of self-denial, which is interpreted to mean fasting. The Rabbinic sages also add more areas of self-denial, such as abstaining from bathing and from sexual relations.[7] Second, no one is to work, as the day is a "sacred occasion."[8] In fact, the Torah is so emphatic about this requirement, it declares anyone who works on that day to be cut off spiritually from the community (a punishment called *karet*), which is compared in severity to the death penalty. Third, certain rituals must be performed to make expiation and become purified.[9] This particular biblical concept grew into what we now understand as asking forgiveness and confessing sins. Finally, there is the special role of the Holy of Holies *(Kodesh Ha-Kodashim)*—the inner sanctum where the chest holding the Ten Commandments was kept. It was the heart of the Tabernacle or *mishkan* (literally, "place of dwelling")—the portable sanctuary used in the wilderness after the Exodus; later it was placed in the Temple in Jerusalem. The Holy of Holies was entered only on Yom Kippur and only by the *Kohen Gadol* (High Priest).[10]

The Torah reading for Yom Kippur morning, found in chapter 16 of Leviticus, is not easy to follow. It describes the procedure for this dramatic Yom Kippur ritual and specifies the duties of Aaron, the *Kohen Gadol,* in the Tabernacle.[11] The ritual is so awesome and complex that there are seven chapters of Rabbinic literature dedicated to elucidating the approximately 42-step process.[12] The practice involves an interweaving of five ritual-bath immersions, four clothing changes of golden and white vestments, three slaughterings of animals, five sprinklings of the blood of the animals, two personal confessions and one confession for the community, as well as several incidents each of burning incense, presenting meal offerings, and burning entrails.[13] To thoroughly appreciate the ritual of the *Kohen Gadol*, however, one must understand that it is no ordinary ritual; it is the once-a-year atonement and spiritual cleansing for the entire community. Such a ritual requires a continual physical and spiritual cleansing of both the abode for the presence of God—the Holy of Holies—and the communal agent of the atonement—the *Kohen Gadol*.

At the heart of the expiation and purification ritual is the drawing of lots for two similar goats. One goat is to be designated for God as a purification offering and one is to be designated for Azazel, an enigmatic name used in the Bible.[14] The goat for Azazel is the one upon which the *Kohen Gadol* confesses the communal sins. The Rabbinic sages explicate this process:

> *[The* Kohen Gadol*] lays his hands upon it and thus says, "I pray on The Name, Your people have transgressed, they have done wrong, and they have sinned before You. I pray by The Name, please pardon the transgressions, the wrongdoings, and the sins that Your people, The House of Israel, transgressed, wrongly committed, and sinned before You. As it was written in the Law of Moses, Your servant,* 'For on this day expiation shall be made for you to purify you of all your sins; you shall be pure before the LORD' (Lev. 16:30)." *And the* kohanim *and the people, who were standing in the Courtyard, when they heard the Ineffable Name come out of the mouth of the* Kohen Gadol, *fell to their knees and prostrated themselves on their faces, saying,* "baruch shem kavod malkhuto le-olam va-ed" *(Blessed be God's glorious sovereignty for all time).*[15]

After all of this, the goat for Azazel is dispatched into the wilderness, taking the communal, spiritual refuse with it.

The Mystery of Azazel

There are two goats used in the Yom Kippur ritual described in Leviticus. These goats act as symbolic agents for the community, each a vessel for a different moral disposition of the community. One is sacrificed to God as a purity offering and the other is designated for Azazel. Oddly, the Torah is ambiguous as to the identity or meaning of Azazel, and this ambiguity raises a question: What does "designated for Azazel" mean, and how do we define Azazel? In trying to resolve this question, we learn that not only are there several answers, they go in three totally different directions.

The first thing Bible scholars do in trying to understand difficult words or concepts is to see how others have translated them. Here we look at four. The Greek translation of the Bible, known as the Septuagint (3rd century B.C.E.), translates Azazel as "the place of sending away."[16] The standard Latin, or Vulgate, version (4th century C.E.) translates it as "scapegoat," which is the origin of the expression "being a scapegoat," or one who takes the punishment for others.[17] The Mishnah (the Oral Law, passed down from Jewish generation to generation, starting with Moses) lines up most closely with the Vulgate, because it interprets Azazel to be *se'ir ha-mishtale'ach,* "the goat that is dispatched." Yet the Talmud aligns with the Septuagint by interpreting Azazel as a "fierce, difficult land."[18] So far, Azazel is either the scapegoat designated for God, or it is *where to send* the goat designated for God.

In another interpretation, the Talmud makes a puzzling and limited statement that "Azazel obtains atonement for the affair of Uza and Aza'el," the names of two demons.[19] Later, two great medieval commentators on the Torah understand Azazel to be not an actual demon, but rather a "demonic angel."[20] They make reference to a verse in Leviticus that says that some people offered sacrifices to goat-demons called *se'irim.*[21] This reference indicates that, in the medieval period, many people were probably aware of a postbiblical legend of fallen angels that is found in the Book of Enoch, part of the biblical canon of the Coptic (Egyptian-Ethiopian) Church.[22] The legend tells of demonic angels arriving on earth, cohabiting with human women, and instructing humans in the ways of prostitution, adultery, weaponry, sorcery, astrology, and the wearing of jewelry and makeup. Azazel, one of the demonic angels responsible for teaching most of the above, was punished by the archangel Raphael, who cast him into a pit in the wilderness and covered him with jagged rocks. There, in the wilderness, Azazel would remain until the day of eternal judgment and the end of the world.[23] It is very possible that through this legend, the persona of Azazel transformed into the aforementioned goat-demon, to which pagans offered sacrifices, because of the association with biblical offerings for sin, which are he-goats. In fact, late midrashic literature and kabbalistic literature both equate Azazel with Satan, who is given sins to consume in order to distract him from his evil work.[24]

Here we can see that Azazel may be understood as a place, the name for the scapegoat, or as some sort of demon. Any interpretation, though, will bring us back to the same issue, one which concerns the way Azazel functions within the Jewish tradition. Judaism teaches that we each have two primal impulses, one for good and one for evil (*yetzer ha-tov* and *yetzer ha-ra*). We learn that we must constantly be aware of these impulses so that we are in control of our lives. Because we are human, we inevitably fail at times and give in to the evil impulse. Being self-aware, however, we recognize that we need to rid ourselves of the stain and guilt from that transgression, but we also know that words are not always enough to do this cleansing. Azazel represents the human need for ritual and for doing something to recompense. In ancient times, doing something to recompense meant intricate ritual and sacrifice. Today it means something else—perhaps it is meditation or exercise, or maybe it is studying and remembering what our ancestors did long ago, as we do in the *Avodah* service of Yom Kippur. Whatever it is, Judaism teaches that, for the sake of our own consciences, we need to do more than apologize when we do wrong.

Pronouncing the Ineffable Name

There is no way for us to know exactly what our ancient ancestors saw, heard, and experienced during the Yom Kippur rites. Still, certain literature and thought provide some insight into the meaning of particular unique features of the Jewish tradition. One is the pronouncement of God's actual name—the so-called Ineffable Name.

From the first time we heard the story of Moses and the burning bush, wherein the name of God is made known as *ehyeh asher ehyeh* (Exod. 3:14), a phrase that is often translated as "I will be that I will be," we have been interested in learning more about God's name. For Jews today, God has no actual name—at least not one that is presently known or that we are able to use in speech. Judaism is firm in its position that God's name itself bears power, a power for which human beings need to demonstrate the utmost respect and caution. In fact, this power is so great that according to the most renowned Jewish commentator, Rashi (born Shlomo ben

Yitzchak in medieval France), when Moses killed the Egyptian taskmaster who was beating a Hebrew slave (Exod. 2:11–12), he did so by uttering God's ineffable name.[25]

The Talmud further explains that during the biblical and early temple periods, the *Kohen Gadol* was the primary bearer of the mysterious and awesome *Shem Ha-Meforash,* the Ineffable Name; only he knew it and was able to say it. On Yom Kippur the *Kohen Gadol* said God's name 10 times at different points during the ritual, and each time it was uttered, it was heard from Jerusalem all the way to Jericho.[26] The Talmud also teaches that once every seven years other *kohanim* were permitted to pronounce the *Shem Ha-Meforash,* but only during the priestly blessing.[27] These utterances could only occur, of course, if there was some sort of indication that the presence of God (the *Shekhinah*) was in the Temple at those moments. The Rabbinic sages recount that after the High Priest Simon the Righteous died in the 4th century B.C.E., those indications were no longer apparent. With this sage of great merit gone, it was as if a portion of God's presence in the community, and favor for it, had gone with him; and no one dared to voice God's real name again, in fear of the outcome.

In truth, the name of God is written all over the Torah in the form of four consonants called the Tetragrammaton (Greek for "four letters").[28] Those consonants are *yud, heh, vav, heh,* which are similar to y, h, v, h; but because no one knows the corresponding vowels to these letters any more, we do not know how to pronounce the name. Instead of saying nothing, Jews speak the word *Adonai,* meaning "my LORD." Some Christian scholars tried to pin down the name of God by applying the vowels for *Adonai* to the Tetragrammaton, a step that led them to erroneously believe the name of God is pronounced as Yehovah or Jehovah. The Jewish tradition teaches us that many secondary names exist for God that we are permitted to use, such as *Makom, Ha-shem, Shekhinah,* and *Emet.* Some kabbalists even believe that the entire Torah is one run-on series of names of God.

Judaism constantly reminds us that we are not equal to God. Were we to use anything other than the permitted words symbolic of God's name (such as *Adonai*—My LORD; *Ha-Shem*—The Name), we would be making a pretentious show of desire to control God. We are meant to understand that we are each unique and special, embodying the image of God; but we should never think that we, or anyone, or anything is on a level with God. We are permitted, however, within the boundaries of ritual structure, to call upon God's Ineffable Name in the process of expiation. This is for one purpose only—self-renewal for the sake of improving ourselves and the world. And so, on the holiest day of the year, the Yom Kippur liturgy provides us with a profound image regarding the use of God's name, without actually using the Ineffable Name. We learn of the *Kohen Gadol* entering the *mishkan,* which was located in the center of the camp wherever the tribes dwelled in the desert. He went alone, deeper into the Holy of Holies, the *Kodesh Ha-Kodashim,* which was in the center of the *mishkan.* There, in the center of the center of the community, one day each year, this one designated person called on the Ineffable Name of God. Today we have no *Kohen Gadol* and no Holy of Holies. We are decentralized, and the only "center" now available is the one found within each of us. Therefore, on Yom Kippur, it is to the center of our being we must go to talk to God—to call upon God for the sake of self-renewal and betterment.

Days of Awe

There are two phrases that refer to the days between Rosh Hashanah and Yom Kippur. One is *Aseret Yemei Teshuvah* (Ten Days of Repentance)[29] and the other is, *Yamim Noraim* or (Days of Awe). The Jewish tradition places people into three moral categories: righteous, wicked, and those who are *beinoni* (in between).[30] The Jerusalem Talmud and the Midrash coined the names of this period with the intention that the time be prayerful and dedicated to serious self-examination and spiritual vigilance.[31] Each *beinoni* receives this grace period to use as an opportunity for tipping the scales of judgment in his or her favor.[32] As it happens, the Rabbinic sages taught that we should always see ourselves as *beinoni* and take responsibility for each moment of the week as if it were the actual tipping point that determines the destiny of the soul.

Because our lives are literally hanging in the balance throughout the Days of Awe, several customs and observances were put into place to make the days as spiritually effective as possible. First of all, additional and substitute phrases were added to the central Jewish prayer, the *Amidah* (literally, "Standing"), also known as the *Shemoneh Esrei* (The Eighteen);[33] and *Avinu Malkeinu* is recited each morning and afternoon, when it is not usually included at all.[34] Most Jewish codes and books of customs, including those of Maimonides (12th-century rabbi, physician, and philosopher), Joseph Karo (16th-century author of the seminal legal guide, Shulchan Arukh), and Jacob ben Asher (14th-century codifier and biblical commentator), recommend adding as many prayers and supplications as possible throughout the week.[35] Other authorities, such as Mordecai ben Avraham Jaffe of 16th-century Prague, even suggest fasting each day (during daylight hours and excluding Shabbat) to add somberness and solemnity to each day.[36]

Although most people do not fast each day of the Days of Awe, a public fast is held the day after Rosh Hashanah, unless that day is Shabbat, in which case the fast is on Sunday. (Except for Yom Kippur itself, fast days never occur on Shabbat.) This fast is called Tzom Gedalyah (Fast of Gedalyah) or Tzom Shevi'i (Fast of the Seventh Month). Tzom Gedalyah, which begins at sunrise and ends at sunset, commemorates the murder of the Jewish governor of Judah, Gedalyah ben Achikam, appointed by King Nebuchadnezzar after the Babylonian conquest of Jerusalem in 586 B.C.E. His assassination destroyed all hope for vanquishing Babylonian control, as it marked the end of any Jewish settlement in the Land of Israel, let alone self-government.[37] Today, while some people see the story of Gedalyah repeating itself throughout history and continue to fast, others choose not to. They believe Tzom Gedalahn memorializes the pain of the destruction and loss of Jerusalem, when we are living in a time when the city is rebuilt.

Erev Yom Kippur: The Threshold of Sanctity

The day preceding Yom Kippur, Erev Yom Kippur, also has particular significance, because the state in which we enter Yom Kippur has an impact upon our spiritual success. This day however is reserved for hope, joy, and festiveness as opposed to the somberness of the surrounding days. Accordingly, it is meritorious to be festive on Erev Yom Kippur, particularly with food and drink, because in doing so, we punctuate the solemnity of Yom Kippur itself.[38] This festivity is extended by omitting the prayer *Avinu Malkeinu,* as well as reciting fewer of the *Selichot* (penitential prayers and poems) that were added during the earlier Days of Awe.[39]

An Erev Yom Kippur custom performed in some Orthodox circles is called *kaparot,* "the expiatory offering." *Kaparot* is controversial today because many people see it not only as a custom with a questionable basis in tradition, but also as a primitive and inhumane one. The ritual of *kaparot* involves lifting a live white fowl (men use roosters and women use hens[40]) above one's head. The person says *zeh chalifati; zeh temurati, zeh kaparati* ("This is my exchange; this is my ransom; this is my atonement") while making one overhead circle with each phrase. Then a ritual slaughterer kills the fowl. Its innards are placed in the street for other birds to eat, and its flesh is given to the poor.[41] Maimonides makes no mention of this custom; and those who do mention it, by and large, object to it because of its pagan connotations.[42] Today, some prefer instead to place money in a handkerchief or in small sack, usually in multiples of 18 for its numerical equivalency to *chai,* meaning "life."[43] After swinging the money around their heads and reciting the short prayer, they give it to charity.

Despite the controversy, the custom of *kaparot* has not died. Four basic reasons are put forth for its practice. The first is the hope that by extending mercy to the birds who feed upon the innards, Jews will be extended mercy by God on Yom Kippur.[44] The second reason involves one of the Hebrew words for fowl, *gever.* Because *gever* also means male person (female, *geveret*), one can infer that if there is a guilty verdict on Yom Kippur, the slaughtered fowl can symbolically serve as a substitute, going to its death instead of the person.[45] The third explanation states that birds are known to acquire their food by stealing, and so by discarding the fowl's innards, people distance themselves from sin.[46] Finally, the fowl provides a form of charity, because the one who performs the ritual either donates the bird's flesh or gives monetary charity in the amount of the bird's worth.[47]

Erev Yom Kippur includes two other unusual features that are an important part of the transition into the harsh self-assessment of Yom Kippur. The first is the daily afternoon prayer service, *Minchah,* which, on this day, includes a special confessional, *Vidui.* During the *Vidui* we beat ourselves on the chest for each transgression listed. This action serves as a symbolic punishment for our hearts, which are ultimately responsible for leading us to sins of greed, lust, and anger.[48] The tradition emphasizes, however, that one must say the confessional prior to eating the meal that precedes the Yom Kippur fast, a meal known as *seudah ha-mafseket* (literally, "the meal that interrupts"). After all, as the Talmud says, one may not feel up to confessing after eating a large meal.[49] Or, God forbid, if a person dies at the meal, they will have died without having made the confession and their divine judgment may be less favorable.[50] That being said, the meal after the *Vidui* should be large and festive, creating a painful distinction between the satisfaction of a full belly and the longing for food experienced during the fast, while at the same time helping us to complete the entire fast.[51]

Before leaving for the synagogue and the Yom Kippur evening services, people partake in other customs that underscore an important Jewish principle: what is sacred extends from the core of the individual, to family and loved ones. Some people make a point of immersing themselves in the *mikveh* (ritual bath), a long-standing purifying ritual[52] for not only women, but also men. Going to the *mikveh* is associated with spiritual transformation (for example, it is used before marriage and before conversion to Judaism) and therefore is a fitting custom to follow as we enter the holiest of holy days. In another custom, parents say a special blessing over their children. To the words of the prayer that is recited on the eve of every Shabbat, they add wishes for their children's welfare in the year to come.[53] It is customary to express hope that they and their children may live upstanding lives, dedicated to acts of lovingkindness, charity, and study.

The manner of dress is important for entering the holiday, as it connects our outward appearance with the proper frame of mind. Therefore, dressing ourselves (and our tables, even though we do not eat or drink until after Yom Kippur) in nice, white apparel is a prominent custom.[54] This sort of dress applies to both men and women. A man who owns a *kitel,* which is the Yiddish word for a long white gown or robe worn traditionally for special days and as his shroud, is encouraged to wear it. Fine white clothing is worn for two primary reasons. The first is that on Yom Kippur we are to consign ourselves symbolically to the status of the ministering angels. Wearing fresh, white attire raises our physical and, in turn, our spiritual character to a purer state, free of sin.[55] Also by wearing white, especially the *kitel,* we are reminded of those who have died and, in turn, of our own mortality, motivating us to greater efforts in our repentance.[56]

Finally, in order to sanctify the day, we light candles prior to Yom Kippur. They are lit in the same manner as on Friday nights, but with the Yom Kippur blessing followed by the *Shehecheyanu,* a blessing said in this case for the new season.[57] Another reason for lighting these candles, according to tradition, relates to Moses' coming down from Mount Sinai on Yom Kippur with the second set of tablets bearing the Ten Commandments (he had destroyed the first set when he found the Israelites worshiping an idol).[58] Because the Torah, which evolved from the tablets, is a light unto the Jewish people, we are lighting candles on this day in honor of the Torah.[59] We light a third candle as well, known as the *ner neshamah,* or soul candle. This memorial or *Yizkor* candle commemorates the souls of our loved ones, traditionally our parents.[60] Lighting candles is often connected with remembering loved ones who have died, as it says in the Bible, "The lifebreath of man *(neshamah)* is the lamp *(ner)* of the LORD" (Prov. 20:27). Furthermore, in Rabbinic literature, Yom Kippur is primarily referred to in the plural—by the biblical *Yom Ha-Kippurim.* It has been taught that Yom Kippur appears in the plural because we not only ask forgiveness for ourselves, but also for those who have already passed on.[61]

Yom Kippur and Self-Denial

Self-denial is one of the most significant characteristics of Yom Kippur, the holiest day of the year. The Torah commands that we should "afflict" ourselves on this day as a part of the purification process (Lev. 16:29–30), and this description has been taken to mean fasting. Chapter 58 of the Book of Isaiah, which is read on Yom Kippur morning following the Torah reading, expands the rationale for fasting. It says that God wants us to fast as a means to improve ourselves, not simply to suffer. Therefore, the self-denial, specifically of the fast, functions as an emotional and spiritual form of expiation, which will lead to our better behavior.

Acts of self-denial, such as fasting, emphasize Judaism's principle that there is much more to the self than the physical. By depriving the body in rituals of abstinence, we undergo a transformative process that redirects our understanding of life to a different perspective. That is, we are forced to confront basic human urges and deal with them through meditative contemplation and prayer, propelling the mind and spirit beyond the ordinary. Consequently, the fast and self-denial on Yom Kippur are not the end to cleansing the self, but an important means by which to achieve spiritual improvement.

Abstinence as practiced in Judaism differs distinctly and importantly from that of other religions. Classic Catholicism, for example, teaches that one should suppress and overpower physical desires, while Judaism teaches that we should repress and consciously set bounds on them. The self-denial expressed in Classic Catholicism, including, for example, sexual abstinence beyond childbearing years, is rooted in the ideology that the body is animalistic and the seat of sin, and the spirit is the only aspect of the human self that is pure and holy.[62] Although there were Jewish thinkers, such as Philo (1st-century Egypt), Solomon ibn Gabirol (11th-century Spain), and Maimonides (14th-century Germany), who were influenced by the Christian notion of bifurcation of body and soul,[63] Judaism understands body and soul as parts of an integrated whole, wherein everything, even physical desire, can be transformed into something holy through proper spiritual intent.[64] This belief is made evident in the etymology of two particular Hebrew words. We see the direct association between the spiritual and the physical in the word for soul *(neshamah)* and the word for breathing *(neshimah)*, the most basic physical act. Furthermore—and particularly germane to Yom Kippur—the Talmud remarks quite directly that "the Holy Blessed One takes the soul, throws it into the body, and judges them as one."[65]

Compassionate Rules

Halakhah, Jewish law, notes certain exceptions to the rules of self-denial, including for pregnant or nursing women, people who are ill, and those who are very delicate or feeble.

Symbolic Footwear

One 19th-century source suggests that the abstention from wearing leather shoes is connected to the first sin committed by Adam,[68] who tasted the forbidden fruit of the Tree of Knowledge of Good and Evil. According to this understanding, people started wearing shoes to avoid having their feet touch the soil that God had cursed after Adam tainted it with his transgression.[69] On Yom Kippur, however, the entire world has a special holiness that does not exist on any other day; and so we may walk upon the ground without shoes—or, as a symbolic gesture, wear something other than our comfortable or stylish leather shoes.

Judaism does not ask a person to abstain for the sake of denial and affliction per se. The Jewish purpose of such self-denial is illustrated in the Bible when the prophet Isaiah describes, in practical terms, what constitutes spiritual improvement. He defines heightened spirituality as being obtained through moral practices, for example, through being selfless rather than selfish. Therefore, the self-denial of fasting experienced on Yom Kippur can be understood as calling upon us to make sure the hungry are fed, the naked are clothed, and the enslaved are freed.

Fasting is not the only form of self-denial on Yom Kippur. The Mishnah discusses four other practices from which one is to abstain: bathing; anointing oneself with soaps, oils, and perfumes; putting on leather shoes; and marital relations.[66] These additional abstinences further the transformative process and force us to focus even more on the relationship between the physical and the spiritual. All together, these five abstinences are meant to help us grow spiritually. Eliyahu Ki Tov, a 20th-century renowned compiler of Jewish customs, claimed that the fact that there are five of them represents other significant aspects of Jewish life and identity, such as the holiness of the five books of the Torah, the five senses that guide our experiences in the world, and the five prayer services of Yom Kippur: *Ma'ariv* (evening), *Shacharit* (morning), *Musaf* (additional), *Minchah* (afternoon), and *Ne'ilah* (closing).[67] Thus, for Judaism, self-denial is part of the spiritual experience, reinforcing a greater humility and gratitude in all aspects of our lives.

Yom Kippur
Pathways Through the Sources

Mishnah
Between God and Fellow

The repentance on Yom Kippur is a repentance that touches all aspects of who we are. We must do everything we can to direct our hearts with proper intention *(kavanah)*. Moreover, we must face specifically how we have wronged others and actually do something to appease them. The Talmud (*Yoma* 87a) points out that, although we must apologize and appease those we have wronged, one need not apologize more than three times.

> If one said, "I will sin and repent, I will sin [again] and repent," he will not be given an opportunity to repent. [If one said,] "I will sin and Yom Kippur will effect atonement," Yom Kippur will not effect atonement. For transgressions that are between man and God *(bein adam la-Makom)*, Yom Kippur effects atonement; for transgressions between a man and his fellow man *(bein adam la-chaveiro)*, Yom Kippur only effects atonement if he has appeased his fellow.... Rabbi Akiva said, "Happy are you Israel. Before whom are you cleansed and who is it that cleanses you? Your father in heaven, as it says, *I will sprinkle clean water upon you, and you shall be clean* (Ezek. 36:25). And it says, *Hope of Israel—Mikveh Yisrael* (Jer. 17:13)—[which teaches that] just as the *mikveh* cleanses the unclean, so too the Holy One blessed be He cleanses Israel."
>
> —Mishnah, *Yoma* 8:9

Maimonides
Perfect Repentance

No one has informed the Jewish tradition on the subjects of repentance and forgiveness more than Maimonides. He organized and elucidated the laws of the Mishnah and Talmud so that there are measurable standards by which to guide our lives. Although we all know we must strive for the highest standards of morality and kindheartedness, when studying this source we may ask whether Maimonides' standards of acceptance and wholehearted forgiveness are realistic.

At this time, when the Temple no longer exists, and we have no atonement altar, there is nothing left but repentance. Even if a man was wicked throughout his life and repented at the end, we must not mention anything about his wickedness to him, as it is written: "A wicked man's wickedness shall not bring about his downfall when he gives up his wickedness" (Ezek. 33:12). Yom Kippur itself atones for those who repent, as it is written: "Atonement shall be made for you this day" (Lev. 16:30).

Perfect repentance is where an opportunity presents itself to the offender for repeating the offense and he refrains from committing it because of his repentance and not out of fear or physical inability.... If, however, one repents only in his old age, when he is no longer able to do what he used to do, his repentance, though not the best, will nevertheless do him some good. Even if a person transgressed all his life and repented on the day of his death and died during his repentance, all his sins are pardoned, as it is written: "Before the sun grows dark, and the light goes from moon and stars, and the clouds gather after rain" (Eccles. 12:2), that is, the day of death. This implies that if he remembers his Creator and repents before death, he is forgiven.

Repentance and Yom Kippur effect atonement only for sins committed against God, as when one has eaten forbidden food ... for sins committed against fellow man, as when a person either injured or cursed or robbed his neighbor, he is never pardoned unless he compensates his neighbor and makes an apology. Even though he has made the compensation, the wrongdoer must appease the injured person and ask his pardon. Even if he only annoyed him with words he must apologize and beg for forgiveness.

One must not show himself cruel by not accepting an apology; he should be easily pacified, and provoked with difficulty. When an offender asks his forgiveness, he should forgive wholeheartedly and with a willing spirit. Even if he has caused him much trouble wrongfully, he must not avenge himself, he must not bear a grudge. This is the way of the stock of Israel and their upright hearts.

—Maimonides[70]

Zohar

The High Priest's Intervention

Although the ritual of the *Kohen Gadol* on Yom Kippur is no longer practiced, the High Priest's actions teach us about the special nature of this day, when heaven and earth come together. This meaning is well illustrated in the ritual of the *Kohen Gadol* entering the Holy of Holies, which the Talmud[71] begins to explain. The core book of Kabbalah, the Zohar, expands upon it, describing the transcendent experience of the *Kohen Gadol,* who was able to ascend into the realm where God makes direct contact with the physical universe through the *sefirot.* (These are the 10 divine emanations of God that constitute a core kabbalistic philosophy whereby God intervenes between the earthly world and the infinite.) Inside the Holy of Holies, the High Priest was able to unify his thoughts with the *sefirot.* The following text explains some of that experience.

> Rabbi Isaac said: A chain was tied to the leg of the Priest as he went in [to the Holy of Holies on Yom Kippur] so that if he died there they could pull his body out. How could they know? They knew it by means of the scarlet thread. For if its color did not change they would know that the Priest had remained there in a state of sin. But if he was to emerge safely they would know it because the thread would turn white. When that happened there was rejoicing both on high and below, otherwise they were all distressed and all would know that their prayers had gone unanswered. Rabbi Judah said: When he entered he closed his eyes so as not to gaze where it was forbidden to gaze. He heard the sound of the cherubim's wings as they sang their praises. The Priest then knew that there was only rejoicing and that he would emerge in safety. In addition he would know it by the manner of his prayers. For if the words of his prayer came out in joy, there was acceptance and blessing. Then there was a joy on high and among those here below.
>
> —Zohar 3:102a[72]

Yehudah Ha-Levi

Attending to the Spirit

Judaism is not a religion of monks, monasteries, and isolation. It is a religion in which even the most pious must participate in the mundane affairs of the world. Yet there is one day, Yom Kippur, when one is supposed to transcend the surrounding world, focusing only on matters of the spirit.

Yehudah Ha-Levi, a Jewish philosopher in 11th- and 12th-century Islamic Spain, was a renowned writer of poetry and prose on both secular and religious topics.

> The pious man attends the Three Festivals and the Great Fast Day, on which some of his sins are atoned for. His soul frees itself from the whisperings of imagination, wrath, lust, and neither in thought or deed gives them any attention. Although his soul is unable to atone for sinful thoughts—the results of songs and tales heard in youth, and which cling to memory—it cleanses itself from real sins, confesses repentance for the former, and undertakes to allow them no more to escape his tongue, much less to put them into practice, as it is written, *I am determined that my mouth should not transgress* (Ps. 17:3). The fast of this day is such as brings one near to the angels, because it is spent in humility and contrition, standing, kneeling, praising, and singing. All his physical faculties denied their natural requirements, being entirely abandoned to religious service, as if the animal element had disappeared. The fast of a pious man is such that eye, ear, and tongue share in it, that he regards nothing except that which brings him near to God. This also refers to his innermost faculties, such as mind and imagination. To this he adds pious works.[73]
>
> —Yehudah Ha-Levi

Kitzur Shulchan Arukh

Observance and Practice

Undoubtedly, when one is unaccustomed to practices of self-denial, they can seem overwhelming. Yet, as we learn in this passage from the 19th-century condensed *(kitzur)* version of the Shulchan Arukh (the standard code of Jewish law, first published in 1565), these practices are certainly not intended to cause unnecessary suffering; participation is meant to be balanced by an awareness of the human condition.

> The following are prohibited on the Day of Atonement: partaking of food, drinking, washing, anointing, wearing shoes, and sexual intercourse. It is also forbidden to do any manner of work and to carry objects, as on the Sabbath. Since it is necessary to add from the profane to the sacred, all these are forbidden shortly before twilight, and also briefly after the appearance of the stars terminating the Day of Atonement.

One who is ill, even if not in danger, may wash in his usual manner. A bride within thirty days of marriage may wash her face so as not to be repulsive to her husband.

The laws pertaining to a woman about to give birth and also a person dangerously ill who may require food, drink, and the desecration of the Day of Atonement by partaking food are in the same status as the laws governing the desecration of the Sabbath. Even though several physicians prescribe that a patient does not necessarily require food and drink and might even suffer ill effects by eating and drinking, if the patient says that, although not yet dangerously ill, he may further jeopardize his health by refraining from food, he is heeded and fed [on Yom Kippur]. In the matter of eating and drinking the patient's judgment is more reliable, since he knows in his heart the bitterness of his symptoms.

Departed ones are memorialized on the Day of Atonement, [first] because remembering our dead invokes a mood of humility, and [second] because even the dead are in need of atonement. It is written in *Sifra* [a compilation of legal midrashim on the Book of Leviticus]: "Atone for Your people Israel—this refers to the living; whom You redeemed—this refers to the dead. This teaches that the departed require expiation; therefore charity should be pledged in their name."

Immediately upon the conclusion of the Day of Atonement, those who scrupulously observe the commandments begin to build a sukkah [temporary hut], to fulfill the verse: *They go from rampart to rampart.* (Ps. 84:8).

—Kitzur Shulchan Arukh 133[74]

The Maggid[75] of Mezritch

Discovering Unity

Teshuvah (repentance) is an extremely important process of spiritual cleansing and healing that we undertake in particular on Rosh Hashanah and Yom Kippur. But its significance extends even further. *Teshuvah* is a method by which we examine the self and its relationship with the entire universe. The Jewish conception of God is one of immanence and transcendence—what is inside, outside, and beyond. Through *teshuvah,* we learn that these qualities are all one and that God is within the self, the selfishness, and the selflessness. Even though one may have arrived at this thought, living the idea requires a lifetime of *teshuvah*.

Rabbi Dov Baer, the Maggid of Mezritch, was an 18th-century leader of the Hasidic movement and a humble follower of its founder, the Baal Shem Tov. As the Maggid would later say, "I found a light in a closet, and all I did was open the door." He left no writings of his own; his students collected his teachings and published them.

> The Maggid of Mezritch was expounding on the Torah verse "You shall make *teshuvah ad Adonai Elohecha,* You shall repent until the LORD your God" (Deut. 4:30).
>
> "What is the meaning of this strange phrasing?" the Maggid asked. "Should Torah not say 'You shall repent *unto Adonai Elohecha,* the LORD your God' rather than *until*? And why say both *Adonai* and *Elohecha* when either one would suffice?"
>
> Answering his own question, the Maggid said, "To understand the first, you must understand the second. What is the meaning of *Adonai*?"
>
> A Hasid replied, "*Adonai* is the four-letter Name of God that signifies the absolute transcendence of the Divine."
>
> "And what is the meaning of *Elohecha*?"
>
> "This refers to *Elohim,* the Name of God that signifies the absolute immanence of God."
>
> "And what is the meaning of *teshuvah*?"
>
> "*Teshuvah* is the process of returning to God by admitting our mistakes and making amends."
>
> "So," the Maggid said. "We are to continue the process of *teshuvah until* we can see *Adonai* manifest as *Elohim,* until we see the one and the many as different aspects of the One and Only."
>
> —Adapted by Rami Shapiro in *Hasidic Tales*[76]

The Rebbe of Lizensk

Forgiving God

Yom Kippur is a holiday of forgiveness—a time when we ask for forgiveness and we forgive others. Interestingly, there is a reciprocal relationship between the two. To receive forgiveness requires our own permission; we have to allow ourselves to be forgiven. In order to allow ourselves to be forgiven, we need to be able to identify with and forgive others and to accept the realities of our natures.

In 18th-century Poland-Galitzia, the Rebbe of Lizensk (Rabbi Elimelech) was a direct disciple of the Maggid of Mezritch, whose followers form the basis of most Hasidic dynasties.

> Rabbi Elimelech of Lizensk was asked by a disciple how one should pray for forgiveness. He told him to observe the behavior of a certain innkeeper before Yom Kippur.
>
> The disciple took lodging at the inn and observed the proprietor for several days, but could see nothing relevant to his quest.
>
> Then, one night before Yom Kippur, he saw the innkeeper open two large ledgers. From the first book he read off a list of the sins he had committed throughout the past year. When he was finished, he opened the second book and proceeded to recite all the bad things that had occurred to him during the year past.
>
> When he had finished reading both books, he lifted his eyes to the heaven and said, "Dear God, it is true I have sinned against You. But You have done many distressful things to me too.
>
> "However, we are now beginning a new year. Let us wipe the slate clean. I will forgive You, and You forgive me."
>
> —Told by Shmuel Yosef Agnon[77]

Franz Rosenzweig

To Stand before God

The prayer service of Yom Kippur is filled with majesty, grandeur, and decorum. Rituals such as the blowing of the shofar, the prostration, and the blessing of the *Kohanim* may only be experienced on Yom Kippur. The ultimate purpose of these rituals, although related to our confession of sins and our atonement, is to address the fact that on Yom Kippur, a Jew's contact with God surpasses that of any other day.

Franz Rosenzweig, a major modern Jewish philosopher, seriously considered conversion to Christianity. But at a small Orthodox synagogue on Yom Kippur, he apparently had an intense mystical experience that influenced his decision not to convert. The exact nature of that experience was never recorded in his subsequent writings.

> The Days of Awe are festivals of a special character, celebrated in the month of that feast which, among the feasts of the community, has as its content: arriving at rest. What distinguishes the Days of Awe from all other festivals is that here and only here does the Jew kneel. Here he does what he refused to do before the king of Persia, what no power on earth can compel him to do, and what he need not do before God on any other day of the year, or in any other situation he may face during his lifetime. And he does not kneel to confess a fault or to pray for forgiveness of sins, acts to which this festival is primarily dedicated. He kneels only in beholding the immediate nearness of God, hence on an occasion which transcends the earthly needs of today. For the same reason the Prayer of the Benedictions [the *Amidah*] said on every Sabbath omits the request for forgiveness of sins. The Day of Atonement, which climaxes the ten-day period of redemption, is quite properly called the Sabbath of Sabbaths. The congregation now rises to the feeling of God's nearness as it sees in memory the Temple service of old, and visualizes especially the moment when the priest, this once in all the year, pronounced the Ineffable Name of God that was expressed by a circumlocution on all other occasions, and the assembled people fell on their knees. And the congregation participates directly in the feeling of God's nearness when it says the prayer that is bound up with the promise of a future time, "when every knee shall bow before God. When the idols will be utterly cut off, when

the world will be perfected under the kingdom of the Almighty, and all the children of flesh will call upon His Name, when He will turn unto Himself all the wicked of the earth, and all will accept the yoke of His kingdom." On the Days of Awe, this prayer mounts beyond the version of the concluding prayer of the everyday service [the *Aleinu*]. On these Days of Awe the plea for bringing about such a future is already a part of the central prayer, which—in solemn words—calls for the day when all creatures will prostrate themselves that "they may form a single band to do God's will with a whole heart." But the concluding prayer, which utters this cry day after day, silences it on the Days of Awe, and, in complete awareness that this congregation is not yet the "single band" of all that is created, anticipates the moment of eternal redemption by seizing on it now, in the present. And what the congregation merely expresses in words in the course of the year, it here expresses in action: it prostrates itself before the King of kings.[78]

—Translated by Francis C. Golffing

Abraham Joshua Heschel

The Unforgivable

The great medieval thinker Maimonides, in his *Mishneh Torah,* gives an eight-element process of forgiveness, among which are the following: acknowledgment of the wrongdoing, a public expression of remorse, compensation to the victim, and not repeating the offense again when confronted the same situation. In certain types of transgression, however, this formula does not work so neatly. Some transgressions seem unforgivable (the Holocaust, for example, or familial abuse). In addition, opportunities to ask for forgiveness from the one we have wronged can be missed (for example, if the person has died). But Judaism still asserts that if we always abide by values inherent in repentance and forgiveness, we will commit fewer transgressions and will ask for forgiveness when we should.

More than seven centuries after Maimonides lived, renowned philosopher Abraham Joshua Heschel emigrated to the United States from Nazi Germany nad became one of the most significant Jewish theologians, professors, and social activists of the 20th century. In this story about him, he expresses the complex reality of both seeking forgiveness from the victims and forgiving wrongdoers.

> …visiting in Germany in the 1950s, [Heschel] was asked the question, when would the Jews forgive the Nazis? Rabbi Heschel told the following story: "There once was a rabbi traveling on a train through Russia. He was shabbily dressed and small in stature and was sitting in a railroad car studying the Mishnah. Two Poles began to make fun of him and deride him. They cursed him, and the rabbi did not reply to them, continuing to study the Mishnah. They then took his suitcase and threw it on the floor. The rabbi maintained his composure, did not rebuke them, gathered all of his belongings, and put them back in the suitcase. They continued to revile him.
>
> "When they reached the town where the rabbi was going, a large crowd was waiting for some important dignitary. The two Poles discovered to their amazement that the little old Jew whom they were taunting was an esteemed and revered rabbi. They later asked him to forgive them for their taunts and jeers. The rabbi said, 'You are asking the rabbi to forgive you, not the little old Jew who was in the railroad car. You have to ask him to forgive you. He is the one you injured by your insults and your jeers.'"
>
> That was Dr. Heschel's answer to the Germans that day. Only the victims can forgive. We do not have the proxy to forgive in their stead.
>
> —Told by Dov Peretz Elkins in *Moments of Transcendence*, Vol. 2[79]

Erich Fromm

No Judgment Without Love

The Yom Kippur process of atonement includes recognition of our relationships with others, the world, and God. Being in a relationship, however, means going beyond the emotional and extends to an interpersonal, creative dynamic. Erich Fromm was a renowned Jewish psychologist of the 20th century who left Nazi Germany and eventually spent most of his career in America. He taught that our relationships should be made up of the elements of care, respect, responsibility, and knowledge. He uses the Yom Kippur story of Jonah to show how human behavior often lacks the elements of care and responsibility.

> [Jonah] is a man with a strong sense of order and law, but without love. However, in his attempt to escape, he finds himself in the belly of a whale, symbolizing the state of isolation and imprisonment which his lack of love and solidarity has brought upon him. God saves him, and Jonah goes to

Nineveh. He preaches to the inhabitants as God had told him, and the very thing he was afraid of happens. The men of Nineveh repent their sins, mend their ways, and God forgives them and decides not to destroy the city. Jonah is intensely angry and disappointed; he wanted "justice" to be done, not mercy. At last he finds some comfort in the shade of a tree which God had made to grow for him to protect him from the sun. But when God makes the tree wilt, Jonah is depressed and angrily complains to God. God answers: "Thou hast had pity on the gourd for which thou hast not labored neither madest it grow; which came up in a night, and perished in a night. And should I not spare Nineveh, that great city, wherein are more than six score thousand people that cannot discern between their right hand and their left hand; and also much cattle?" God's answer to Jonah is to be understood symbolically. God explains to Jonah that the essence of love is to "labor" for something and "to make something grow," that love and labor are inseparable. One loves that for which one labors, and one labors for that which one loves.[80]

—Erich Fromm

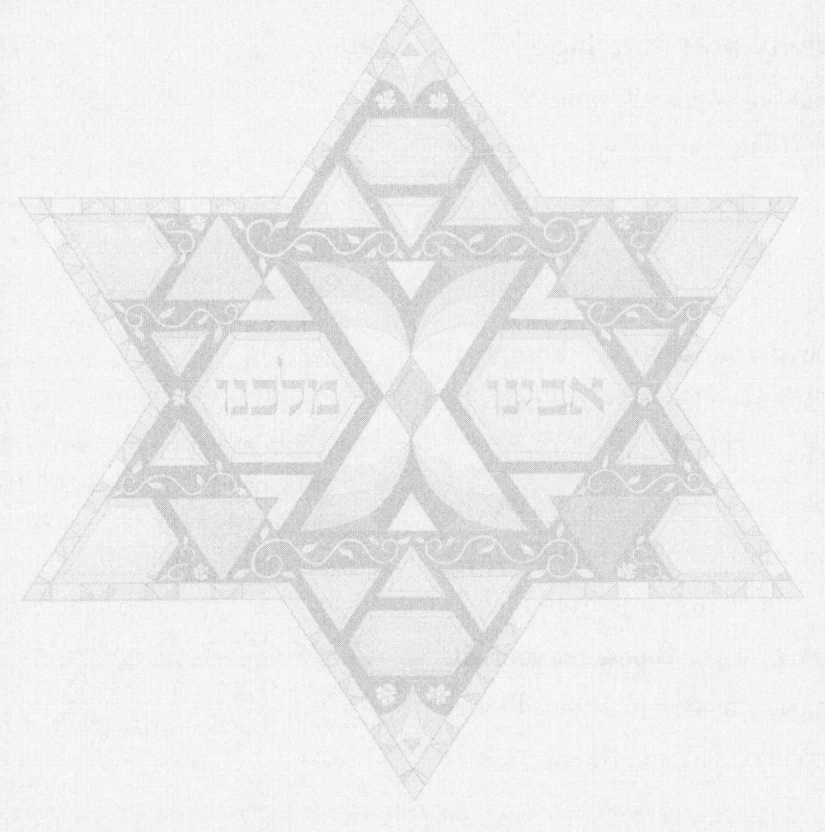

Yom Kippur
Interpretations of Sacred Texts

The texts studied in these pages are from the Mishnah, the *machzor,* and the Bible. The Mishnah, a body of Jewish law that had previously been oral only, was written down about 200 C.E., largely in response to the dispersion of the Jews. The *machzor* is a special prayer book, in this case for Rosh Hashanah and Yom Kippur. It contains not only the basic liturgy, but also *piyyutim* (liturgical poems) specific to each holiday. The Book of Exodus*, found in the Five Books of Moses, recounts the Israelites' escape from Egyptian slavery, while the Book of Jonah, found in Nevi'im ("Prophets"), describes Jonah's God-given mission to save the city of Nineveh. Each of these texts is accompanied by multiple levels of study.

THE THREE LEVELS
Peshat: simple, literal meaning
Derash: historical, Rabbinic inquiry
Making It Personal:
contemporary analysis and application

Festivity and Marriage

Rabban Shimon ben Gamliel** said:[81] "Israel had no better days than the 15th of Av (Tu b'Av) and Yom Kippur, when the young women of Jerusalem would go out dressed in borrowed white clothes—[borrowed] so as not to embarrass those that did not have.... The young women of Jerusalem would go out and dance in the vineyards. And what would they say?—'Young man, raise your eyes and see what you choose for yourself. Don't pay attention to beauty. Don't pay attention to family lineage. *Grace is deceptive, beauty is illusory; it is for her fear of the LORD that a woman is to be praised.*'" (Prov. 31:30).

—Mishnah, *Ta'anit* 4:8

Peshat

This last paragraph of the Mishnah that deals with solemnity and occasions for fasting *(Ta'anit)* concludes with a discussion of festivity and joy. It introduces us to Tu b'Av, the Jewish "Lovers' Day," which usually falls in the heat of August. Apparently, on both Tu b'Av and Yom Kippur, there were celebrations with dancing, where unmarried young people would go to find romance.[82] All were invited to participate, regardless of social status, as the girls (even the most wealthy) would wear borrowed clothes.[83] This piece also teaches that one should not judge a woman on the basis of beauty or wealth, but for what is in her heart.

Derash

The Rabbinic sages of the Talmud offer six different reasons why Tu b'Av is celebrated, the most compelling being that it was the only day of permitted intertribal marriage, showing compassion to those who fell in love with someone from another Israelite tribe.[84] Most interesting, however, is the association of festivity with Yom Kippur. The association is primarily based upon a midrash, which tells us that the first set of tablets were broken on the 17th of Tammuz (a solemn fast day) because of the sin of worshiping the Golden Calf; and it was on Yom Kippur that the new set was brought down.[85] Our being given the second tablets epitomizes God's forgiveness and mercy and is therefore a reason to celebrate. In addition, just after Yom Kippur ends we celebrate the verdict of our judgment, under the assumption that we were judged with mercy and compassion throughout the Ten Days of Repentance.[86]

Making It Personal

At first glance, it makes no sense that Yom Kippur and Tu b'Av, a celebration of love, would be linked together. However, there are two powerful lessons that we can derive from this text. One is that Judaism values introspection and thoughtfulness in our romantic relationships. That is to say, in our 21st-century world, saturated with media whose underlying message is that sex, beauty, youth, and wealth are the ultimate values, Judaism calls upon us to ask the bigger questions and go deeper, beneath the surface. The people we love are not merchandise, and we must behave in accordance with the values of one who "fears the LORD," including honesty, sincerity, and appreciating the unique humanity—the divine image or *tzelem Elohim,* as it were—of the ones we love.

The second lesson is that our relationship with God, which is in the forefront of our consciousness on Yom Kippur, is similar to a marital relationship.[87] Both comprise blessings and successes to enjoy, as well as challenges and obstacles to overcome. Just as in marriage, we cannot always foresee each and every matter in our relationship with God. All we can do is take a realistic look at ourselves, have courage, and take a leap of faith. We can have such faith because of the ability we have to think, learn, pray, teach, and love. This ability enables us to know that we can overcome the hurdles that cause us to falter. Ultimately, we can find a blessing in any test God gives us.

---

* The Book of Exodus ("Going Out") was so titled when translated into Greek because it describes the Israelites' departure from Egypt. In the original Hebrew the title is focused differently: the book is called *Shemot* ("Names"), taken from the first verse, "These are the names of the sons of Israel who came to Egypt with Jacob. . . ."

** Rabban Shimon ben Gamliel II (circa 135–170 C.E.) was the head of the Usha academy in Palestine. He was among the greatest of the sages of the Mishnah and the father of Yehudah Ha-Nasi, compiler of the Mishnah.

THE THREE LEVELS
Peshat: simple, literal meaning
Derash: historical, Rabbinic inquiry
Making It Personal:
contemporary analysis and application

Sin and Confession

Al het she-chatanu lefanecha. . . .
We have sinned against You
purposely and by mistake. . . .
We have sinned against You by
speaking badly of others. . . .
We have sinned against You by
greed and oppressive interest. . . .
We have sinned against You by
rashly judging others. . . .
For all these sins, forgiving
God, forgive us, pardon us,
grant us atonement.
Ve-al kulam Elo-ha selichot, selach lanu,
mechal lanu, kaper lanu

—The *Al Het* Confessional,
High Holiday *Machzor*

Peshat

These few lines of the Yom Kippur *Al Het** confessional represent just a fraction of the 44 sorts of transgressions committed daily. They are detailed in an alphabetical acrostic within the Yom Kippur liturgy, listing two sins for each of the 22 letters in the Hebrew alphabet.

Confessing, like fasting and self-denial, is one of the most significant mitzvot (commandments) Jews fulfill on Yom Kippur. It is based upon the biblical account of the confession of the High Priest (see earlier section, "Yom Kippur in the Bible") on behalf of the community. Once the Temple was destroyed, however, sacrifices and the formal role of the Priests ended. Therefore, personal and communal prayer became the primary Jewish expression for relating to the Divine.

The manner in which Jews confess marks an important distinction between Judaism and other religions. Unlike classic Christianity and Catholicism, where the priest acts as a divine intermediary, receiving the confession of each individual, Jews pray and confess directly to God. In fact, Jews perform a confessional during daily prayer. The Yom Kippur confessional is much more comprehensive, providing a stunning account of the imperfection of humanity within which all cannot help but find themselves.

Derash

The Talmud notes that we deliberately say "We have sinned" in contrast to "I have sinned."[88] For in Judaism, we all must acknowledge what it is to be a human being, namely, that we are all imperfect. Each of us must individually atone for personal transgressions yet also remain aware that everyone is flawed, while we stand amidst the entire community. No one is, or ever was, perfect; even the Bible is blunt in its description of the improprieties of our great ancestors, such as Abraham, Jacob, and King David.

The tradition also asserts that the source of human imperfection lies in our emotional instability. When we allow our fears and desires to dictate our impulses, without an overlay of reason, we are more likely to do wrong. Emotional response without thoughtfulness leads to transgression. With this concept in mind, we actually beat our hearts in remorse, as the heart symbolizes the seat of sin.[89]

Making It Personal

It is of great significance that the *Al Het*, the Yom Kippur prayer asking forgiveness for a multitude of sins, only lists moral transgressions. After all, Judaism takes a legal approach to religious practice, and the list could have included all of the religious infractions people commit, such as breaking Shabbat or eating nonkosher foods. This is not because the sages of the tradition, who wrote this prayer, did not value such observance; they understood that ethics and ritual go hand in hand. Rather, the moral infractions listed in this prayer are those committed between human beings—*bein adam lechavero.* Religious transgressions such as breaking Shabbat or neglecting kashrut (Jewish dietary laws) are purely between man and God—*bein adam la-Makom*—and their exclusion from *Al Het* shows the sages' conviction that God surely forgives.[90]

Yom Kippur is the opportunity that Judaism provides to evaluate our behavior, as this prayer teaches, especially in regard to our behavior toward others. The combined act of living righteously and treating others well is portrayed in our tradition as a craft and art form that requires study and practice. Public confession eliminates a degree of our shame and facilitates a sense of forgiving, as everyone admits that they are not yet masters of this craft. As aspiring moral artists, we can now wipe clean the slate of our souls and begin again, echoing the words of Rabbi Solomon Schechter (architect of the Conservative movement), "the great saintly souls are lovely to look at just as a great piece of art is."[91]

---

* *Al Het*, loosely translated, is the beginning of the phrase "We have sinned against You." The prayer is one of the best-known Yom Kippur *viduim* (confessionals).

THE THREE LEVELS
Peshat: simple, literal meaning
Derash: historical, Rabbinic inquiry
Making It Personal:
contemporary analysis and application

Truth versus Mercy

From the Book of Exodus

So Moses carved two tablets of stone, like the first, and early in the morning he went up on Mount Sinai, as the LORD had commanded him, taking the two stone tablets with him. The LORD came down in a cloud; He stood with him there, and proclaimed the name LORD. The LORD passed before him and proclaimed: *Adonai! Adonai! El rachum ve-chanun, erekh apayim ve-rav chesed ve-emet notzer chesed la-alafim, nose avon va-fesha ve-chata'ah ve-nakeh....*[92] "The LORD! The LORD! A God compassionate and gracious, slow to anger, abounding in kindness and faithfulness [truth],[93] extending kindness to the thousandth generation, forgiving iniquity, transgression and sin..."

—Exod. 34:4–7[94]

From the Book of Jonah

This displeased Jonah greatly, and he was grieved. He prayed to the LORD, saying, "O LORD! Isn't this just what I said when I was still in my own country? That is why I fled beforehand to Tarshish. *Ki yadati ki atah El chanun ve-rachum, erekh apayim ve-rav chesed, ve-nicham al ha-ra'ah...* For I know that You are a compassionate and gracious God, slow to anger, abounding in kindness, renouncing punishment. Please LORD, take my life, for I would rather die than live."

—Jonah 4:1–3[95]

Peshat

On Yom Kippur, before the Torah is removed from the Holy Ark *(Aron Kodesh)* we chant three times from the *machzor* the Thirteen Attributes of God (also known as the Thirteen Attributes of Mercy). Taken from *parashat Ki Tissa*[96] in the Book of Exodus, chapter 34, these 13 attributes reflect back upon us and tell us what we are to learn about and strive for in our lives.[97] God came down in a cloud and pronounced these attributes at Mount Sinai, after the Jews had experienced extreme moments there of both glory and despair. These included God's giving of the tablets of the Pact (on which the Ten Commandments were written); the sin of the Golden Calf and subsequent punishment; God's threat to destroy Israel; and the creation of the second set of tablets, (which, according to Rabbinic tradition, occurred on Yom Kippur).

Jonah also experiences many ups and downs, including fleeing from God, being thrown into the sea, getting swallowed by a fish, and finally conceding to God's wishes that he pronounce the destruction of Nineveh—only to have God renege on the plan. At this point Jonah repeats the Thirteen Attributes of God; however, he omits the word *emet* (truth). Therefore, we are left with this question: is it possible that Jonah does not understand God as a God of truth?

Derash

When Jonah repeated the attributes, he was upset for two possible reasons. One 13th-century commentary says that Jonah was upset because he actually knew all along that God was not going to punish the people of Nineveh and that is why he fled to Tarshish. Jonah knew that he would be the false prophet described in Deuteronomy (18:21–22).[98]

Another medieval commentator says that Jonah did not agree with God's display of compassion.[99] In other words, Jonah questioned how God could be so merciful with such an evil people, yet be so strict and vengeful with the Israelites. Accordingly, Jonah could not accept the Ninevites' repentance. After all, these were the Assyrian people who would destroy and conquer Israel in 722 B.C.E.[100]

Both of the commentaries portray Jonah as angry with God. The omission of *emet* in his prayer may be a sign of despair and anger with God and the world, or perhaps of his own inability to feel compassion; and so he begs for death.

Making It Personal

Jonah is symbolic for all of us. Jonah wants truth—and consequences. So too we want to see people pay for their crimes, to watch ethical consequences *(middah ke-negged middah)* exacted before our very eyes. This would help us make sense of the world. We know, however, that this is not how life works. People are often given second chances (or even more). This circumstance creates a reality supporting our tradition's claim that compassion and mercy are stronger than justice.[101]

On Yom Kippur, we acknowledge our sins; and, in the hope that God listens to us and sees our truest intentions, we pray that we too may be given a second chance. The story of Jonah challenges us to have such hope not only for ourselves, but for others as well. Thus, the book leaves us all with a question. God asks Jonah (and by implication us) whether or not God should care about the sinning Ninevites, who also prayed for mercy. In other words, where is the boundary between forgiving people and exacting strict justice?

Yom Kippur

Significance of the Holiday: Some Modern Perspectives

An Evolution in Rite and Prayer

by Cheryl Peretz

Yom Kippur is the holiest day of the Jewish year and, although always deemed as such by the Jewish people, adherence to it changed throughout the ages. We see significant evolution and adaptation in how the holiday has been practiced from the time the Torah was given until today.

The Biblical Period

According to the biblical tradition, the Day of Atonement, known as the Sabbath of all Sabbaths and designated to be observed on the 10th day of the seventh month, was one in the cycle of holidays announced by Moses after his return from Mount Sinai. Like the other occasions in the cycle of holidays, the Torah calls for the offering of a special sacrifice on Yom Kippur. This day, however, is distinguished by the phrase *te'anu et nafshoteikhem … ki bayom ha-zeh yekhaper aleichem letaher etkhem mikol chatoteikhem,* "you shall practice self denial … for on this day atonement shall be made for you to cleanse you of all your sins" (Lev. 16:29–30). This statement is, of course, attached to the priestly ritual through which atonement and forgiveness were achieved. Therefore, although we think of Yom Kippur as a time for each of us to participate in our own individual atonement, in its earliest rites as described in the Torah, it was primarily an endeavor limited to the High Priest in the Temple.

As the Israelites wandered in the desert, Moses' older brother, Aaron, assumed the role of High Priest, whose job it was to purify himself, his family, and the nation on Yom Kippur. In addition to the ordinary morning rites, the High Priest would dress in special vestments and enter the Holy of Holies, the curtained-off area of the tabernacle housing the original set of broken tablets over which God's sheltering presence hovered. In an unusual, yet powerful ritual, the High Priest would select one of two goats provided by the people and place his hands on the head. This act would serve to transfer the burden of the people's sins onto the animal. The goat was then taken to a high cliff and pushed off the side to its death.

The purpose of killing an innocent animal was not to blame it for the collective sins of the people; rather it served as a vehicle through which one could transport those sins and transgressions far away. When accompanied by the congregation's acknowledgment of its behaviors and its genuine remorse, divine forgiveness became possible.

THE SECOND TEMPLE ERA

Much is written in the Mishnah (tractate *Yoma*) about Yom Kippur in the period of the Second Temple. There we are provided with a description of the holiday that is more familiar to us, yet little is mentioned as to how this evolution occurred. Expanding beyond priestly rituals of purity, the Mishnah (1st to 3rd centuries C.E.) records several significant changes in the observance of Yom Kippur.

The Mishnah tells us that the High Priest would begin his preparation one week prior to Yom Kippur, entering the Temple and assuming all temple responsibilities himself. As the week wore on, the preparation would intensify, laying the groundwork for the awesome holiness of the day itself. In addition, he would study two Torah portions and learn one by heart in order to ensure that he did not err. For the High Priest, however, the night preceding Yom Kippur held the most special significance, as he would remain learning Torah all night, engaging in meditative and spiritual preparation. If he fell asleep, the younger Priests would wake him by reciting psalms. If necessary, the High Priest was forced to stand all night on a cold, stone floor.

During the Yom Kippur ritual itself, the High Priest recited three specific confessional formulas and on three different occasions he would pronounce the four-letter name of God (the Tetragrammaton). The temple ritual also included reading the Torah's account of the day (Lev. 16) and the passage describing the sacrifice for the day (Num. 29). This was accompanied by a series of blessings and prayers, all of which continue to find their way into our service today (Mishnah, *Yoma* 8).

It is also during the Second Temple period when the role of the congregation is increased and expanded. Just as there were prayers for the Priest in biblical times, we witness the emergence of the entire people engaging in prayers in the temple era. The most distinguishable of these prayers is the famous line that silently follows the *Shema*—the central statement of God's oneness and Jewish faith. According to the Mishnah, the people would assemble outside in awe of the moment and, after the High Priest uttered the Ineffable Name, they would prostrate themselves, saying, *barukh shem kevod malchuto le-olam va-ed,* "Blessed be the name of the glory of His kingdom forever and ever," a phrase even toda, is only said aloud (rather than in an undertone) on Yom Kippur.

By this period it is also already evident that Yom Kippur was observed as an entire day filled with prayer and meditation. Interestingly, however, despite the unique nature of the morning rites for Yom Kippur, the afternoon temple service maintained its regular format, only marked by the High Priest washing and changing his clothes again, lighting the menorah, and burning incense. When he finally went home, well-wishers, who spent the day praying and fasting, would accompany the High Priest and thank him for a successful Yom Kippur. The High Priest would then host a feast for fellow Priests and other dignitaries. The remnants of this tradition are still practiced today with the "break-the-fast" meal enjoyed by family and friends.

Post Temple Era

The destruction of the Second Temple in 70 C.E. brought many difficult challenges for the rabbis in preserving the service and rituals of Yom Kippur. Because the temple rites could no longer be performed, the rabbis had to reconstruct the day without the pageantry associated with temple life. Weight and meaning shifted from sacrifices and priestly rituals to prayer, repentance, and the giving of charity. Furthermore, the responsibility for atonement shifted from the High Priest and the congregation to the individual, and, rather than through sacrifices, the actual day became the means for atonement (Mishnah, *Yoma* 8).

We also see this period develop and expand the statement of the Torah's depiction of the day, namely that it is a day that "you shall practice self-denial." The rabbis defined this phrase by way of prohibitions against not only eating and drinking, but also washing, anointing, wearing shoes, and having sexual relations. Finally, the prayer service is firmly established, including the five different times of prayer that continue until today (evening, morning, additional, afternoon, and closing). Because of the historic importance of the day, and the collective memory of the Jewish people, the Rabbis created the *Avodah* service, which made sure that the service retained descriptions of Yom Kippur's ancient priestly rituals.

In the centuries that followed, the liturgy in the *machzor* (the High Holiday prayer book), as we know it, continued to develop, especially throughout the Middle Ages. Today we discover liturgical poems *(piyyutim)* by medieval scholars such as Eleazar Kalir,

Meshullam ben Kalonymous, and Rabbi Meir of Rothenburg. In the end, the *machzor* brings us back to the very origins of the holiday, where we find the Israelites in the wilderness. It brings us back to the elaborate priestly rites of the great Temple in Jerusalem and to our Rabbinic sages, who advanced the survival of the holidays by unearthing and teaching their most fundamental meanings. As we encounter the year's most holy day, we come to confess and pray as participants in the Jewish present, evoking an eternally evolving Jewish ritual of the distant Jewish past.

Repentance, Confession, and Atonement

by Bradley Shavit Artson

Yom Kippur, the pinnacle of the Days of Awe, displays a quantumlike quality of reconciling two distinct but crucial modes of being. Atonement—the public need to make good for collectively falling short, for communal manifestations of greed, wrongdoing, impiety—jostles with the need for repentance—the individual's return from having veered off the narrow path of righteousness.

At its earliest layer, the biblical Yom Kippur is a day of atonement—a day when the entire people Israel come together to cleanse the temple sanctuary of the residue of a year's worth of sin:

> And this shall be to all of you a law for all time: In the seventh month, on the tenth day of the month, you shall practice self-denial; and you shall do no manner of work, neither the citizen nor the alien who resides among you. For on this day atonement shall be made for you to cleanse you of all your sins; you all shall be clean before the LORD. It shall be a sabbath of complete rest for you all, and you all shall practice self-denial; it is a law for all time.
> —Lev. 16:29–30

The core of the Torah reading for the day of Yom Kippur emerges from the heart of the priestly codes, detailing the regulations for purifying the altar and the sanctuary from the defilement of having absorbed another year of Israel's sins. Surely, this day is more filled with ritual than any other, more swollen with poetry, pomp, a rich musical and liturgical rite, than any other. Yom Kippur is the high-water mark of the priestly conviction that rite makes right, that Israel's relationship to God demands adherence to the public practice established by Torah and by Rabbinic code. On Yom Kippur, we return *as a people* to the path of mitzvot and prayer. It is as a people that we are cleansed.

Yet Yom Kippur is also intensely personal, a day of introspection and repentance on an individual level too. That focus on *teshuvah* is reflected in the ancient words of the prophet Isaiah, selected as the haftarah reading on this most ritually laden day of all:

> Is such the fast I desire,
> A day for men to starve their bodies?
> Is it bowing the head like a bulrush
> And lying in sackcloth and ashes?
> Do you call that a fast,
> A day when the LORD is favorable?
> No, this is the fast I desire:
> To unlock fetters of wickedness,
> And untie the cords of the yoke
> To let the oppressed go free;
> To break off every yoke.
> It is to share your bread with the hungry,
> And to take the wretched poor into your home;
> When you see the naked, to clothe him,
> And not to ignore your own kin.
> Then shall your light burst through like the dawn
> And your healing spring up quickly;...
> —(Isa. 58:5–8)

On the very day when we come together to enact such a complex choreography, at the time when we attend to an endless ritual script—it's at that exact moment that we read the piercing charge of Isaiah, who condemns ritual that is not the outer reflection of real inner work. Ritual is beautiful when it is the manifestation of ethical rigor and spiritual depth. Then observance can become an art form of the body, almost a dance. But ritual severed from ethical or spiritual moorings is worse than mere inaction—it is hypocrisy institutionalized, it is abomination!

The key to both atonement and repentance is confession, the Torah's simple requirement that the sinner (individual or the people) confess the sin publicly, "Aaron shall lay both his hands upon the head of the live goat and confess over it all the iniquities and transgressions of the Israelites, whatever their sins...." (Lev. 16:21), reminding us to confess for the ways we, as a people, have failed to live up to the highest standards of Torah, failed to answer God's call to be a light to the nations, failed to become our truest selves. At the same time as the Priest confesses our collective wrongdoing, we also confess our individual shortcomings and betrayals, "When a man or woman commits any wrong toward a fellow man, thus breaking faith with the LORD, and that person realizes his guilt, he shall confess the wrong that he has done...." (Num. 5:5–7). The communal ritual traces an inner awareness—as we contemplate the gap between our potential and our deeds, between what we could have been and how we actually acted, we muster the courage to repent.

According to Rav Sa'adia Ga'on, great philosopher and talmudic sage of medieval Baghdad, repentance entails four things: the renunciation of sin, the feeling of remorse, the quest for forgiveness, and the assumption of the obligation not to relapse into sin.[102] The day stands, therefore, on the edifice of honest self-scrutiny, on the optimism that human beings can grow toward the light, that we can discipline our errant behavior to express our highest ideals. Yom Kippur is a day in which the sanctuary of our heart, as well as the institutions we have established as a people, are held to a very high standard (God's) and judged by that standard, not for the sake of smug self-congratulation, but because the work is great, and the master is waiting to forgive.

Moral Freedom and Responsibility

by Elliot N. Dorff

Fasting and services all day long. That, unfortunately, is all that comes to mind when most Jews think of Yom Kippur, the Day of Atonement. It is definitely a "downer," and flies in the face of what American culture has taught us to value—namely, individual freedom and happiness.

The irony is that the Jewish tradition believes in individual freedom and happiness too. The Torah includes 613 commandments, by traditional count, and the Rabbis added many more; but none of those commandments make any sense unless we have the ability to obey or disobey them. That is, the Torah presumes that we are not automata forced to do whatever we are programmed to do; we are instead people with free will, who can and do decide whether to obey any of God's commandments and, if so, how. That is the theme of one of the very first stories of Genesis: Adam and Eve eat of the fruit of knowledge of good and bad, a mythic way of asserting that human beings know the difference between right and wrong and can act on that knowledge if they choose to do so. The many biblical stories in which God and the Israelites are at odds because the Israelites have chosen not to obey God's commandments, together with the stories of Abraham, Moses, Jeremiah, and Job all arguing with God as to what God should do and demand of Israel in the first place, make it crystal clear that the Jewish tradition puts heavy emphasis on individual freedom. In fact, only one of the major medieval Jewish philosophers, Gersonides, interprets Judaism in a deterministic way; all the others assume, along with the Bible and Talmud, that we have free will. This is the polar opposite of religions like Islam that assert instead that our actions are determined by God, the Fates, or something else.

Similarly, unlike Calvinist Christianity and some other religions, most Jewish texts presume that we should strive to be happy in life, that indeed one reason to follow the dictates of Jewish law in the first place is because they will lead us to a wise, fulfilling, and happy life. So, for example, Moses says this to the Israelites:

> See, I have imparted to you laws and rules, as the LORD my God has commanded me, for you to abide by in the land you are about to enter and occupy. Observe them faithfully, for they will be proof of your wisdom and discernment to other peoples, who, on hearing of all these laws, will say, "Surely, that great nation is a wise and discerning people."
> —Deut. 4:5–6

Wisdom, in biblical Hebrew, means *savoir faire,* knowledge of how to handle oneself in life in order to succeed, "street smarts." Thus in saying that Jewish law will make us wise, the Torah is asserting that it will help us succeed in living our lives fruitfully and successfully, such that we can avoid problems and feel fulfilled. Similarly, at the very beginning of the Book of Psalms, the psalmist declares that obeying Jewish law will make us happy:

> Happy is the person who has not followed the counsel of the wicked or taken the path of sinners or joined the company of the insolent; rather, the Teaching of the LORD is his delight, and he studies that Teaching day and night. He is like a tree planted beside streams of water, which yields its fruit in season, whose foliage never fades, and whatever it produces thrives.
> —Ps. 1:1–3

Furthermore, Yom Kippur is the only biblical holy day on which we fast; on all the rest, including the weekly Sabbath, we are supposed to rejoice with sumptuous food, conjugal relations, and time spent with family and friends. Hence the element of *oneg Shabbat,* the joy of the Sabbath, that the Rabbis built into its observance in these ways. With regard to the biblical festivals the Torah is even more explicit: "You shall rejoice in your festival,..." (Deut. 16:14), it tells us.

So why is Yom Kippur different? Why does Jewish law require us to observe it each year with solemn and long services and with fasting? It is because the Jewish tradition is convinced that along with freedom comes responsibility. That is, precisely because we have knowledge of good and evil and the ability to act on that knowledge, we are responsible for our actions. And that responsibility is not just theoretical; it adheres to each and every one of our actions. What the Days of Awe, beginning with Rosh Hashanah and ending with Yom Kippur, thus beckon us to do is to engage in a process of reflection about what we have done in the past year; to ask forgiveness of any individuals we may have hurt and to take the steps of remorse and repair that are required in making up for what we have done wrongly to others; and now, during the Ten Days of Repentance culminating on Yom Kippur, to ask God for forgiveness as well for the ways that we have acted against God's will.

As the Jewish tradition perceives this process, it is a very serious business. Indeed, as the liturgy has it, our very lives are at stake. Hence the music of the services skips octaves to alert us to the gap that separates us from God and from what God wants of us. Hence also the long services: it takes an awful lot to get us out of our self-satisfied and egocentric stupor to see ourselves as God does and to make the changes in our lives that would make us better people, more in line with what God would have us be. That is also why we fast on this day—both to show our remorse for what we have done wrong and also to make us focus on our spiritual and moral lives rather than our physical lives. Furthermore, nobody is perfect; that is why we need Yom Kippur each year. Indeed, three times each weekday, Jewish liturgy has us ask God for forgiveness for our sins; this theme of our imperfection and our need to change is highlighted during this season of the year, but it certainly is not restricted to it.

And yet this is "the white fast," in contrast to the Ninth of Av, when we commemorate the tragedies of Jewish history, which is "the black fast." Yom Kippur is white—that is, joyous, because God knows that He created us imperfect and thus uses mercy as well as justice in judging us. Ultimately, the Jewish tradition is convinced that "repentance, prayer, and righteous deeds will avert the severity of the decree,"[103] that if we are sincere in our efforts to change, God will wipe away the taint of our past sins and work with us in the future to be better human beings.

May we manifest that level of sincerity on Yom Kippur, and may we make the changes necessary to live our lives more closely in accordance with God's will so that we may attain the freedom, wisdom, and happiness that it brings.

Accepting the Decree

by Miriam Burg

"Let us proclaim the holiness of this day—a day of awe and terror."

So begins *U-netaneh Tokef,* perhaps the most haunting prayer in all of Jewish liturgy. The prayer confronts us—in stark and unabashed language—with the truth of our own mortality. In many ways, Yom Kippur itself is a rehearsal for dying, a day of "make-believe" so real that, among other practices, we do not eat or drink (the dead have no need for sustenance) and we dress in a *kitel* (the same garment in which Jews are buried). *U-netaneh Tokef,* recited in traditional synagogues during the *Musaf Amidah* on both Rosh Hashanah and Yom Kippur, challenges us to stare death in the face and to arise from that experience with renewed commitment to what matters most in life.

The High Holy Day prayer book is distinguished by multitudes of *piyyutim,* liturgical poems written throughout the centuries that express the spiritual sensibilities of their authors. *U-netaneh Tokef* is one such *piyyut.* Though its historical origin remains uncertain, the prayer has been attributed to the 11th-century rabbi Amnon of Mainz (11th century C.E.). According to legend, Rabbi Amnon uttered the words immediately before tragically dying for his refusal to convert to Christianity *(Or Zarua, Hilkhot Rosh Hashanah).*

U-netaneh Tokef proclaims that God judges every human being on Yom Ha-Din, the Day of Judgment, and decrees the fate of each person. Whether or not one agrees with this theological perspective, listening to the litany of possible endings is nothing short of haunting, because it reminds us that, ultimately, life and death are not in human hands.

On Rosh Hashanah it is written, and on Yom Kippur it is sealed:

> How many shall leave this world, and how many shall be born; who shall live and who shall die, who in the fullness of years and who before; who shall perish by fire and who by water, who by sword and who by a wild

> beast; who by famine and who by thirst, who by earthquake and who by plague; who by strangling and who by stoning, who shall rest and who shall wander; who shall be serene and who disturbed; who shall be at ease and who afflicted; who shall be impoverished and who enriched, who shall be humbled and who exalted.[104]

It is a condition of our humanity that, no matter how "good" we are, our time in this world is finite. We will die and, though we can make lifestyle decisions that help or hinder the length of our days, we do not have complete control over when or how our end will come. This difficult reality, however, so nakedly revealed in these lines, is not the end of this poem; what follows is both comforting and hopeful. It reads, "But repentance *(teshuvah)*, prayer *(tefillah)* and acts of righteousness *(tzedakah)* remove the bitterness of the decree."

There is a very similar statement in the Jerusalem Talmud that helps to elucidate the possible meaning of these words. The Talmud reads, "Three things annul the evil decree: prayer, acts of righteousness, and repentance" (J. Talmud, *Ta'aniyot* 2:65b). There is, of course, a noticeable difference between the two. Do repentance, prayer, and acts of righteousness annul the decree, or do they remove the bitterness of the decree?

Part of the answer to that question lies in answering another question: what exactly is "the decree"? The simplest interpretation, given the preceding paragraphs of the *piyyut,* is that the decree is a particular pronouncement of death or suffering for a given person. However, we know that people who repent, people who pray, and people who do acts of righteousness still die. Even the noblest effort does not ensure that a tumor will disappear or that an earthquake will spare someone. Even the "best" people die. We do not have an obvious power to rescind such decrees.

More broadly, "the decree" has another meaning: human mortality. Whether or not we believe in a God who, quite literally, writes each of us in the book of life or death every year at this season, we know that at some season, in some year, death will find us. We cannot annul that decree. So, what can we do? According to the author of *U-netaneh Tokef,* we have the remarkable capacity to "remove the bitterness" of the decree. How? By repenting, praying, and doing acts of righteousness. A person who repents is someone who constantly reflects on his or her life and makes changes to live it with increasing integrity. A person who prays is someone who maintains an active and personal relationship with God. A person who does acts of righteousness is someone who makes it a priority to care for others. Taken together, then, the person who does these three things honors the self, the other, and God; the person who does these three things lives a life of great value.

In his book *Man's Search For Meaning,* Viktor Frankl, the great philosopher and Holocaust survivor, wrote, "Ultimately, man should not ask what the meaning of his life is, but rather he must recognize that it is *he* who is asked. In a word, each man is questioned by life; and he can only answer to life by *answering for* his own life; to life he can only respond by being responsible."[105] The bitterness of the decree can be sweetened by living responsibly, by living a worthwhile and sacred life. The poem teaches that when we do so, we can die knowing that we did not waste God's precious gift—life—bestowed so generously upon us. *U-netaneh Tokef* declares: though we do not have control over the quantity of our days, we do have control over their quality.

This powerful *piyyut* concludes by telling us how much God values our lives. Even so, the poet is compelled to remind us that our lives here are temporary.

> Our origin is dust and our end is dust. At the hazard of our life we earn our bread. We are like a fragile vessel, like the grass that withers, the flower that fades, the shadow that passes, the cloud that vanishes, the wind that blows, the dust that floats, the dream that flies away. But You, Sovereign of All, are the living and everlasting God.

We are not God. We are human, and humans are mortal. We are "flowers that fade," but before that, we can be vibrant and beautiful, we can shoot up toward the sun, bringing sweet aromas and dazzling visions into God's world. It is the prayer of this prayer that the reality of death will inspire us to life.

Yom Kippur

Alternative Meditations

Elul

by Judith Sarah Schmidt

the colors of the flowers
are becoming quiet
a ripe apple falls gently
like love
into my hands
bees gather their last
honeyed harvest
all is wrapped in stilled tenderness

crossing over to the mainland
the ferry master cautions to
hold our ears
as the horn blasts through
the morning fog
I do not cover my ears
I let it be a shofar sound
circling me
in these last days of summer
toward the harvesting
of my heart

to search and weigh and sort
golden songs dark silences
flowerings fallen seeds
the lost and found
and never to be found
of this year this life

hesed hands raise up
the shofar's cry

lift the heart
like a white lamb
bleating prayers of praise
for the plentitude
of these days
bleating prayers of tears
for the starving, sick bodies
the senseless bloodshed
of this year

awaken me please Your sleeper
remember me please Your forgetter
spare me
prepare me
unshutter my heart
naked to open
toward the first star
to offer myself
at the neila gates
receive me into Your hands
as seed offering

plant me anew
into the new year
and as evening descends
on the last night
as the gates of heaven
begin to close
wrap me just a little longer
in the lingering scent
of Your unending love

The Ritual of the Scapegoat

by Ellen Frankel[106]

The Sages in Our Own Time explain: Azazel was a goat-demon, a popular mythological figure in the ancient world. According to the apocryphal Book of Enoch, the angel Raphael, in order to punish Azazel, along with several other angels, for sleeping with the "daughters of men," banished him to the desert. From this outpost he controlled acts of harlotry, war, and sorcery. Using "sympathetic" magic—that is, fighting fire with fire—the High Priest would dispatch the sin-laden goat once each year to cancel the goat-demon's sinful influence on the people.

The Rabbis add: We learn in the Mishnah that a priest was appointed to accompany the goat to make sure it did not return to inhabited lands; later, it was driven off a cliff.

Miriam the Prophet suggests: Although nowadays we only *read* about this ritual as part of the Yom Kippur liturgy, we might consider—given our experience as a people, and as Jewish women in particular—designating during this period our own totem figures: symbolic images, words, or objects that we could release against those demonic forces that scapegoat us or encourage us to stray.

Dinah the Wounded One declares: Imagine how liberating it would be to exorcise the stereotype of the JAP (Jewish American Princess) from popular culture. Or our own internalized anti-Semitism, which makes us hate our bodies, our names, our men, and ourselves. How healthy it would be to drive these demons off a nearby cliff!

Meditation before Yom Kippur for One Who Cannot Fast

by Simkha Y. Weintraub

Ribbono shel Olam/Master of the Universe;
Creator of All, Source of All Life,
Who Knows What is Deep in Human Hearts,
Who Nurtures Every Living Being:

As You know, dear God,
Yom Kippur is fast approaching, and because of my condition,
I am not able to keep the traditional fast—
I cannot abstain totally from eating.

On this Day of Atonement, this Sabbath of Sabbaths, this year and every year, it is so central to join the people of Israel in denying ourselves food and drink for one day so that we focus on correcting our misdeeds, on knowing our mortality; on reaching for a life of Torah, mitzvot, and lovingkindness; on You.

You know, dear God, that it is not my intent
to be apart from our people and our tradition.
My current state of health makes it unsuitable for me to fast

So, dear God, I turn to You now in sincerity and openness:
Help me in the coming year to do my best in guarding my health.
Help us, Your children, learn how to protect our bodies from harm.
Help us support others in caring for their *tzelem Elokim,* their Image of God.
Teach us to help one another grow and thrive in Body, Mind, and Spirit.

Guide caring family and health care professionals in their partnering with you
to bring healing if not cure, support and strength if not an end to symptoms.
And if there is an opportunity for me to help others who suffer
by doing something they need or by being attentive company—
Grant me the ability to do this mitzvah with love and devotion.

Rofeh khol basar/Healer of all living creatures:
I thank You for the breath that is in me
for the community of Israel that lives
for the possibilities of today and tomorrow.

A Carnival at the Gates: Jonah and Laughter on Yom Kippur

by Rachel Adler[107]

A Chasidic saying declares in a paradoxical pun: *Yom kippurim yom kepurim.*[108] Yom Kippur is a day like Purim. A powerful paradox! Here are two holidays that seem to be each other's antithesis. Yom Kippur is a fast, a day of tears and introspection. Purim is a feast, a day of laughter and carousing. Yom Kippur demands bodily deprivation. Purim mandates bodily pleasure. Whereas Yom Kippur reinforces traditional laws and values, Purim stands them on their heads. Boundaries are eroded. Roles are reversed. For men to dress as women is in some communities a traditional Purim masquerade. Even the daily services lack their usual solemnity; they are punctuated by jokes, interruptions, and, in some communities, irreverent parodies of other liturgies. "Purim Torah" caricatures the study of sacred texts. Satires mock teachers and communal leaders. The rules require unruliness: "Raba said, on Purim, one is obligated to drink until one does not know *[ad shelo yada]* the difference between 'cursed be Haman and blessed be Mordecai'" (Megilla 7a).[109]

Viewing Purim as the inverse of Yom Kippur brings us closer to understanding their likeness, for an inversion is merely a likeness reversed. Yom Kippur is a fast preceded by a feast, while Purim is a feast preceded by a fast. Purim is a celebration tinged with somberness, whereas Yom Kippur is a solemn occasion pervaded by celebration. Hence, Yom Kippur's liturgical structure closely resembles festival liturgies. Sanctuary and Torah Scrolls are decked in white. Worshipers wear their best clothes. Only their feet, in nonleather shoes, bespeak fasting and mourning. This amalgam of joy and mourning is also expressed by the *kitel,* a white garment worn by the service leader and by traditional worshipers, a white garment that also serves as both wedding robe and shroud.

The central liturgical performance of Purim is the reading of the Book of Esther, whose laughter is frequently undercut by mourning, dread, and violence. Traditionally, at certain points in the narration, its lively cantillation slides into the haunting melody in which the Book of Lamentations is chanted, suggesting the tenuousness of all escapes. Texts, as Paul Ricoeur says, "explode the worlds of their authors."[110] Our judgment and our laughter are dynamic responses altered by changes in the world, the community, and the self we bring to every reading or ritual enactment. Layered upon the text of Esther are memories of the Holocaust, the story in which Haman won; of the terrible Purim celebration of 1994, at the Cave of Machpelah in Hebron, where Baruch Goldstein reenacted upon the bodies of praying Muslims the revenge of the Jews of Persia upon their enemies; and the 1996 terrorist retaliation against Israeli teenagers. These shadows upon an already shadowed text are manifestations of Yom Kippur amid the uproar of the carnival. We are forced to recall the reality and finality of death, the sins of vengeance, and the terrible repetition compulsion to which they shackle both victor and vanquished.[111]

Death and justice are central themes for both Purim and Yom Kippur. On both we acknowledge that existence, individual and communal, is precarious, and human power and knowledge are limited. We have responsibility but little control. We figure in patterns that are beyond our discernment and can be hurt by forces and currents that are beyond us as well as by the repercussions of our own acts.

Purim commemorates a narrowly averted holocaust decreed through a perversion of justice. Falsely accused, the Jewish people are abandoned by a king who hands over his authority to a biased and greedy official. Justice reinstated expresses itself as another kind of favoritism: salvation for the Jews but pitiless retribution for their enemies. Life and death, justice and injustice, are arbitrarily dealt out to winners and losers in the great game of power. A palace bureaucracy riddled with cabals is checkmated by an even more mysterious opponent: the divine strategist whose name is never mentioned in the Book of Esther.

On Yom Kippur, life and death and the administration of justice are equally central concerns, but there are tensions and ambivalences in their definitions. One set of liturgical themes derived from the book of Kohelet (Ecclesiastes) radically and reductively articulates human impermanence and ultimate insignificance: "What are we? What is our life? What is our piety? What is our righteousness? What is our attainment, our power, our might?[112] Human beings are no different from animals, for all are fleeting and futile *[ki hakol hevel]*."[113] There is no favoritism in Kohelet's account of divine justice. An imperfect humanity must account for itself before an impersonal, impartial, and omniscient deity. In a second set of themes, however, justice is personal, flexible, and leavened with compassion. The cornerstone text for this theology of justice is the declaration of God's mercy as proclaimed by God to Moses after the sin of the Golden Calf (Exod. 34:7) and by Moses back to God after the spies return with their false report and the people lose faith in God's promise of the land (Num. 14:18): "YHWH YHWH God, showing-mercy, showing-favor, long suffering in anger, abundant in loyalty and faithfulness, keeping loyalty to the thousandth [generation], bearing iniquity, rebellion and sin."[114] The rabbis heighten this theology of justice-as-compassion by an audacious undermining of the text. They repunctuate the final clause of the verse, so that instead of the literal reading "and clearing, he surely does not clear [the guilty], but visits the iniquity of the parents upon children and children's children to the third and fourth generations," they obtain the reading we use liturgically: "and clearing even the guilty."[115] This formula, which we recite over and over, expresses the tacit subversion of retributive justice at the heart of Yom Kippur.

Purim belongs to those festivals that invert or subvert rules and norms overtly rather than covertly. Many cultures have such festivals. The ancient Romans called them Saturnalia. Medieval Europeans called them feasts of fools and carnivals. Such festivals glorify bodily pleasure and celebrate the comic, the grotesque, and the excessive. These characteristics of the carnivalesque have in recent years attracted the attention of literary scholars and anthropologists.[116]

It is late in the day of Yom Kippur that the carnivalesque bursts into our liturgy.[117] At the afternoon service, with blood sugar at low ebb and self-congratulation for our asceticism on the rise, we read what may be the funniest book of the Bible, Jonah.

The custom of reading Jonah on Yom Kippur is very old. Its first written source, interestingly, is in Megilla 31b, the tractate of the Babylonian Talmud whose major topic is the laws of Purim.[118] These ancient liturgical associations with Purim can serve as a portal into a book that is rather off-putting for women. The fictional world of Jonah is devoid of feminine presences. God and prophet, Jew and non-Jew, land and sea, animals and plants, represent difference in Jonah, but the difference of women is absent. Understandably it is easier for women to read themselves into the Book of Esther, where sexuality and the difference of Jew and non-Jew are the tensions that move the plot, and heroes and villains are both male and female. Yet some primary tenets of feminist spiritualities inform the womanless world of Jonah: a profound tenderness for others, even others wholly different from ourselves, and a moral universe brimming with forgiving laughter. Laughter, provoked by burlesque and by the carnivalesque, is the bridge that connects Jonah with Purim.

Jonah is a parody, burlesquing other Biblical stories and punning outrageously.[119] It is also the most carnivalesque of Biblical books, rich in monstrosities, curiosities, spectacles, and monkeyshines. The star of this freak show is the world's most recalcitrant prophet. Ordered to Nineveh, he hops a ship to the other end of the known world. In the violent storm that ensues, everyone else is on deck, praying. Jonah has to be dragged to his devotions by the captain. After the lot falls on Jonah, and he acknowledges that he is the cause of the storm, it is Jonah who suggests that he be heaved overboard; the sailors are shocked. First they attempt to get back to land, then they pray not to be condemned for shedding Jonah's "innocent blood." Reluctantly they toss in the prophet, and when the sea miraculously calms, they hold a regular revival meeting, complete with sacrifices, testimonials, and vows to YHWH. This demonstration of faith presages Jonah's inexplicable conversion of Nineveh. Although he lacks any discernible gifts either of evangelism or of charm, wherever this curmudgeon of a prophet goes, he leaves a trail of people beating their breasts and shouting hallelujah.

After the reluctant evangelist's own purifying immersion, we encounter the most impressive beast in the carnival's menagerie: a giant fish that can swallow prophets but just can't digest them. Our sympathies are with the fish; Jonah, as the audience has begun to discover, is pretty hard to stomach. After three days and nights, Jonah capitulates. In a stunning and lyrical psalm of repentance, he both apologizes and recounts his excellent adventure as the world's deepest diver. The travelogue features such exotic locales as the belly of *Sheol,* the heart of the seas, the primal abyss, the roots of the mountains, and the barred gates that hold the sea back from the earth. God's response to Jonah's effusion is brief and businesslike; He speaks to the fish and it throws up, a literal demonstration of "return" to a prophet unclear on the concept. Spat out onto dry land, to receive his prophetic mission a second time, Jonah does turn himself around to make tracks for the gigantic metropolis to which he has been ordered, a city it takes three days to cross. Ambling a mere third of the way into the city, Jonah begins racking up more world records. First he gives the world's most laconic prophecy, a mere five words in Hebrew: "Forty days more and Nineveh will be overthrown" (3:4).

To Jonah's intense distaste, this curt and uninviting oracle is monumentally and unprecedentedly effective. Isaiah, Ezekiel, Jeremiah, pour floods of eloquence, indignation, passion, and pleading upon God's chosen people to no effect whatever. Jonah dumps the naked facts of doomsday on an unpromising bunch of *goyim,* and they fall all over themselves rushing to do *teshuva.* To add insult to injury, the second marvel in the carnival menagerie reveals itself: in this burg, even the dumb animals fast in sackcloth and ashes, a sly hint, perhaps, that even they are better at *teshuva* than the folks on Jonah's home turf.

Inadvertently Jonah has produced a howling success, and, characteristically he immediately begins howling. He flings in God's face a blasphemous version of the very litany the Yom Kippur liturgy has been repeating all day: "This is why I hurried to run away to Tarshish!" he complains. "Because I knew that you are a God showing-mercy, showing-favor, *[El chanun verachum],* long-suffering in anger and abundant in loyalty *[erekh apayim verav chesed],* and indulgent of evil *[venicham al hara'a].*"[120] Jonah's unorthodox ending to the verse traduces God for the very quality we have been imploring God to exercise: clearing the guilty. Jonah is also at cross-purposes with the Yom Kippur worshiper in his surly rejection of life. "Remember us for life," we plead repeatedly in High Holy Day prayers. We reiterate such passages as Deuteronomy's "Choose life so that you may live" (30:19) and Isaiah's "Turn from your evil ways; why should you die, house of Israel?" (55:6). Jonah tells God, "Go ahead, kill me. I'd rather be dead than alive." To which God, like the perfect therapist, replies, "Should you really be this angry?"

Still hoping for a replay of Sodom and Gomorra, Jonah builds a sukkah outside the city so he can anticipate Nineveh's downfall in comfort. God roofs the structure with a shade plant that shoots up like Jack's magic beanstalk but also equips it with an equally speedy worm to chomp it down, the last beast in the marvelous menagerie. When Jonah, seared by sun and scorched by wind, again begs for death, God responds therapeutically once again: "So you're really angry about losing the plant?" That sets God up for the punch line: "You cared about the plant though you did not cultivate it or grow it. Shouldn't I care about a city where there are hordes of people who don't know their right from their left [and hence, unlike the People of the Book, may just not know any better] and besides [a final dig in the ribs] there are all those terrific animals!" The liturgy appends its own gentle joke to the ending, two verses from Micah (7:18–20) praising God, the forgoer of retribution and acceptor of *teshuva.* God "hurls our sins into the depths of the sea"; unlike the recalcitrant prophet, we do not have to be hurled in bodily along with them.

The afternoon Yom Kippur prophetic reading of Jonah, like the morning prophetic reading from Isaiah 57–58, balances the religious teaching offered by the Torah portion it follows. After a Torah portion detailing the priestly ritual for Yom Kippur, the Isaiah reading attacks the sanctimonious for commodifying religious ritual and consuming it at the expense of those they exploit and oppress. In the afternoon, a Torah portion enumerating a variety of sins of the flesh is followed by Jonah, in which the sins of the spirit are exposed, a narrative in which the official representative of godliness is rigid, pitiless, and oblivious of the wonders and oddities popping up all around him.

Probably the most religious response to the reading of Jonah would be a hearty guffaw. That guffaw would distance us enough to see in comic perspective the bodies we are so righteously afflicting and the spirits we are so assiduously burnishing. It would indicate that we understand the Book of Jonah's answer to the question posed by Isaiah's nettled audience: "Why do you not notice when we fast? Why do you not heed when we afflict ourselves?" (Isaiah 58:3). God's answer in Jonah is: "Because when you posture and preen yourselves on your temporary bodily deprivations without attaining an iota of concern for the needs and sufferings of other living beings, I find you shocking and ridiculous. This time, my gambit is to laugh at you and tease you into compassion." By mocking the sins of the spirit, Jonah sends us back into our afflicted bodies to be made whole, to know ourselves as bodies flooded with spirit. If we have understood, we will be able to extrapolate from our own growling bellies, aching heads, boredom, and weariness to the infinitely precious and vulnerable spirit-flooded bodies of other living creatures. Leaving behind us both self-abasement and self-congratulation frees us to see ourselves as God sees us, with amused tenderness and persistent hope.

This brief moment of illumination is the carnival prize waiting to be won. Snatch it up quickly, before the curtain falls and the tents are struck and the monsters bedded down. The lights of the carnival are dimming fast. At the far end of the field loom a pair of great gates, and those gates, ladies and gentlemen, are closing.

PART 5

Sukkot

Hashkiveinu. *Help us, God, to lie down in peace and awaken us again to life, our Ruler. Spread over us Your sukkah of peace, guide us with Your good counsel. . . . Praised are you God, who spreads the sukkah of peace over us, over all of God's people Israel, and over Jerusalem.*

—From the evening prayers for Shabbat and festivals[1]

A Merging of Worlds

TRANSCENDING TIME AND SPACE, Jewish observance goes beyond the linear manner with which we view history and our current world. Every ritual and every holiday in the Jewish tradition is intended to break down the psychological and physical constructs of our lives to evoke a true existential response. They frame each thought and feeling that touches our essential humanness and help us to see ourselves amidst the continuum of God's universe. No holiday accomplishes this more than Sukkot, as it forces us to unite what is otherwise divided—merging ancient history with the present, the natural world with the manufactured world, and the transient with the permanent. During Sukkot, it is within the context of this experience that we are commanded to be joyful.[2]

Sukkot (literally, "Booths") is one of the three pilgrimage festivals, along with Passover and Shavuot that were originally agricultural celebrations.[3] Also known as the Feast of Booths or Feast of Tabernacles, Sukkot marks the fall harvest. Its significance, however, goes beyond being a holiday of thanksgiving for the harvest. In the *Amidah* (the central prayer said daily and on Shabbat and holidays), Sukkot is described as *z'man simchateinu,* "the time of our rejoicing." The Bible, in one place, simply calls it *he-hag,* "the festival" (I Kings 12:32) and, in another, denotes it as the most important celebration—*hag Adonai,* "festival of God" (Lev. 24:39,41). The special significance and joy of Sukkot cannot be removed from the fact that it falls on the heels of the *Yamim Noraim,* the 10-day period of introspection and repentance beginning with Rosh Hashanah and ending with Yom Kippur, to which it brings a sense of completion and spiritual gratification.

The days after Yom Kippur leading to Sukkot, as well as the eight days of Sukkot themselves, always seem to move quickly, blasting forcefully in and out of the calendar. One cannot, however, miss their distinctive experiences and sensations. These include acclimating to nature through the aromas of the outdoors; savoring the physical aspects of the *lulav* and *etrog* (palm branches and a citrus fruit that are used ritually); finding joy in decorating the sukkah (temporary booth or hut for the holiday); relishing the prolonged singing and dancing in synagogue; and experiencing the importance of hospitality through hosting visitors and meals in the sukkah. For us today, Sukkot's most apparent complexity and richness, however, lie in its disparity: we are drawn out of the security of our own homes and ease of our modern lifestyle, yet simultaneously comforted by reconnecting with nature and our community.

Sukkot culminates with the holiday of Simchat Torah, a celebration of all that God gave us. (It falls on what is counted as the eighth day in Israel, but is the ninth day elsewhere.) We conclude the annual cycle of Torah reading and then immediately begin again, starting with the story of Creation. On this day we literally dance with the Torah scrolls to celebrate both the Torah itself and Sukkot's messages about the essence of humanity, the beginnings of civilization, and the meaning of living in God's world. It is the holiday that compels us to look upward, through the cracks of impermanence, toward the same night sky and stars upon which our earliest ancestors gazed. Here we stand, humbled, and filled with awe and gratitude for all there is, simply celebrating life.

Sukkot in the Bible

Unlike the other fall holidays, Sukkot receives numerous references (approximately 10) in the Bible. When viewing all of these references together, we see that understandings of the holiday vary considerably. For example, only in Exodus (23:16) is Sukkot called *hag ha-asif,* "feast of ingathering [of the fruits of the harvest] at the end of the year."[4] In other biblical references, it is called *hag ha-sukkot,* "feast of booths." Beyond such variations are more complex seeming discrepancies. For example, in Deuteronomy (31:10–12), it says that the Torah is to be read on Sukkot every seventh year; while in Nehemiah (8:1–18), it states something different—that the Torah is read on Rosh Hashanah and then studied on Sukkot for seven days. Another example contrasts the text in Leviticus (23:33–44), the chief biblical source for Sukkot, to the text in Nehemiah, which differs in its description of the *arba minim* (literally, "four species"—the *lulav* and *etrog*); Nehemiah includes olive branches and omits the willow branches found in Leviticus. Nehemiah also suggests that after the return from the Babylonian exile, the Israelites had to relearn the Torah commandment to observe Sukkot. Explicitly, it says that they had not "dwelt in the booths" since the time of Joshua (from circa 1200–538 B.C.E.—roughly 700 years). All of these oddities raise more questions about Sukkot than they resolve. Nonetheless, consistencies do occur as well, and the primary text in Leviticus gives a definite description of Sukkot as both a sacred occasion and a time of great joy.

The Bible consistently emphasizes two aspects of Sukkot's sacredness: its agricultural importance and its historical importance. Sukkot is a celebration of the fall harvest, a crop-gathering event that must have been a major occasion, because it came at the end of a period of doubt about having enough food for the winter months. As a harvest festival, Sukkot joins Passover and Shavuot as one of the three festivals for which ancient Israelites would journey to the Temple in Jerusalem to offer their choice fruits.

The significance of Sukkot grew from its being an agricultural observance into its being a part of Jewish historical identity, as described in Leviticus (23:41–43).[5] The sukkot (plural of sukkah), played a key role in what is usually considered the most important event in Jewish history, the Exodus: "You shall live in booths [sukkot] seven days; all citizens in Israel shall live in booths, in order that future generations may know that I made the Israelite people live in booths when I brought them out of the land of Egypt, I the LORD your God." As a physical and spiritual reconstruction of our historical past, the holiday serves well as one of our ways to commemorate the Exodus.

The Bible also specifically defines the holiday, which is to occur for eight days, as filled with joy. Rabbinic authorities elaborate upon this description, explaining that we show this feeling by singing *Hallel*, the liturgical expression of joy and thanksgiving, on all days of Sukkot—both the holiest ones (the first, second, seventh, and eighth) and the intermediate days, *hol ha-mo'ed* (the third, fourth, fifth, and sixth).[6] In fact, one could say that the anthem of the holiday is the poetic phrase that envelops Deuteronomy 16:14–15, *Ve-samachta be-chagekha ... ve'hayita akh same'ach*, "You shall rejoice in your festival ... and you shall have nothing but joy." Considering the celebratory mood and historical meaning of the holiday, it is no wonder that King Solomon made Sukkot the period for the dedication of the Temple in Jerusalem (I Kings 8:2).

A postbiblical text (Jubilees 16:16–31), however, may best convey the joyful spirit of Sukkot.[7] This beautiful text indirectly associates Sukkot with biblical stories studied on Rosh Hashanah and Yom Kippur, which describe Abraham's reaction after hearing the joyous news that his childless wife Sarah had finally become pregnant at 90 and after years of infertility.[8] Moved by gratitude and inspired by the blessings of life, Abraham established a "festival of joy." In a gesture of thanksgiving, he built booths—sukkot—and celebrated the gifts of God's natural world with willows, palm branches, and beautiful fruit.

Symbols of Sukkot

Religions and cultures are made up of symbols, which are concepts or objects that carry a greater context and meaning than what is plainly evident. Sigmund Freud and Carl Jung, distinguished psychoanalysts, and Joseph Campbell, expert on comparative religions and mythology, have written seminal works about people and symbols. They demonstrate that, through symbols, the mind can keep in place a distinct piece of information while free-associating with various other symbols; organize them in multiple ways; and also hold the connected meanings between and within them all.[9] A one-word symbol, for example, could comprise volumes of thought patterns and recollections. Religion, we could say, is essentially the language of symbols that express human spirituality. For Judaism, Sukkot is a holiday in which we are surrounded by very profound religious symbolism, especially regarding the sukkah itself, the *arba minim* (four species), and the *ushpizin* (heavenly visitors).

The Sukkah

A sukkah is a temporary shelter of at least two-and-a-half sides, with a roof made from organic materials, ideally, cut branches. Although the roof must provide more shade than exposure, it should be open enough that someone inside can see the stars.[10] The Talmud tells us to decorate it,[11] eat in it, and even sleep in it, unless rain is falling hard enough to make it impossible to enjoy ourselves.[12] Why build a sukkah? Because the Bible says that it reminds us of the Exodus from Egypt and our wandering for 40 years in the desert.[13] But how, exactly, does a sukkah remind us of this desert journey? And of which aspects in particular? And finally, what does such a reminder offer us today?

There are hundreds, even thousands, of arguments recorded in the Talmud, only a few dozen of which have ever been resolved. The significance of the sukkah remains a subject of debate that affects our modern perspective on the holiday. In particular, the Talmud briefly notes two opposing understandings held by sages Rabbi Eliezer ben Hyrcanus, a 1st- and 2nd-century scholar, and his student Rabbi Akiva ben Joseph (50–135 C.E.), an authority on Jewish tradition.[14] Rabbi Eliezer understands sukkot figuratively, describing them as *ananei kavod,* "clouds of glory." More than 1,000 years later, medieval rabbis and sages, such as Rabbi Jacob ben Asher (circa 1270–1340; Germany and Spain), who was known as Baal Ha-Turim, would expand upon what Rabbi Eliezer said by explaining that this divine cloud cover led the Israelites in the desert day and night and protected them from sun, rain, and wind.[15] Later, Rabbi

Yaakov Culi (1685–1732; Turkey), author of an anthology of customs and midrashim,[16] describes the six clouds as enclosing the Israelites—one in each compass direction, one above, and one below, along with a seventh cloud to lead the way.[17] According to such interpretations, these clouds—these sukkot—were manifest representations of God's presence. They were what guarded and guided the Israelites, as this desert generation, enduring tremendous physical hardship, transformed spiritually from being slaves into being a free people.[18]

Alternatively, in the original talmudic debate, Rabbi Akiva understands the sukkot differently from his teacher Rabbi Eliezer—not as clouds of glory that guard a precious holy nation, but as *sukkot mamash,* actual booths. He believes that we are to remember the earthly sukkot and the actual physical experience of living in the desert. In examining his argument, we can shift our focus from the relationship God had with the Israelites who left Egypt to a focus on later generations, such as our own, which reenact at Sukkot the deprivations of desert life.[19] Perhaps we can understand Rabbi Akiva's position by looking at a different place in the Talmud, in a discussion about who will get to the world to come. Rabbi Akiva believes the generation of the desert (*dor ha-midbar*) to be so lowly that it would not have a place in the world to come (*olam ha-ba*).[20] Apparently he considered its members to be unworthy, because they continuously argued for returning to the slavery and moral filth of Egypt, rather than struggling with life in the Exodus and accepting the responsibility of God's freedom. This perspective may explain his understanding of the booths as they pertain to our celebration of Sukkot—a holiday in which we experience a certain amount of humility remembering the harsh time in the desert, despite the joyousness of the occasion.

In the end, we are left with both perspectives and their distinct differences. We often seesaw back and forth, espousing at one moment Rabbi Eliezer's understanding and at another Rabbi Akiva's, without even realizing how they are different. Rabbi Eliezer portrays a time when the Jewish people were literally embraced and sheltered by God. Sukkot is thus the holiday that brings us to the spiritual place where we experience the world with pure faith. Rabbi Eliezer wants us to feel God's direct presence in our lives. While sitting in the sukkah, we feel everything is going to be all right, because God is with us now, just as God was there in the camp with our ancestors. For Rabbi Eliezer, we have just completed self-examination and judgment at Rosh Hashanah and Yom Kippur; for him, Sukkot is the time to allow ourselves to be hugged by God.

In contradistinction, Rabbi Akiva emphasizes not the security of God in the sukkah, but the insecurity and transience of life that our ancestors must have experienced in the desert. He is rigorously preaching that we need to continue to reexamine ourselves. True appreciation of what our creature comforts and luxuries mean—our big houses, soft beds, refrigerators, air conditioners, and entertainment centers—can only come from contemplating what it is to be without them; and this we do by dwelling inside the open and fragile sukkah. Stepping out of our homes and looking back objectively at what we have is an important spiritual experience—similar to the moments of reflection we have when setting out for home after weeks in a foreign country. Rabbi Akiva believes that on Sukkot we should take an objective look at our lives by using the physicality of the sukkah to continue the path of self-improvement and introspection laid down by Rosh Hashanah and Yom Kippur.

The Talmud shows great wisdom in not resolving this debate between Rabbi Eliezer and Rabbi Akiva, for both of their understandings are right, both are true.[21] We need Rabbi Eliezer's conviction of God's protection and guidance in our lives, symbolized by the sheltering aspects of the sukkah. And we need Rabbi Akiva's belief in the importance of abandoning any complacency in our lives and of constantly seeking spiritual progress, symbolized by the temporariness of the sukkah. Therefore, we may adopt both approaches for our conception of the sukkah and simply conclude, as the Talmud does in many well-known places, "These [Rabbi Eliezer's] and these [Rabbi Akiva's] are the words of the Living God," *Elu v'elu divrei Elohim Chayim.*[22]

Building a Sukkah

Even though exhausted by the hunger pains of the Yom Kippur fast and the all day prayer-a-thon, once that day ends, the Jewish tradition is already looking ahead to the mitzvot and observance of Sukkot, which is only four days away. Therefore, right after Yom Kippur ends, and as soon as they've eaten something, many Jews begin putting up their sukkah, driving in at least the first nail. In doing so they abide by the maxim of *de-mitzvah ha-ba'ah le-yado al yachmitzena*—when the opportunity for the next good deed is at hand, do not let it sour.[23] Because dwelling in the sukkah for a week has great spiritual import and weight, erecting a sukkah is surely a good deed.

Most of the customs for Sukkot primarily revolve around the sukkah itself (its construction and decoration) and how one is to spend time in it. These considerations are actually more complicated than they may sound, because the Talmud (*Sukkah* 28b) understands the sukkah in two almost contradictory ways. On one hand, the sukkah is a booth, a word that connotes temporariness; and on the other, the Torah dictates that we are to dwell in it. Consequently, the Talmud ruled that the sukkah must have the features of a regular dwelling place, by being decent enough for someone to live in, yet also a temporary, somewhat insecure hut. Maintaining the paradoxical nature of the sukkah is the underlying premise for detailed rules surrounding its construction.

Basic Guidelines for Construction

- The sukkah must be built in an open space under the sky, so that it is not indoors or under dense foliage or the roof of any other structure.[24]
- As a temporary dwelling, it should be sturdy enough to sustain a normal wind, but just unstable enough so that it would not withstand a very strong gale.[25]
- The roof *(s'khakh)* must be made of plant material, such as cut branches, bamboo, or straw, but not grasses or leaves that dry quickly or have an unpleasant odor.[26] Most people today use large palm fronds or reusable slatted palm mats.
- The walls are less important than the *s'khakh* and can be made of any materials.[27] There should be at least two-and-a-half walls, but most sukkot have at least three. The walls should also be no higher than 20 cubits (approximately 37 feet), no shorter than 10 handbreadths (approximately 36 inches), and have an area of at least 7 by 7 handbreadths, which is thought to be the necessary space for one person (approximately 26 inches squared).[28]
- The *s'khakh* must assume the principle of *tziltah merubah me-chamatah,* which means the sukkah must be more shaded than sunlit.[29] Yet the *s'khakh* must be permeable enough for heavy rain to penetrate the sukkah and holey enough for us to look up and see the larger stars in the night sky.[30]
- The walls must be fully built before the *s'khakh* is applied. Because the roof is the most significant aspect of the sukkah, we finish with that element. In fact, the walls may remain up from Sukkot to Sukkot, as long as the roof is newly applied.[31]

Because we are to spend a considerable amount of time in the sukkah—eating, reading, studying, praying, and even sleeping,[32] we should establish a moderate sense of permanence by decorating the interior and by using the utensils, dishes, and linens that we normally use for festive occasions.[33] Essentially, the sukkah is to serve as our home. And how does the Jewish tradition define home? Home is the place where one eats and drinks, of course. Accordingly, on the first night of Sukkot we are to bring the holiday inside the sukkah, where we make *Kiddush* (the ceremony in which we recite a blessing over wine) and have a meal. If the weather conditions are bad (perhaps very cold and windy), it is fine to have just a bite of bread and then go inside; we are to rejoice in the sukkah, not suffer in it.[34] In fact, according to Moses Isserles, an Askenazic, 16th-century legal authority, if it is raining "too hard," we should not insist on remaining.

The Four Species

The season, the land, and the climate each play a part in one's experience of the world and, therefore, in one's spiritual life. On no other Jewish holiday is this idea better expressed than on Sukkot. And with no other symbols is it better experienced than with the four species, the *arba minim.* The Torah says, "… on the fifteenth day of the seventh month [Sukkot] … you shall take the product of the *hadar* trees, branches of palm trees, boughs of leafy trees, and willows of the brook, and you shall rejoice before the LORD your God for seven days" (Lev. 23:40). The Rabbinic sages of the Mishnah (1st to 3rd centuries C.E.) identify these four species as *etrog* (citron, the fruit of the *hadar* tree); *lulav* (branch of the date-palm tree); *hadas* (branch of the myrtle bush); and *aravah* (branch of the willow tree).[35] With the *arba minim,* the Rabbis emphasize the significant part that nature's beauty plays in Sukkot ritual.

Why these particular species? The Midrash and the Rabbis, throughout Jewish tradition, offer a great many explanations, of which the following three are most often discussed. In the first one, a midrash teaches us that the four species represent the four different types of Jews in the world. As each of the species potentially possesses the good qualities of taste and fragrance, so too do Jews potentially possess the desirable qualities of knowledge and good deeds. In this analogy the *etrog* is the most important species, possessing both taste and fragrance, and so it represents Jews who have both knowledge and good deeds. The dates of the palm tree have taste but no fragrance; that tree stands for those who have knowledge but lack good deeds. The myrtle has no taste, but it has fragrance; it stands for those who have no knowledge but do have good deeds. With neither taste nor fragrance, the willow represents people who are without knowledge or good deeds. The midrash concludes with God stating, "Let them all be tied in one band and they will atone one for another."[36] In other words, the more virtuous will complement those who lack virtues.

In the second midrash, we learn that each of the species represents a different part of the human body, associating them by shape: the *etrog* is like the heart, *hadas* is like the eyes, *aravah* is like the mouth, and *lulav* is like the spine.[37] As all four species are taken together in devotion to God, so should we all devote every part of ourselves, in every way we express ourselves—for example, through our hearts, eyes, mouths, and posture—toward God's will.

Finally, the third midrash says that each of the four species requires rain to thrive; and, with our gathering of them all, we show gratitude for our past welfare and demonstrate our hope for blessings in the coming year.[38] Holding them in our hands, we pray that there will be rain enough for the four species and implore God to provide a healthy and bountiful agricultural year for all.

The four-species ritual is called "waving, or shaking, the *lulav*." This expression names only the most prominent element, but actually refers to waving all four species. Many laws and customs—an almost overwhelming set of specificities—surround the *arba minim*. For example, the *lulav* must be about a foot long and cannot have a severed tip; each *hadas* must be free of split or broken leaves; the majority of *aravah* leaves must be free of shriveling; and the *etrog* must be blemishfree and bigger than an egg.[44] The three branches are to be bound together as a group consisting of one *lulav*, three *hadas*, and two *aravah*. Each

Precious Citrus

Of the four species, the *etrog* has grown to be the one most frequently imbued with symbolism. Stories and even a movie script[39] have been written about the *etrog*, and many people continue to be meticulous about acquiring a perfect fruit. Much material exists in the Midrash and in folklore, especially associating the *etrog* with women and fertility. The association seems to stem from the legend that the *etrog* is the fruit that Adam and Eve consumed in the Garden of Eden, against God's command.[40] One tradition advises women to bite off the *pittam* (the nipplelike end) once the *etrog* is no longer needed for Sukkot.[41] By waiting a week, they demonstrate their difference from Eve, who could not resist temptation.[42] Thus this ritual may serve as a reward that facilitates conception. The Talmud echoes the link among Eve, birth, and the *etrog* by asserting that women who eat the *etrog* will have "fragrant" children.[43]

person who waves the *lulav* should have a personal set of the four species; if someone needs a set, it should be transferred as a gift rather than lent.[45] After the destruction of the Second Temple, the tradition specified that the *arba minim* are "to be taken" (the ritual performed) each day of Sukkot except Shabbat. (Most people bring the four species from home, and a prohibition exists against carrying on Shabbat.) This pattern serves as a remembrance of the daily Sukkot practice in the Temple.[46]

How to Wave the Lulav

- In the left hand,[47] hold the *etrog* with its *pittam*—the bump on the pointed end—facing down. (Sometimes the *pittam* is gone, having fallen off early in the etrog's growth cycle;[48] just choose the end opposite the end where the stem was attached.)
- In the right hand, hold the cluster of branches, with the green spine of the *lulav* facing toward you.
- With the *etrog* touching the cluster, recite the blessing called *al netilat lulav,* "to take the four species." This blessing recognizes God as the one who commands us to take the *lulav* and perform this ritual act. On the first day of Sukkot, we also recite the *Shehecheyanu* blessing, thanking God for sustaining us and helping us reach this season.
- Turn the *etrog* so that the *pittam* is pointing up.
- Shake the four species together in six directions: east, west, north, south, above, and below.[49]

The gentle shakes or waves of the *lulav* are called *na'anuim,* and each one consists of three shakes. In other words, with arms outstretched, make three shakes to the east, return to center; three shakes to the west, return to center; and so forth—until all six directions are completed. The *na'anuim,* which take place throughout the seven-day holiday, may be done in a sukkah or in a synagogue. Customarily, the initial time is at the first morning service, right before *Hallel* and also during *Hallel.*[50]

We shake the *lulav* in every direction because the Talmud proclaims, "We wave toward the four points of the world in honor of God, for they are His dominion" (*Sukkah* 37b). The tractate also says that this action is a way of warding off evil, as in evil winds and evil waters from above and below. Another reason we wave the *lulav* is to uplift our spirits after the anxiety of such extensive spiritual work on Yom Kippur. As it says in the Bible, "... then shall all of the trees of the forest shout for joy" (Ps. 96:12).[51] Yet another reason, which may seem to be in opposition to the one just mentioned, states that rather than proceeding from Yom Kippur with anxiety and trepidation, we emerge from Yom Kippur uplifted in delight. Therefore, we wave the *lulav,* our baton of victory, for having just triumphed, through atonement, in our internal battle against the forces of sin and evil.[52]

Mysticism of the Number Four

Jewish mystics see an enormous amount of hidden meaning in the *arba minim,* most of it derived from the number of species in the ritual—four. Judaism has long found symbolic meaning in words, things, and phenomena through a system of number-letter equivalencies called *gematria.* Four is a very special number in the Jewish tradition. There are four corners of the earth; four corners on a tallit (prayer shawl); four compass directions; four elements composing the physical universe; four seasons; four Matriarchs (Sarah, Rebecca, Rachel, and Leah); four traditional ways of interpreting Torah (*peshat,* simple; *derash,* explained; *remez,* hint; and *sod,* secret); and four worlds of Kabbalah (*asiyah,* doing; *yetzirah,* feeling; *beriah,* thinking; and *atzilut,* existing). Most importantly, four is also the number that represents the oneness of God and God's presence in this world, expressed by the four letters of God's name: *yud, heh, vav, heh* (the Tetragrammaton). All the "fours" in the universe and the four letters of God's name fuse together in one collaborative, peak moment of symbolism. This moment occurs in daily prayer with the gathering of the four corners of the tallit during the recitation of the words of the *Shema*—the statement of God's oneness.

Hasidism, through kabbalistic interpretations, expands the four-species representation of the four letters of God's name into the number seven—the total number of pieces in the *lulav.* In Kabbalah the number seven symbolizes God's seven core manifestations in the universe.[53] Therefore, each wave of the *arba minim* literally draws God into the world and into the self.[54] Rabbi Zalman Schachter-Shalomi, the spiritual leader of the modern Jewish Renewal movement, explains just how the *arba minim* serve as a conduit between the individual and the sublime, according to Hasidic understanding.

> We become wielders of magic when we shake the four species in all directions. ... we are extending God to *eyn sof*—the place of infinity. This is

a primitive act with many layers of symbolism, the most obvious being the joining of phallus *(lulav)* and womb/cervix *(etrog)*. In the language of the kabbalistic *sefirot* [the 10 emanations of God], the three myrtles are *hesed, gevurah,* and *tiferet* [lovingkindness, strength, and harmony]; the two *aravot* are *netzah* and *hod* [eternity and glory]; the *lulav* is *yesod* [foundation]; and the *etrog* is *malkhut* [kingdom]. The meaning of the ritual is so important that even those worshippers without the four species should stretch themselves in the six directions in order to make manifest the rule of the Holy One.[55]

The Heavenly Guests

Sukkot begins in the sukkah. This is where we light the ritual candles; we make *Kiddush;* we recite *leshev ba-sukkah,* which is the blessing that sanctifies the commandment to dwell (literally, "sit") in the sukkah; and we say the prayer *Shehecheyanu,* in which we thank God for sustaining us and bringing us to this special day.[56] In addition, we do something not done on any other holiday. We insert a prayer before *Kiddush,* one that involves a mystical custom of inviting *ushpizin* (literally, "visitors")—our heavenly guests—to join us. The central text of Kabbalah, the Zohar, instituted the custom of inviting into the sukkah the poor of the community, as well as seven *ushpizin:*[57] Abraham, Isaac, Jacob, Joseph, Moses, Aaron, and David.[58] All seven are guests each day of Sukkot, but one is singled out, in a traditional order, for special honor. By summoning our ancestors through prayer, we draw upon the special blessings that each imparted to the world and upon the *sefirot* (varying aspects of God) that each represents.

The act of welcoming our ancestral guests into the sukkah has several layers of meaning. First, Sukkot is a holiday of hospitality: we invite not only family and friends to eat in the sukkah, but also the destitute and the needy. Such hospitality is an expression of caring, openness, and compassion. As we open our homes and give of ourselves to the guests of flesh and blood, so too we welcome those who make up our historical and spiritual identity. In doing so, we are not merely receiving the *ushpizin* into the sukkah, but into our innermost hopes, desires, and sentiments.

Second, Jews are in a covenant with God through these ancestors. Every day in prayer, by calling upon the God of our ancestors, we hearken back to the foundation of the relationship between Israel and God. Recounting the origins of our eternal covenant with God forces us to return to our intended purpose and mission, that of creating a life of holiness, justice, and compassion. The lives of our ancestors help us to see our true vision of what we are as human beings and Jews and to remember what we are supposed to do in the world. They represent the fulfillment of that vision. Each one, in individual and special ways, contributed to building the Jewish relationship with God and, in turn, to bettering God's world. Therefore, by inviting these guests into our sukkot, we are simultaneously reminded of where we came from, who we are now, and what we aspire to be.[59]

Third, we invite these particular guests into the sukkah to reinforce our awareness of their tremendous dedication to God and their deep contribution to humankind. Abraham, Isaac, and Jacob demonstrated hospitality, sacrifice, humility, passion, and loyalty; Moses and Aaron, throughout the Exodus, exemplified intense devotion to God; and David taught courage by establishing a kingship guided by the principles of the Torah.

Adding to the Guest List

Many people today, especially in the liberal strands of Judaism, have argued that women should be included in the list of *ushpizin* because, although often unrecognized, they have been dedicated to God and have contributed to the world in ways as meritorious as those of men. It is believed that their inclusion could only add more blessing and meaning to this custom. For people who have decided to add women to the list, uncertainty may exist about which *ushpizot* (female ancestral guests) should be included. The Rabbinical Assembly of the Conservative Movement has been helpful by selecting a woman to pair with each man, based on common symbolic themes.[60]

Ushpizin and Ushpizot

EVENING	*USHPIZIN*	*USHPIZOT*	THEME
First	Abraham	Sarah	Parents of Faith
Second	Isaac	Rebecca	Transmitters of the Legacy and Foundation
Third	Jacob	Leah	Progenitors of Israel
Fourth	Joseph	Rachel	Nurturers of the Past and Caretakers of the Future
Fifth	Moses	Miriam	Leaders of Freedom
Sixth	Aaron	Deborah	Harbingers of Peace
Seventh (Hoshanah Rabbah)	David	Ruth	Living Legacies of Israel for the Past, Present, and Future

Another grouping for *ushpizot,* based upon a medieval kabbalistic source, claims that we should invite into the sukkah the biblical prophetesses that the Talmud specifically identifies,[61] including Sarah, Miriam, Deborah, Hannah, Abigail, Huldah, and Esther.[62] This grouping, however, is separate from and does not pair with the traditional males.

Other alternative practices include inviting important Jewish men and women throughout history—men such as Judah Maccabee, Maimonides, Albert Einstein, or Yitzchak Rabin; and women such as Emma Lazarus, Henrietta Szold, or Hannah Szenesh. Some people even invite great contributors to world history and social justice, regardless of religion, such as Abraham Lincoln and Martin Luther King, Jr. No matter who is invited, however, the hosts of the sukkah use these encounters to try to become better people. They take inspiration from the spiritual presence of those who offer examples of hope, faithfulness, and the pursuit of freedom.

The Water Ritual

During the time of the two temples (from the beginning of the first in 950 B.C.E. to the end of the second in 70 C.E.), sacrifices were often accompanied by the pouring of a prescribed amount of wine on the altar. For Sukkot, in a unique ritual, *nisukh ha-mayim* (literally, "pouring of the water"), the Priests also poured water on the altar each day, to accompany the morning sacrifice.[62] (Although this joyous ritual is not explicitly mentioned in the Torah, it was accepted by the sages as a prescribed law.) Because Sukkot is associated with nature, with the change in seasons, and with human reliance upon water for survival, this ritual probably was a request for healthy winter rains.

To obtain the water, each day of Sukkot, except for the first day and on Shabbat, our ancient ancestors would go to the banks of a stream near the temple grounds called Shiloah. The Priests would then perform an extraordinary ritual using golden vessels and candelabras. During the drawing of the water, people sang psalms,[63] played musical instruments, and danced. The Talmud tells of the sages having a deliriously happy time at this ritual, drinking wine and doing acrobatics, such as juggling torches, knives, eggs, and glasses of wine.[64] This ceremony was called *simchat beit ha-sho'evah,* the rejoicing at the Place of Water Drawing.[65] Today certain Hasidic sects dance and sing in the streets in remembrance of the ceremony, which has not been performed since the Second Temple was destroyed nearly 2,000 years ago.

Three "Last" Days

Hoshanah Rabbah

The seventh day of Sukkot is called Hoshanah Rabbah. The word *hoshanah* is a Hebrew call for help (literally, "please save"); *rabbah* means "great." If we were to come up with a loose translation, it would be something like "The Day of the Great Call for Salvation." The Torah did not mention or distinguish this day from the others of Sukkot. The name,[66] as well as the specific identity, began to develop in the Second Temple period and blossomed in the Rabbinic period (the talmudic era). During the medieval period,[67] Hoshanah Rabbah was given even greater weight and grew into a day of divine judgment, reflective of Yom Kippur.

The ancient Israelites celebrated Sukkot through the sixth day with tremendous merrymaking, *simchat beit ha-sho'evah;* but on the seventh day, Hoshanah Rabbah, the mood became solemn. As a special ritual, people took a third branch of willow and added it to the two that were already part of the *arba minim* for use in the extra sacrificial service, *Musaf.* At one point during this service, everyone walked seven times around the altar in circuits called *hakafot.* During the *hakafot,* members of the congregation recited paragraphs of appeals for salvation called *Hoshanot,* while holding their *arba minim* and the additional branch of willow. At the end of the sevenfold circuit, they beat[70] their willow branches on the ground, watching the leaves fall from the stems,[71] most commonly explained as a symbolic representation of the frailty of human life, especially at a time when we rely upon God's graces. This beating of the willow, a tree that grows only near water, is called *chibbut aravah* and may possibly be a remnant of an ancient pagan rite that called on the "waters below" to respond to the "waters above."[72] Today we still practice *hakafot* and recite *Hoshanot,* by taking the Torah scrolls from the ark and circling the *bimah* (platform from which the Torah is read) seven times before performing *chibbut aravah.*

Going in Circles

Circling, in the Jewish tradition, symbolizes protection and completion. For example, at Ashkenazic weddings, the bride traditionally circles the groom seven times; and Honi the Circle Maker, in a famous Rabbinic story, draws circles in which he stands while asking God for rain.[69]

In the medieval period, the Rabbis added an even more serious note to Hoshanah Rabbah, which they identified as the third and last day of judgment, following Rosh Hashanah and Yom Kippur. Three weeks of self-examination and repentance culminated in this day, primarily because of Rashi's comment in the Talmud regarding Yom Kippur, which says that God's final verdict is given on Hoshanah Rabbah.[73] Also, the central text of Kabbalah, the Zohar, which was very much a part of normative Judaism throughout much of Europe, proclaimed, "the seventh day of the festival [Sukkot] is the conclusion of judgment of the world, and articles of judgment are issued forth from on high."[74]

There are a number of explanations for the great significance of Hoshanah Rabbah; the three most commonly given come primarily from medieval sources. The first one states that in the heavenly world, a case can be heard more than once, not unlike the way a case can be heard again on earth, where fair-minded societies provide courts of appeal. Thus on Rosh Hashanah, one verdict is given; on Yom Kippur, another opportunity for success occurs. Hoshanah Rabbah represents one last opportunity to gain acquittal from on high, and so we take drastic measures by repeating and reciting *Hoshanot.*

The second explanation derives from a midrash. It tells of God's giving Abraham one day to atone for his sins and completely wipe the slate clean. God explains to Abraham that he and his descendants have Yom Kippur, but if they really need another chance, one is given on Hoshanah Rabbah. Why? Because just as Abraham is the 21st generation from Adam—the first human to sin—so is Hoshanah Rabbah the 21st day of the new year.

The third explanation begins with Sukkot. As the festival of the fall harvest and the beginning of the rainy season, Sukkot is understood as the holiday when God judges the world and determines the rainfall for the coming year. With water the most precious commodity in the desert of Israel and the "source of life," being judged for our year's supply of water is the same as being judged for life. Because Hoshanah Rabbah is the actual time during Sukkot when this judgment is made,[75] it is appropriate that we would make an extra effort to cast off our sins, as we do during the beating of the willows, *chibbut aravah.*[76]

We in the modern world experience Hoshanah Rabbah from a different perspective than our early ancestors did. Even though no one can specifically pinpoint its origins, we cannot help but see the ancient or even pagan connotations of the day.[77] Anthropologist Theodor Gaster points this out about the particular customs of Hoshanah Rabbah in his book on the Jewish festivals: "[T]here is one ancient 'functional' rite which has indeed survived almost unaltered, though so different a meaning is now read into it that its original purport can no longer be recognized. This is the custom of 'beating hosannas'—that is, of taking extra twigs and beating off their leaves upon the lectern during the recital of the Hosanna litanies on the seventh day. The conventional explanation of this practice is that it symbolizes the frailty of human lives, which fade and fall, 'thick as autumnal leaves which strew the brooks in the Vallombrosa.' The truth is, however, that it harks back to a primitive and fairly universal belief that the willow is a symbol of fertility and to the consequent custom of beating people with branches of that tree in order to induce potency and increase."[78] We participate in this ritual today and must ask how beating the ground with willows can be assimilated into our modern, intellectual sensibilities.

Symbolic rites work in more than one way; they are not only intellectually symbolic. That is, the physical aspects of symbolism are just as important as the inherent meaning. The smell of things, the look, and the actual activity—each plays a part in our emotional and spiritual experiences by evoking a particular human response, such as wonder, apprehension, delight, and even aggression.[79] The value of drawing upon and becoming aware of such human responses is what lies at the core of mysterious, esoteric experiences. Our ancient ancestors understood this concept well; they understood that there is inherent wisdom derived from the unspoken. As Eliyahu Ki Tov, the 20th-century authority on customs, wrote: "The custom of beating the *aravos* [willows] on the ground has great mystical meaning known only to the very wise who merit the knowledge of those secrets. Those who have no understanding of the esoteric should have the intent of following the custom of the prophets and sages of all generations. Their reward for emulating these actions is that God will regard them as if they had indeed acted with the proper, profound intentions."[80]

These wise people knew that sometimes, to elicit certain effects, we have to completely change our standard behavior. The rites of Hoshanah Rabbah provide such opportunities. To grasp the magnitude and significance of a fall harvest holiday and a symbolic prayer for the nourishment of rain, it is important for Jews today to completely change their frame of experience. Part of spirituality is to avoid being bogged down by an intellectual snobbishness and, instead, allow ourselves to participate in the visceral aspects of human existence.

Shemini Atzeret

Another "last day" is Shemini Atzeret. Distinguishing it from the rest of Sukkot is actually a complicated matter. In fact, distinguishing it from Simchat Torah, the day that follows, is even more complicated. Although Hoshanah Rabbah may technically be the "last day" of Sukkot, the Rabbis decided to treat Shemini Atzeret (and Simchat Torah, *see* below) as a part of Sukkot, because its significance is unequivocally informed by Sukkot itself.

Two cryptic references in the Torah cause the confusion about the status of Shemini Atzeret. In both Leviticus and Numbers, God commands that the eighth *(shemini)* day—referring to Sukkot—is to be a "sacred occasion" and an *atzeret,* generally translated as "solemn gathering."[81] The inherent problem is that no one really knows exactly what *atzeret* means. Possibly it comes from the word *atzar,* meaning "stop," and thus implies that we are to refrain from work. On the other hand, *atzeret* may also be defined by its textual context, which implies that it is some sort of deliberate extension of the prior seven days.[82] This lack of verbal clarity is likely the reason why the Rabbinic sages seemed to struggle with the precise meaning of the holiday.

The earliest Rabbinic reference to Shemini Atzeret calls it *yom tov acharon shel ha-hag,* the last day of the festival.[83] The Talmud, however, declares, "The eighth day is a festival in its own right."[84] At the same time, the Talmud attempts to distinguish it from Sukkot, as there are 70 temple sacrifices given throughout Sukkot, compared to only one given on Shemini Atzeret.[85] (This distinction was only theoretical, as the Temple had been destroyed five centuries prior to the redaction of the Talmud.) Cutting through this puzzle, the most appealing depiction of the holiday may be that of Samson Raphael Hirsch, a 19th-century Orthodox rabbi who lived in Germany. He infers the meaning of the holiday from the word *atzeret,* which he renders as "to gather" or "to store up."[86] Accordingly, on this eighth day *(shemini)* of Sukkot, the final day of celebration, we must store up the sentiments of gratitude and devotion acquired throughout the entire fall holiday season; nearly two months will pass until we celebrate another holiday, that of Hanukkah.

Although the observances of Shemini Atzeret generally share the characteristics of the rest of Sukkot, there are four significant differences. The first is that there is no more shaking of the *lulav* and *etrog.* Second is that although we have our meals and recite *Kiddush* in the sukkah, we no longer say the blessing to sanctify us through the commandment to dwell in it, as we did the previous seven days.[87] The third is that in the synagogue, after the Torah reading, we recite the memorial prayer *(Yizkor)*.[88] And finally, the special payer for rain *(Geshem)* is added to the repetition of *Musaf*, and thus begins the period of an additional call for rain in our prayers, which lasts until Passover.[89] It is customary for the leader of the *Geshem* prayer to wear a *kitel* as was done during the divine judgment of the High Holidays. Wearing the garment indicates that this is the season of divine judgment for the future year's rainfall, the time when we pray that God's goodwill may afford us the appropriate amount.

Simchat Torah

> Every seventh year ... at the Feast of Booths [Sukkot] ... you shall read this Teaching aloud in the presence of all Israel
> —Deut. (31:10–12)

In much of the Diaspora (the Jewish communities outside the Land of Israel), Shemini Atzeret (the eighth day of Sukkot) is followed directly by a second special day, Simchat Torah (literally, "joy of the Torah"). In Israel and in most Reform congregations, however, all of the observances for Simchat Torah are held on Shemini Atzeret, combining the two holidays into one day and making them almost indistinguishable. Simchat Torah itself is the celebration dedicated to both completing the yearly cycle of public Torah reading and starting it again.

The first mention of such a cycle appears in the Bible, in Deuteronomy, where Moses instructs the tribe of Levi and the elders of Israel to gather all the people for a public reading from portions of the Torah once every seven years.[90] The need to read the Torah publicly intensified after the destruction of the Second Temple in 70 C.E.; Jews were dispersed into other parts of the Middle East, into North Africa, and into Europe; and their earlier religious and cultural world became decentralized. Because a reference in the Mishnah (the first effort to permanently record Jewish custom and law, compiled in the 3rd century C.E.) supported Deuteronomy's prescription,[91] we understand that Jews were continuing to read the Torah publicly; and we also know that there were Torah readings for festivals, special *Shabbatot* (plural of Shabbat), and fast days.[92] But it was not until the talmudic era, about the 6th century C.E., that the Jews in the Land of Israel began to read the entire Torah in public and do so until all the Five Books of Moses were completed. At that time, the cycle took three years in a pattern called the Palestinian triennial, beginning the first year with the first book, Genesis, and finishing, at the end of the third year, with the fifth book, Deuteronomy.

The Jews of Babylon, however, followed a different custom, established by the beginning of the 7th century C.E., and completed the entire cycle each year, which they did by dividing the Torah into 54 weekly portions. (Because the number of portions exceeds the number of weeks in a given year, more than one portion is read during certain weeks.)[93] In Hebrew, the word for portion is *parashah* (plural, *parshiyot*).

In the 19th century, a reintroduction of the Palestinian triennial cycle was attempted at the West End Congregation in London, but was unsuccessful. In the middle of the 20th century, various congregations in the United States (primarily Conservative ones) were seeking ways to modernize the service and also to spend more time on Shabbat on Torah study. They too attempted to revive the Palestinian cycles[94] with the argument that reading only a section of the weekly Torah portion would make Torah study more concentrated and thus enhanced. The reintroduction failed for two reasons. First, in the pattern of the Palestinian triennial cycle, the weekly reading would have differed from what the rest of the Jewish world was reading. Second, Simchat Torah celebrations would only occur one out of every three years, instead of annually.

Finally, in 1988, the Committee on Jewish Law and Standards of the Conservative Movement passed a legal responsum that put into practice a new American triennial cycle.[95] This new triennial cycle, rather than dividing the entire Torah into thirds, as was done in the Palestinian cycle, divides each of the individual 54 portions into thirds. Therefore, a congregation can be reading within the same portion as those who follow the annual cycle, but will only read one-third of each portion per year. In addition, this pattern enables the congregation to read from Genesis through Deuteronomy each year, providing for an annual celebration of Simchat Torah. There is an obvious drawback to this system: only one-third of each conventional Torah portion is actually read per year; and the readings, because incomplete, do not flow smoothly into the portion of the following week. Nonetheless, the vast majority of American Conservative and Reform congregations prefer this new cycle. All Jews in Israel, however, and Orthodox Jews in America continue to follow the annual cycle with the full portion read each week.

Whichever cycle a congregation may follow, observance of Simchat Torah begins in the same way, with the evening service. It provides, in addition to the regular festival liturgy, a special Torah service in which the final *parashah* of the year is read. Before the reading itself begins, selected congregants take all of the Torah scrolls from the ark and parade them around the synagogue. They make seven of these *hakafot* (circuits), which are performed with joy and accompanied by drinking, singing, and dancing.[96]

The festivities for Simchat Torah continue the next morning with seven more *hakafot.* Children are particularly involved in this merrymaking and are often given paper flags to carry in the processional. The Torah reading that day is drawn from three scrolls. From the first scroll, we read the last parashah of Deuteronomy and from the second, the first parashah of Genesis. Thus, when we end the Torah with the final book, Deuteronomy, we immediately begin again with the first book, Genesis, to symbolize that Torah never ends and that we never complete our learning. From the third scroll we read the *maftir* (the passage that concludes the Torah reading). For Simchat Torah, the *maftir* is from Numbers (29:35–30:1), about observing Shemini Atzeret.

An *aliyah* (plural, *aliyot*) is the honor of being called upon to make one set of the blessings said before and after each section of the Torah reading. Customarily, on Simchat Torah, everyone in the congregation receives an *aliyah;* and so it is common to have both individuals and groups of people called up at once. Three of the *aliyot* are particular honors. The first of these most-honored *aliyot* is the next-to-last one for the reading of Deuteronomy that completes the annual cycle of Torah readings. This *aliyah* is identified as *Kol Ha-Ne'arim* (literally, "All the Children"), because it is given to a distinguished member of the community, joined on the *bimah* by all of the children present. The adult honoree holds aloft a prayer shawl forming a canopy above the children. In unison, the honoree and the children say the blessings before and after this reading. Then the entire congregation blesses all the children by reciting the blessing Jacob gave to his grandchildren.[97] In this moment of Simchat Torah, we see a parallel between the unbroken cycle of Torah reading and the never-ending transmission of Torah from generation to generation.

The second very special honor is the final *aliyah* for this reading from Deuteronomy. The *aliyah* is designated as the *Hatan Torah* (literally, "Bridegroom of the Torah"), and the honor is reserved for someone of great distinction in the community, such as the rabbi. The third special honor is the *aliyah* for the Torah reading that begins the new annual cycle—the one at the very beginning of Genesis. The recipient of that *aliyah* is designated *Hatan Bereishit* (literally, "Bridegroom of Genesis"). Some congregations have a custom to spread a tallit over the *Hatan Torah* and *Hatan Bereishit,* similar to making a canopy over the children.

Reading Kohelet

> A season is set for everything, a time for every experience under heaven:
> A time for being born and a time for dying.
> —Eccles. 3:1–2

On the intermediary Shabbat of the festival of Sukkot, it is an Ashkenazic custom to read the Book of Ecclesiastes. The book's Hebrew name, Kohelet, is taken from the self-ascribed name of its author in chapter 1, verse 1. The English name, Ecclesiastes, is taken from the Greek meaning "the one who assembled," which is also how the word Kohelet is translated in the Septuagint (the Greek translation of the Bible). Traditionally, Kohelet is said to be King Solomon at the end of his life, when he is reflecting upon the wisdom he has gained. After all, Solomon is the archetype of Jewish wisdom, given that he was granted a "wise and discerning mind" by God (1 Kings 3:12). King Solomon or not, the content of Kohelet has historically been quite controversial; some Rabbinic sages disqualified it as unsacred and claimed it should be removed from the biblical canon.[98]

Kohelet speaks to a range of topics, including wealth, friendship, the cycles of life, the limitations of wisdom, and the enjoyment of existence. Overall, Kohelet maintains that human beings are incapable of totally understanding the purpose of the world and that it does not really matter what we do, for both the good and the bad ultimately suffer and die. Kohelet repeatedly states that all is futile, *hevel* (literally, "vapor"), which is clearly an argument against the more conventional Jewish theology of reward and punishment set forth in Deuteronomy. The Deuteronomistic philosophy claims that one who acts rightly will be rewarded in this lifetime and one who acts badly will be punished.[99] By comparison, aside from Kohelet's final two verses, which in fact seem out of place and are probably editorial additions,[100] it fully dismisses the philosophy found in Deuteronomy. For example, Kohelet argues that since your behavior, good or bad, has no effect on how life treats you, the goal of life should be to enjoy it and be carefree.[101]

Why do we read Kohelet on Sukkot? The most practical explanation is one of default: The Rabbis had already assigned four of the five *megillot* (literally, "scrolls")—a series of books in the Bible section called Writings—to other holidays, each with a measure of thematic connection. Kohelet was just a leftover;

and Sukkot, despite having no clear relationship to the book, got it.[102] The most commonly understood symbolic correlation is that both the holiday and the book speak to the transitory nature of life. Kohelet is clear in its message that material wealth is meaningless because we all die anyway. Sukkot teaches us, through our time in the sukkah, that our material possessions are not the true source of our security. Moreover, Kohelet and Sukkot share the message that joy is a profound and important part of life.

Yet, although Kohelet speaks to joy in life, most of what it says does not seem to coincide with what so much of Judaism (and, for that matter, so much of most religions) supports. How can Judaism be a proponent for viewing life as "utter futility"? How is the sentence "For the only good a man can have under the sun is to eat and drink and enjoy himself" (8:15) consistent with the piety, prayerfulness, and spirituality that Judaism proposes in so many places? The answer is simple: Judaism does not support most views of Kohelet. It supports only the central theme, which is that human beings do not have all the answers.

Kohelet may have been canonized, despite its blatant disregard for Deuteronomy, because those who made such decisions were humble enough to realize that the truth exists in many forms. Jonah and Job are also responses to the Deuteronomistic philosophy, and they too have much to teach us about life and death and about good and evil. The Rabbinic sages who passed the Jewish tradition on to us did not see themselves as intercessors between God and people, but as thinkers and teachers serving the Jews on the streets—people who often were subjects of torment and deprivation. The sages understood that a holy life could be conceived in many different ways, as we all are given different lots with which to start.

About halfway through Sukkot, we are nearing the end of the most intense part of the year, one that is filled with the most extreme holiday manifestations of theology, ritual, and observance. At this point we may find ourselves more than ready to reenter the world of the mundane. Many of us feel we have had enough; we are tired of being judged. Perhaps we admit to ourselves that we are still struggling with our beliefs. At this moment, on Shabbat, we encounter the philosophy of Kohelet. If we disregard the more usual image of the wise King Solomon, we realize that Kohelet is also tired; and he is sure of only one thing—there is no logical explanation to how the world works. So what does Kohelet do?

He searches. Kohelet experiments with life; he is in fact a spiritual seeker. He concludes that he has not found the answer, and therefore he is not going to worry about not having answers; he will simply live life to its fullest.

Thus the message of Kohelet may actually be not for Sukkot itself, but for after Sukkot. It is a message of comfort, allowing us to return to the commonplace aspects of life, to come down from the lofty heights of the *Yamim Noraim* and the clouds of glory. Judaism does not say that one has to have all the answers, and faith is not its rallying cry. Rather, Judaism supports a life of seeking, in all facets, whether it be through the intellect or whether it be through the heart.

Sukkot

Pathways Through the Sources

Midrash

A New Reckoning

Midrashim function in wondrous ways. In the following midrash a question is posed about a particular literary point in the Torah. An answer is provided in the form of a parable. The author, concerned about misinterpretation, goes on to explain exactly how the parable addresses the question. All the while, we the readers are given an elaborate portrait of the intricate connection between Judaism and the spiritual cycle of the calendar. We receive a theological discourse on the innate imperfection of humankind and the compassionate relationship between God and Israel. This midrash also provides a definition of the purpose of Sukkot and an explanation of how the holiday fits within the greater context of Jewish practice and spirituality.

> A comment on the verse *On the first day you shall take* (Lev. 23:40). Can the words *first day* mean the first day of the month? No, for Scripture has fixed the day as *the fifteenth day of the seventh month* (Lev. 23:39). But why should Scripture have shifted over from counting by days in the month to counting by days in the festival? R. Mani of Shaab and R. Joshua of Siknin citing R. Levi replied as follows: The matter may be explained by a parable—the parable of a city that owed the king its tax. The king sent collectors to take up the money, but the people of the city would not pay what they owed the king. Thereupon the king said, "I will go myself and collect it." When the people of the city heard that the king was on his way to collect the tax, the notables of the city went out to meet him a distance of 10 parasangs and said to him, "O king, our lord, we acknowledge that we owe you money. But right now we have not the means to pay the entire amount. We entreat you, have pity on us." The king, seeing that they were seeking a peaceful settlement with him, remitted a third of the sum the citizens owed.
>
> When the king came to within five miles of the city, the city councillors came out, prostrated themselves before him and said, "O king, our lord, we have not the means to pay." So the king remitted another third of the sum the citizens owed. Then when he entered the city, the very moment he entered it, the

entire city, everyone in it, men and women, grownups and little ones, came out, prostrated themselves at his feet, and pleaded with him. The king said, "Suppose I ask no more than one part in four of what you owe." They replied, "Our lord, we have not the means." What did the king do? He remitted the entire amount and wrote off their debt in full. What did all the people of the city do then? They went, the grownups and the little ones, and brought myrtles and palm branches and sang praise to the king. The king said, "Let bygones be bygones; from this moment on we shall commence a new reckoning."

The application of the parable is as follows: Throughout the days of the year, Israel sins. Then on New Year's Day the Holy One [goes up on His throne and] sits in judgment. What do the People of Israel do then? They gather and pray in synagogues, and after reciting the 10 verses asserting God's sovereignty [*Malkhuyot* in the High Holiday *machzor*], the 10 verses asserting God's remembrance of His creatures [*Zikhronot* in the *machzor*], and the ten verses alluding to the shofar [*Shofarot* in the *machzor,* which speaks to revelation], they blow the shofar. Thereupon the Holy One remits one-third of the punishment for Israel's iniquities. Between New Year's Day and the Day of Atonement those men who are notable for their piety fast as they avow penitence. Thereupon the Holy One remits another third of the punishment for Israel's iniquities. Then when the Day of Atonement comes, all Israel fast as they avow penitence, men, women, and children. Indeed they avow complete penitence, for they put on white garments, even though they are bare of foot like the dead. They say to Him: Master of the universe, we are two things at once: in our white garments we are like the angels who are eternal, but bare of foot we are like the dead.

When the Holy One sees Israel resolved upon complete penitence, He forgives all sins and writes off Israel's debt to Him, as it is written, *For on this day atonement shall be made for you to cleanse you of all your sins* (Lev. 16:30). When Israel sees that the Holy One has made atonement for them and has written off their debt, what do they do? During the four days between the Day of Atonement and the Feast of Tabernacles they go and fetch myrtle and willows and palm branches and build booths and sing praises to the Holy One. The Holy One says to them: Let bygones be bygones. From this moment on commences a new reckoning. Today is the first day in the new reckoning of iniquities. As Scripture says, *On the first day* (Lev. 23:40).

—*Pesikta Rabbati* 51:8[103]

Midrash Rabbah

Prolonging the Celebration

The Torah (Lev. 23:36) states that the eighth day of Sukkot is a special day, a holiday in its own right. The sages of the Jewish tradition wanted to understand why the holiday extended for eight days, rather than spanning a conventional seven-day week? And why should the eighth day, known as Shemini Atzeret, be more significant than any of the others? In truth, the observance of the Jewish holidays from the beginning of Rosh Hashanah through Sukkot is tiresome, and by the eighth day many of us are ready for the holidays to be over. However, as this midrash teaches, rather than rush to end them we should learn to preserve and savor them, for it will be another year before we are able to be so intimate with God.

> Rabbi Joshua ben Levi said: By rights, Shemini Atzeret should have followed Sukkot after an interval of fifty days, as Shavuot follows Passover. But since at Shemini Atzeret summer passes into autumn, the time is not suitable for traveling. [Therefore, God could be compared to] a king who had several married daughters, some living nearby, while others were a long way away. One day they all came to visit their father the king. Said the king, "Those who are living nearby are able to travel at any time. But those who live at a distance are not able to travel at any time. So while they are all here with me, let us make one feast for all of them and rejoice with them."
>
> —Midrash, *Song of Songs Rabbah* 7:2[104]

Rashi on Kohelet

The Joy of Now

It is customary to read the Book of Ecclesiastes (Hebrew name, Kohelet) on the Shabbat of the intermediate days of Sukkot, known as Shabbat Shemini Atzeret.[105] Kohelet is famous for teaching that everything has its season to die and that all is ultimately in vain. These are not the most optimistic of themes! They are, however, appropriate for Sukkot, as the sukkah represents our own impermanence on earth and, ultimately, our dependence upon the will of God.[106] Sukkot turns the transience of life, of which Kohelet speaks, into one of life's beautiful mysteries. Furthermore, Kohelet's conclusion to enjoy life while it is here connects directly to Sukkot, because he believes that rejoicing is the truest form of wisdom. Rashi, who was born in the 11th century and remains our greatest Bible commentator, eloquently elucidates these points for us.

"[God] has made everything beautiful in its time;[107] He also puts eternity in their mind, but without man ever guessing, from first to last, all the things that God brings to pass" (Kohelet 3:11).[108] Also, the wisdom of the world that God instilled in the hearts of mankind, He did not instill in each one's heart, rather a little to this one and a little to that one, in order that man should not fully grasp the workings of the Holy One, Blessed is He, to know it; [and thereby] he will not know the day of his visitation [death] and on what he will stumble, in order that he put his heart to repent, so that he will be concerned and say [to himself], "Today or tomorrow I will die." ... [This verse] expresses what is "hidden," for if man knew that the day of his death was near, he would neither build a house nor plant a vineyard. Therefore, [Kohelet] says that "He has made everything beautiful in its time." The fact that there is a time for death is a beautiful thing, for a person optimistically says [to himself], "Perhaps my death is far off," and he builds a house and plants a vineyard; and it is beautiful that it is concealed from people.... Now, since the time of visitation [death] is concealed, that there is nothing better for man than to rejoice with his portion and to do that which is good in his Creator's eyes, while he is yet alive.

—Rashi on Kohelet (Ecclesiastes) 3:11–12[109]

The Zohar

Hosting the Divine

Sukkot is a holiday in which there is an overt concern for the poor. The Zohar institutes a ritual of hospitality, meriting those who dwell in the sukkah with the privilege of welcoming both God's presence *(Shekhinah)* and our great ancestors *(ushpizin)* into the sukkah. For the Zohar, each of the *ushpizin* draws a divine quality or emanation *(sefirah)* into the community. For example, Abraham is *hesed* (lovingkindness); Isaac is *gevurah* (strength). It is clear from the text, however, that if one has not also invited the poor, the celebration is meaningless and the table is "not of the Holy One." Therefore, the observance and spiritual expression of Sukkot is directly linked to *tzedakah* (literally, "righteousness"—charitable giving) and care for the poor.

Whoever sits under the shadow of faith inherits freedom for himself and his children for ever and is blessed.... But whoever removes himself from the shadow of faith inherits exile for himself and his children.... When a man sits in this dwelling [the sukkah], the shadow of faith, the *Shekhinah* spreads out Her wings over him from above and Abraham and five of the righteous and King David stay there with him.... When Rav Hamnuna the Elder was about to enter the sukkah he would rejoice and would stand by the door of the sukkah saying: "We invite our guests." He would arrange the table and recite the benediction and then he would say [twice]: "Ye shall dwell in Sukkot. Please be seated, O ye supernal guests, please be seated...!" He would then wash his hands and would rejoice, and would say: "Happy is our portion. Happy the portion of Israel, as it is written: 'For the portion of the LORD is His people'" (Deut. 32:9). And he would sit.... Therefore, a man has to make the poor happy since the portion of those guests he invites belongs to the poor. But if a man sits under this shadow of faith and he invites these supernal faithful guests without giving them their portion [by not inviting the poor to his table], they all go away from him, saying: "Eat no the bread of him that hath an evil eye" (Prov. 23:6). That table is ... not of the Holy One, blessed be He.

—Zohar 3:103a-b[110]

Sefer Ha-Hinnukh

The Power of Four

Each of the symbols for Sukkot carries an extraordinary amount of meaning. We are taught that the *arba minim* symbolize four very important, yet very different, things. As a group, they symbolize joy; they symbolize the harvest; they symbolize nature; and they symbolize the human being. *Sefer Ha-Hinnukh* (The Book of Education), attributed to a talmudist in medieval Spain, teaches us that all of these things are ultimately cues to remind us of the beauty of the world and the joy of life, which are credited to God.

God ordained a festival at this time [of natural rejoicing in the harvest] in order to direct their principal joy to Him. Since such rejoicing has a tendency to lead men after material desires and to divert them from spiritual thoughts at that time, the Almighty commanded us to take in our hands things that would remind us that all joy should be turned towards Him, to pay Him homage. It was His will that the objects reminding us of our spiritual obligations should also evoke joy in keeping with the joyous time.... And it is well known that the Four Species by their nature make the hearts of all who gaze on them to rejoice.

> Moreover, these Four Species are symbolic of something else. They are likened to the principal human limbs: the *etrog* resembles the heart, the seat of the mind, alluding to the service of the Creator with the mind; the *lulav* to the backbone, intimating that the entire body should be engaged in His service, may He be blessed; the myrtle is the eyes to warn that one should not let his eyes stray on the day of rejoicing of his heart; and the willow resembles the lips, signifying that one should control his speech and fear God even in the time of joy.
>
> —*Sefer Ha-Hinnukh* 285[111]

Moses Chaim Luzzatto

Engulfed in Light

Judaism teaches that God is one and God is everywhere; the world is filled with God. This is an awe-inspiring thought because it implies that we are constantly interacting with God and surrounded by God's presence. For the pious throughout history, certain holy symbols have brought this concept to the forefront of consciousness. By examining the "spiritual history" of these symbols, we too can be aided in fostering faith and motivating self-improvement. The sukkah and the *lulav* have certainly served as powerful agents of spiritual awareness.

Moses Chaim Luzzato, also known by the Hebrew acronym Ramchal, was a prominent rabbi originally from 18th-century Italy. While living in Amsterdam, he wrote *Derekh Ha-Shem* (The Way of God), a philosophic text about God's purpose in Creation, justice, and ethics, from which this selection comes.

> The essence of the sukkah and the *lulav* is directly related to the Clouds of Glory with which the Holy Blessed One surrounded Israel. Besides the physical benefits of sheltering and protecting them, they also provided tremendous spiritual benefit. It is these clouds that raised Israel and set them apart from the world, as they were wrapped in Illumination.… It was through this that Israel attained the high level that was meant for them, which continued to be passed on from one generation to the next. This is the Holy Light of which the Blessed One is immersed and which surrounds the righteous, separating them from others, and elevating them above all; the sukkah serves to renew this on each Sukkot. This is the Light of the Blessed One that illuminates all of Israel and engulfs them when they take the *lulav* and its species.
>
> —Moses Chaim Luzzatto[112]

The Rabbi of Kamionka

The *Etrog's* Glow

Throughout the Jewish tradition, the *etrog* has been a symbol and object of high worth; great emphasis is placed on acquiring a beautiful *etrog* for the holiday, even at much expense. Because the *etrog* is one of the four species shaken with the *lulav* on Sukkot, it is understood to be an object of contemplation and, in turn, spiritual transformation, as we see in this mystical Jewish tale from Prague, first published in 1937.

> One year the Reb [rabbi] of Kamionka came to the city of Belz for Sukkot in order to be with his master, Reb Sholem of Belz. As he walked into the House of Prayer, he heard Reb Sholem's voice praying the Hallel prayer. He looked up, expecting to see the rebbe at the *bimah,* but he was not there. The Rabbi of Kamionka looked around the synagogue in confusion, for he could still hear the rebbe's voice ringing out, as clear as ever.
>
> The visiting rabbi looked around again slowly, ever so slowly. Surely Reb Sholem was there somewhere. And at last he saw him where few would think of looking. For somehow Reb Sholem had entered entirely into an etrog, an etrog so perfect that it could only have been a gift from heaven. Barely able to believe such a miracle was taking place, Reb Sholem stared at that etrog, so doubly blessed. As he peered at it, the etrog began to glow. It became transparent in his vision, and he saw that the source of its light was within, and that it was the light of Reb Sholem, who filled the shell of the etrog.
>
> The Rabbi of Kamionka closed his eyes for an instant and still saw the glowing etrog as clearly as when his eyes were open. He marveled at this, and when he opened his eyes again, he saw Reb Sholem standing before the Ark, with the light of the etrog glowing from his face and the fruit itself cradled in his hand.
>
> —Retold by Howard Schwartz in *Gabriel's Palace: Jewish Mystical Tales*[113]

Samson Raphael Hirsch

Minding What We Share

The modern world challenges us in so many ways. So often we are consumed with the surface of things, emphasizing unsettling differences rather than noticing the deeper similarities. We look on magazine racks and see people who are thinner, more beautiful, younger, wealthier, and sexier than we are. We watch television and see people who live in bigger houses and drive more comfortable cars than we have. As a tragic result, some of us work as hard as we can, taking hardly a moment for our loved ones and ourselves, and, all too often, fail to find the satisfaction that appears to be "out there." Sukkot comes to tell us that all of this is temporary and insignificant. What is eternal, however, is the divine blessing of the Holy One, the blessing that is with us at each moment.

Rabbi Samson Raphael Hirsch, considered the founder of contemporary Orthodox Judaism, traveled a complex path in this lifetime. Given both a secular and a traditional Jewish education, he eventually became totally opposed to Reform Judaism, which was developing in Germany in the 19th century. For him, Western culture combined with Orthodox Judaism would serve modern people as "the way of the world."

> The building of the [sukkah] teaches you trust in God. Whatever may be your station in life, whether you are richly or poorly endowed with goods of this world, you are neither dazzled by abundance nor frightened by want. The goods of the earth are not your goods. It is with that which others reject and despise that you build this tabernacle of your life. You know that whether men live in huts or in palaces, it is only as pilgrims that they dwell; both huts and palaces form only our transitory home....
>
> We may in the quantity of our possessions be divided into a thousand grades. One may build his walls of hewn stones and the other modest planks.... But in respect to our actual protection, of that which covers and shields us—the *s'khakh* [roofing]—we are all equal. This is not anything which bespeaks human craftsmanship, not anything which has to fear the breath of transitoriness. In the walls we may differ, but in the *s'khakh* we are all equal. For it is not human wealth or strength or skill, but the grace and blessing of God which protects us and covers palaces and huts with the same love....
>
> [The] sheltering love of God is everywhere and constantly with you ... where it protects you, there you dwell, were it only for a moment, in the most fleeting and transitory dwelling, as calmly and securely as if it were your house forever.
>
> —from Samson Raphael Hirsch, *Judaism Eternal: Selected Essays*, translated by Isidor Grunfeld[114]

Elie Wiesel

Joy under Adversity

How can the Torah "command" us to be joyous on a certain holiday? Can we be forced to dance and sing? These are legitimate questions, yet the Jewish tradition still insists that we rejoice on Sukkot, no matter what else we may be experiencing. Joy is one of the most essential expressions of the human spirit, for song and dance are the shield and sword of the Jewish spirit that have been instrumental in our survival through millennia of horror. Highlighted by Simchat Torah, Sukkot is the embodiment of that expression, calling upon the spirit to rejoice no matter the pains of life.

Elie Wiesel was raised as an Orthodox Jew in Romania. Incarcerated during the Holocaust in four different concentration camps, he witnessed the Jewish experience under the most extreme circumstances. He eventually became a renowned author, worldwide political activist, and winner of the Nobel Peace Prize.

> The Gaon of Vilna said that *ve-samachta be-chagekha* (You shall rejoice in your festival) is the most difficult commandment in the Torah. I could never understand this puzzling remark. Only during the war did I understand. Those Jews who, in the course of their journey to the end of hope, managed to dance on Simchat Torah, those Jews who studied Talmud by heart while carrying stones on their back, those Jews who went on whispering *Zemirot shel Shabbat* [Hymns of Shabbat] while performing hard labor—they taught us how Jews should behave in the face of adversity. For my contemporaries one generation ago, *ve-samachta be-chagekha* was one commandment that was impossible to observe—yet they observed it.
>
> —Elie Weisel[115]

·◆— Sukkot —◆·

Interpretations of Sacred Texts

Studied at multiple levels in these pages are one text from the biblical Book of Zechariah and two from the Mishnah. Found in Nevi'im (Prophets), Zecahariah has two thematic sections: the prophet's exhortations for a speedy return to Jerusalem (chapters 1–8) and his prophecies about the "end of days" (9–14). The Mishnah, a body of Jewish law, is divided by subject into six "orders"; *Mo'ed* is the one that deals with the Sabbath and festivals. Two of *Moed's* tractates are *Ta'anit* ("Fasts"), a treatise that includes discussions about prayers and fasts for rain, and *Sukkah,* a discussion of the laws of the holiday Sukkot.

THE THREE LEVELS
Peshat: simple, literal meaning
Derash: historical, Rabbinic inquiry
Making It Personal:
contemporary analysis and application

Materialism and Redemption

Lo, a day of the LORD is coming
when your spoil shall be divided in
your very midst! For I will gather all
the nations to Jerusalem for war:
The city shall be captured, the
houses plundered, and the women
violated; and a part of the
city shall go into exile. …

All who survive of all those nations
that came up against Jerusalem shall
make a pilgrimage year by year to
bow low to the King Lord of Hosts
and to observe the Feast of Booths.
Any of the earth's communities that
does not make the pilgrimage to
Jerusalem to bow low to the King
Lord of Hosts shall receive no rain.

—Zechariah 14:1–2,16–17

Peshat

Each Shabbat and on festivals and holy days, a passage is read from one of the books of The Prophets (Nevi'im). Called the haftarah (from the root for "complete"), these passages are related either thematically or tangentially to the Torah portion. In this haftarah for Sukkot, Zechariah's "doom and gloom" prophecy for the final day of divine judgment ends on a hopeful and interesting note. The first two lines begin with capture, plunder, and rape, underscoring a feeling of powerlessness before God. The conclusion of the chapter describes, in somewhat of a paradox, the survivors' celebration of Sukkot.

Derash

The festival of Sukkot and the sukkah itself commemorate redemption, that of the Jewish people from slavery in Egypt. This haftarah expands upon the role Sukkot plays, as it will be the central holiday after the final redemption of the Jews.

Perhaps this prophecy places Sukkot as the fulfillment of the final redemptive process because of its place in the calendar. Rosh Hashanah and Yom Kippur are paradigms for judgment; therefore, it makes sense for Sukkot to follow the judgment as a symbol of reward for those who survive—a festival of abundance and joy. Certainly, if there is a holiday of abundance, it is Sukkot. As Kohelet* teaches, [there is] "a time for every experience under heaven" (Eccles. 3:1); and Sukkot is definitely the time to feast rather than fast, to reap rather than sow, and to rejoice rather than mourn. From this perspective, Sukkot embodies the final redemptive stage and subsequent freedom.

Making It Personal

Judaism surely encourages the organic life expressions of abundance and joy, as they signify an inherent peacefulness and prosperity. That being said, Judaism is careful not to get carried away with joy and abundance and always ensures a balance with spirituality on life's scale. Balance is a must because human fallibility in the form of lust, desire, and greed often turn joy into vanity and abundance into materialism. In Ecclesiastes, Kohelet's words act as a sobering warning, "A lover of money never has his fill of money, nor a lover of wealth his fill of income. That too is futile" (5:9).

For Judaism, abundance and joy are spiritual terms, not material experiences by which we spoil ourselves while turning a blind eye to the suffering that happens around us. Sukkot calls for us to invite the poor into the sukkah; because joy is found in lovingkindness.

Spending time in the sukkah—this poor man's hut—we release ourselves from all that enslaves us and we see the depth of the world. The sages describe the sukkah as a protective "cloud of glory." Alternative symbolism offers that the sukkah erases whatever clouds our view of life. We are beings of light, not just crude matter. Once we accept that our spirits are eternal, we can experience mature joy by choosing meaningful lives of struggles and accomplishments, and appreciation of the simple gifts. Sukkot teaches us to find the joy in our limits and imperfections, in our dependency (such as our need for rain to live), and in our mortality.

* Kohelet is the name of the book that is translated in the Septuagint (the Greek translation of the Bible) as Ecclesiastes. Traditionally, Kohelet is said to be King Solomon at the end of his life. The word may mean "the Assembler," as in assembler of sayings

THE THREE LEVELS
Peshat: simple, literal meaning
Derash: historical, Rabbinic inquiry
Making It Personal:
contemporary analysis and application

Prayer and the Powers of Rain

When [do we begin to] mention the [prayer over] the Powers of Rain *(Geshem)*?

Rabbi Eliezer says, "On the first day of the Festival [i.e., Sukkot]."

Rabbi Joshua says, "On the last day of the Festival [i.e., Shemini Atzeret]."

Rabbi Joshua [challenges] Rabbi Eliezer, "Since rain on [Sukkot] is nothing but a curse, why should one mention rain [on Sukkot]?"

Rabbi Eliezer replies, "I did not say that one is to request [rain during Sukkot], rather only to mention [God's rain giving power] in its season [which starts at Sukkot]."

Rabbi Joshua then says, "If that is so [since it is not a request for God's power, but merely a mention of it], shouldn't one mention it all year round!"

[The Mishnah, however, specifies that] we only request rain immediately before the rainy season [i.e., on the last day of Sukkot—Shemini Atzeret]

—Mishnah, *Ta'anit* 1:1–2

Peshat

Each year on Shemini Atzeret, a line is added to the *Musaf Amidah* (the extra *Amidah* said on Shabbat and holidays), which is then included in the daily *Amidah* until the first day of Passover. The line praises God as the One who causes the wind to blow and the rain to fall *(mashiv ha-ru'ach u'morid ha-geshem)*.[116] It is inserted into the second of the 19[117] blessings of the *Amidah*—the one referring to God's power. The *hazzan* (leader) introduces the line with great ceremony and with poetry in the form of an alphabetic acrostic[118] that is added to the second recitation of the *Musaf Amidah*.

The inclusion of this line in the *Amidah* becomes a matter of a debate, which considers timing and purpose. The sages of the Mishnah clearly agree that we should include the line in the season of Sukkot, but an argument ensues over whether that should occur before or after the festival. For them, the timing is ultimately dependent upon the function of the line: Is it a request for rain or simply a statement about God?

Derash

In this Mishnah, Rabbi Joshua argues not to include the line during Sukkot because it is a curse to us. The other rabbis accept this argument because the Talmud teaches elsewhere (*Sukkah* 28b–29a) that if it rains into a sukkah, there is an exemption from eating in it. In other words, with rain, the mitzvah of dwelling in the sukkah is no longer necessary. Asking for rain during Sukkot is thus an indirect rejection of the mitzvah of dwelling in the sukkah; and even Rabbi Eliezer agrees that no one should request rain on Sukkot, solely to mention God's rain-giving power.

In the Diaspora,[119] 60 days after the fall equinox, we do insert a specific request for rain (*tal u'matar livrachah,* "dew and rain for blessing"). It is placed elsewhere in the *Amidah*—in the ninth blessing, the one that calls for annual prosperity. According to medieval legal codes, the insertion should take place on this date for two reasons. By then, rain is absolutely necessary in Israel, and Sukkot pilgrims have had time to return home from Jerusalem.[120] Therefore, we now insert this request from December fifth until Passover, when the seasons change.

Making It Personal

Prayers of request, especially those for rain and for survival, are taken very seriously in Judaism. Although we live in a post-Holocaust world, when some may doubt the efficacy of prayer, it remains one of the pillars of Jewish practice. The sages did not question whether or not to pray, rather they were concerned with how to pray, whether to ask for something, and, if so, what and how; they believed in the power of prayer. The intent of a request, however, was and is the most sensitive aspect, as personal appeals easily become disgraced with coveting and self-centeredness. Jewish liturgy certainly speaks to the importance and worth of each of us, but it also demands that we humble ourselves to the point of being something greater than our individuality. It rarely includes requests specifically for oneself; in other words, we ask God to understand or forgive "us" rather than "me." Even in the traditional liturgy, prayers of healing are made on behalf of other people rather than for ourselves. Judaism teaches that through our mental and spiritual intent and through the godliness that is within each of us, we affect God by what we say and what we truly mean when we say it.

THE THREE LEVELS
Peshat: simple, literal meaning
Derash: historical, Rabbinic inquiry
Making It Personal: contemporary analysis and application

The Law and the Lesson of Fragility

If a sukkah is higher than twenty cubits[121] it is invalid . . . . if it is not 10 handbreadths[122] high or if it does not have three sides,[123] or if its unshaded part is more than its shaded part—it is invalid.

If one dragged a vine or a gourd or ivy over the sukkah for a cover—it is invalid. But if he covered it with more than just them or if he cut them—it is kosher. This is the general principle [for the covering, *s'khakh*]: whatever may be contaminated and does not grow from the earth may not cover it.

A reed mat made for the purpose of covering a sukkah, may be used. If one makes a sukkah on top of a wagon or on top of a ship, it is kosher and they may go into it on *yom tov* . . . . This is the general principle: if a tree is removed and it could stand by itself, it is kosher and they may go into it on *yom tov*.

—Mishnah, *Sukkah* 1:1,4,11 and 2:3

Peshat

The halakhic (legal) requirements for a sukkah are no small matter. Chapters upon chapters have been written about how to put up this flimsy hut and with what materials. It should be built before the holiday. It cannot be too high or too low. It has to have at least three sides, but not be fully enclosed by four. Indeed, each year synagogue bulletins around the world send out instructions to remind congregants of such details.

The most important aspect of the sukkah is the roofing, the *s'khakh*. The *s'khakh* must be organic material (evergreens, bamboo, and palms are the most common) and detached from the growing plant. Lightweight wooden slats may be used as support beneath them, but nothing heavy should be used, nor should any roofing be nailed into place. The *s'khakh* should cover the roof well enough to create plenty of shade, but be spread out enough that one can see the stars from inside.

Derash

The sukkah is definitely understood to be a temporary residence, not even requiring a mezuzah (B. Talmud, *Yoma*

10b). Still, we are meant to dwell in the sukkah for the seven days of Sukkot—eating in it, sleeping in it, making ourselves as comfortable in it as possible. Rabbis and scholars through the ages understood the sukkah and the laws that surround it as being symbolic. The sukkah symbolizes the freedom first experienced in the desert. On one hand, it is to remind us of the physical conditions experienced by our ancestors. On the other hand, it is to remind us of the emotional and spiritual conditions experienced by our ancestors. In sum, it is to remind us of the impermanence and instability they endured, entrusting their lives to the one God, the true master who connects each and every feature of desert life, from the stars above to the soil below.

Making It Personal

During the spring holiday of Passover, with its story of the Exodus, we explore the meaning of freedom. The unleavened bread, matzah, is its primary symbol. On Sukkot, the sukkah is the symbol of our ancestors' freedom; and we test our understanding of that freedom through more extreme measures, posing real challenges to modern Jews. We are commanded to eat and sleep in the sukkah, a backyard hut—can we do it? Can we leave the luxuries and security of a home for the insecurity of a half-built tent? Are we able to take just one week out of 52 and spend it away from material comfort? Although some of us are physically unable to do so, many of us today simply never consider it, or outright refuse it. Thus, we are humiliated by comparison to the faith and strength of our ancestors. The sukkah defies us by asking if we are slaves and, if so, to what? The truth is, renunciation is the key to freedom and self-mastery, and the sukkah facilitates such growth and healing.

Sukkot

Significance of the Holiday: Some Modern Perspectives

History and Tradition Interwoven

by Joel Roth

Piecing together the history of the festivals of the Jewish calendar is a very complex undertaking and remains the subject of much disagreement.

It is agreed by all that the three festivals which are today commonly called the *Shalosh Regalim* (three pilgrimage festivals: Pesach, Shavuot, and Sukkot) were, indeed, pilgrimage festivals even in the biblical period, as evidenced by the fact that they are each called *hag* (festival) in the Torah, at least sometimes (Exod. 23:12–19, 34:18–23; Lev. 23: 6,34; Num. 28:17, 29:12; Deut. 16:10,13).

In Exodus 23:16 and 34:22, Sukkot is called *hag ha-asif,* the festival of the ingathering. No date is stipulated, and no length is mentioned. Rather, it is defined as "at the end of the year, when you gather in the results of your work from the field" and "the turn of the year." There is no mention of either dwelling in booths or the use of what is now called *etrog* and *lulav.*

In Leviticus 23:33–43, the references to Sukkot are different. The holiday is called *hag ha-sukkot,* the festival of booths; its date is set on the 15th day of the seventh month; and it is designated to last for seven days with the eighth day being an *atzeret* (a concluding assembly). Verses 37–38 appear to be a conclusion to the entire chapter, which has outlined all of the holidays of the Jewish year. Then, in verses 39–43, we have what appears to be a postscript about Sukkot. It says we are to observe a festival during which we gather the four species (*etrog* and *lulav*) and we sit in booths for seven days to remember that God caused the Israelites to live in booths when they were taken out of Egypt.

In Numbers 29:12–38, in a list of required sacrifices for each day of the holiday, the holiday is nameless, though its date is stipulated as the 15th of the seventh month. There is no mention of any other type of requirement such as *etrog* and *lulav* or booths. Since the chapter lists the sacrifices of each of the eight days of the holiday (seven plus *atzeret*) separately, it is clear how long the festival should last.

Deuteronomy 16:13–15 mandates a seven-day pilgrimage called *hag ha-sukkot* to take place "after the ingathering from your threshing floor and your vat." No specific date is mentioned, nor is there any specific mention of dwelling in sukkot (except as implied by the name of the festival) or of the use of *etrog* and *lulav.* There is a requirement that "you rejoice in your festival." Verse 15 stipulates that the seven-day observance take place "in the place that the LORD will choose."

Noted biblical scholar H. L. Ginsberg (1903–1990) proposed a convincing theory that accounts for the evolution and history of all three of the biblical pilgrimages. Regarding Sukkot he hypothesized that it was originally celebrated as a one-day pilgrimage on the day of the full moon of the ingathering period (i.e., the 15th of the seventh month), and that it took place at a local shrine. It was possible for the people to take one day off during the ingathering for a local pilgrimage. It was purely an agricultural festival.

With Deuteronomy's insistence on centralized worship, it was no longer possible to observe the festival at a local shrine. It had to be moved until after the completion of the ingathering and the processing of the produce ("after the ingathering from your threshing floor and your vat"), and since it was now possible to take off time, the pilgrimage became a seven-day festival. It was known as *hag ha-sukkot* because of the temporary housing structures that were needed to accommodate the pilgrims on a seven-day pilgrimage. It remained an agricultural festival entirely.

Leviticus 23 (and Numbers) retains the seven-day structure of Deuteronomy, but deems it unnecessary to postpone the festival until after the completion of the ingathering and restores its date to the full moon of the seventh month and speaks again of the ingathering, rather than the processing, of the produce. The booths are reinterpreted as a reference to the wandering in the desert, and the four species seem to be a method of "rejoicing" that is mandated by Deuteronomy and retained by Leviticus.

The Rabbinic, i.e., talmudic, tradition, of course, perceives of the entire Torah as a single, divine document. It is not conceivable that the type of historical development reflected in the research of modern scholars would find echoes in the Rabbinic tradition. In the Rabbinic tradition, the passages in the Torah are understood to complement each other, and the differences between them are not taken to imply disagreement between them.

In the Rabbinic tradition, therefore, the dwelling in sukkot and the utilization of the four species are not afterthoughts, but integral and original parts of the observance of the holiday. Nor was there ever a period in which Sukkot was observed for any fewer than seven days, plus the *atzeret.* As was the case with each of the other pilgrimages, Sukkot too had both an agricultural and an historical dimension, both of which are equally important in the festival's observance.

The Rabbinic tradition defines in great detail the requirements of the booths, both in terms of their construction and the obligation to "dwell" in them. Similarly, the four species are defined in a way far more precise than in the Bible itself, and details of imperfections that would disqualify them from use on the festival are explicated. The obligation to "take" the four species could be fulfilled at any time of the day or night, but the Mishnah also records that they were "shaken" at specific points in the recitation of what we call *Hallel* today. This practice continues to this day.

The temple service and worship on Sukkot included far more than the offering of the sacrifices mandated by the Torah. There were circuits around the altar made daily with large willow boughs, and seven circuits on the seventh day of the holiday. These have their remembrance today in the *hoshanot,* the circuits made around the synagogue with *etrog* and *lulav* in hand once on each day of Sukkot (except Shabbat), and seven times on the seventh day. The temple service of Sukkot also included a water libation—the only one of the year—which accompanied the offering of the daily *Tamid* sacrifice, in addition to its normal wine libation. The water libation has no explicit biblical source, though it was traced to the Bible by Rabbinic interpretation, as support for an ancient practice.

For six of the days of Sukkot there was a joyous celebration called *simchat beit ha-sho'evah,* which took place in the Women's Court of the Temple. This was in fulfillment of the mandate to "rejoice." Lighted torches played a large part in the celebration and, in addition, there were *menorot* set up in the court from which the light could be seen, according to the Mishnah, throughout Jerusalem. It is told of Rabban Shimon ben Gamliel that he would hold, or juggle, as many as eight lighted torches at once.

Clearly, the observance of Sukkot as it is practiced by observant Jews today is far more Rabbinic than it is biblical. That, of course, is no surprise since it is Rabbinic Judaism which has become normative Jewish practice.

Harvest and New Seed

by Arthur Waskow

Full moon, full harvest, history fulfilled, full hearts. As the sabbatical month—the seventh month, the moon of Tishrei—grows to fullness, we are ready to celebrate Sukkot, the Festival of Huts.

At Rosh Hashanah, the moment of new moon, we have already experienced the moment of rebirth, the rediscovery of our true identity, the reexamination of ourselves, the return to our true path. In the swelling of the moon at Yom Kippur, we have already brought our renewed selves into intense contact and reconciliation with God. And now at the full moon we celebrate Sukkot—the festival of fulfillment, of gathering in the benefits that flow from this encounter between God and ourselves, the blessings that flow from repentance and forgiveness. The harvest that takes the form of joy and *shalom,* harmony, in the world.

Sukkot is not only the fulfillment of the moon of Tishrei. It is also the fulfillment of the yearly cycle of the sun's impact upon the earth. All the sun's work comes to fullness as the harvest ripens and is gathered in. In the solar cycle, Pesach has celebrated the earth's rebirth, the birthing of lambs, the sprouting of barley, the birth of a people, and the birth of freedom. Shavuot has marked the peak of earthly power and the encounter of the newborn people with God, as spring moves into summer. Sukkot celebrates the glory of the earth fulfilled. As the moon has rewarded our celebration of her birth and growth by bursting into a glowing perfect circle, so the earth rewards our care of seed and stalk by bursting into ripened fruit and grain. And Sukkot also represents fulfillment in the aspect of the year as a lesson plan in history. In that lesson plan, Pesach reminds us of the moment of liberation from slavery in *Mitzrayim;* Shavuot reminds us of the moment of transcendent contact with God at Sinai. And Sukkot is the reminder of the fulfillment of this work of liberation and encounter; for Sukkot reminds us of the time of traveling in the wilderness under God's close protection, making camp in temporary huts. Just as we ourselves grow from our first spiritual awakening—an awakening to the possibility of freedom, creativity—into the passionate, awe-filled reality of contact with God, so we are now rewarded in our spiritual lives with the ingathering of spiritual riches. Our relationship with God bears psychic fruit.

We walk into the sukkah—the fragile field hut, open to the light of moon and stars that our forbearers lived in while they gathered in the grain. We dangle apples and onions, oranges and peppers, from its leafy roof. And we feel the joy that for a moment life is so safe, the world so loving, that we can live in these open-ended huts without fear.

Seed for Winter: Shemini Atzeret

After the moon of Tishrei has been celebrated in its birth, its swelling, and its fullness, the moon begins to wane, prophesying its own disappearance. At the same moment, in the solar cycle of the year, the fields stand bare and the seed is stored away. In the Land of Israel, farmers begin to sniff the smell of rain. Winter looms, the fourth season of the year. The earth prepares to hibernate, go underground, build up reserves of strength to make new life.

The waning moon and the fourth season need a fourth festival, for we need to welcome winter in the world and in ourselves. Mechanical symmetry might have required that a fourth festival stand on its own at the outset of winter, as Shavuot stands at the outset of summer. But Rabbi Joshua ben Levi explained that when the Temple stood, we could not wait till winter to make the pilgrimage to the Temple in Jerusalem. Torrential rains, muddy roads—these meant that we must stay home. So the winter festival was placed immediately at the end of the fall festival, when the pilgrims were still at the Temple.

Just as the spring festival of new life and liberation was not complete till we had counted seven weeks plus one day to the summer festival of fullness and revelation, so the fall festival of ingathering and redemption was not complete till we had counted seven days plus one day to the winter festival of sleeping and inwardness. When the pilgrims returned home, they needed just behind them not the boisterous joy of the sukkah and the water pouring, but the quiet celebration of a sense of inner peace.

So to meet this need we had Shemini Atzeret. Some translate this as the Eighth Day of Completion, others, the Eighth Day of Assembly. For *atzeret* means putting a boundary, restraining, collecting—either the days (and so, completion of the festival) or the people (and so, assembly of the multitude).

We can understand the restraint as inward, too. While the Temple stood, we turned from the expansive week of the multiple sacrifices of Sukkot to the minimum: one bull, one ram. The Talmud teaches that this reduction of the sacrifice from 70 bulls to one represents God's turning from concern with the 70 nations—the whole world—

to a quiet tête-à-tête alone with the People of Israel. The approach fits well with seeing Shemini Atzeret as the inward, wintry holy day, the festival of self-restraint.

Not only was the explicit message of Shemini Atzeret a measure of constriction, retreat, quiet—so was its medium, the implicit message of its form. For by tacking Shemini Atzeret right on to Sukkot, the Torah made sure that it would almost disappear from sight. Sukkot presents the fruitful earth in all its colorful and showy boldness; by Shemini Atzeret, the fleshy fruit has rotted away and what remains is tiny, almost invisible seed that must disappear into the ground to bear the crucial nucleus of new life, quiet until it sprouts in spring.

The Torah made sure that the tradition would speak of the three pilgrimage festivals—Pesach, Shavuot, and Sukkot—while almost forgetting the fourth. Almost—but never quite. For Shemini Atzeret appears as an independent festival in two—but only two—of the Torah's four recitations of the festival cycle. In accord with its role as seed for plunging deep into the earth, this pattern makes it the Festival of Now-you-see-it-now-you-don't.

It is as if this shadowy festival, this miniature celebration, was the *yud*—the tiny letter of the four in God's most holy name. The *yud* is the first letter of the Name, but suppose we see the Name as a continuing process, a spiral in which the end is (like seed) a new beginning and the beginning (like seed) stands also at the end. Then the *yud* is a tiny seed at the end of the Name, the concentrated lesson of its flowering, the seed that carries meaning forward to begin the next saying of the Name: *yud, heh, vav, heh.*

Open to the Earth and All Humanity

by Arthur Waskow

What is a "sukkah"? Just a fragile hut with a leafy roof, the most vulnerable of houses. Vulnerable in time, since it lasts for only a week each year. Vulnerable in space, since its roof must be not only leafy but leaky—letting in the starlight, and gusts of wind and rain.

In our evening prayers throughout the year, just as we prepare to lie down in vulnerable sleep, we plead with God—"Spread over us Your sukkah of *shalom*—of peace and safety."

Why does the prayer plead for a "sukkah of *shalom*" rather than God's "temple" or "fortress" or "palace" of *shalom,* which by most conventional standards would surely be more safe and more secure?

Precisely because the sukkah is so vulnerable.

For much of our lives we try to achieve peace and safety by building with steel and concrete and toughness:
Pyramids,
Air raid shelters,
Pentagons,
World Trade Centers.

Thick skins and tough hearts.

But the sukkah comes to remind us: We are in truth all vulnerable. If as the prophet [Bob] Dylan sang, "A hard rain's a-gonna fall," it will fall on all of us. We all live in a sukkah.

Even the widest oceans, the mightiest buildings, the wealthiest balance sheets, the most powerful weapons do not shield us.

The planet is in fact one interwoven web of life. There are only wispy walls and leaky roofs between our different cultures and nations. The command to love my neighbor as I do myself is not an admonition to be nice: it is a statement of truth like the law of gravity. However much and in whatever way I love my neighbor, that will turn out to be the way I love myself. If I pour contempt upon my neighbor, hatred will recoil upon me.

And today our "neighbors" means not only all human communities, but all the life-forms on our planet and those beings that only now are we coming to see as part of "Life": the ozone layer, the percentage of carbon dioxide in the air, the rivers, the oceans, the wetlands.

Sukkot teaches us this as well. For anciently, on the first day of Sukkot we poured water at the altar of the Holy Temple to remind God to pour water in the form of the rainy season. On the seventh day, anciently, we beat willow branches on the earth near riverbanks lined with willows, the trees that need so much water that they must grow near rivers. Again, imploring God for sacred rain. Today these ceremonies have become desiccated, literally dried up. And without them, what we learn is that our planet is a dry, dead thing, merely an object. The more we act this way, the more we turn the planet indeed into what we think it is—a dry, dead thing that endangers us, rather than sustains us.

Yet even now, there are aspects of Sukkot that could transform our worldview. The sukkah itself beckons us into the earth, leaving the houses that shield us from wind and rain to spend a week reminding ourselves that we are part of earth, not separate from it. And we still act out the last remnant of the wave-offering that was so important when the Temple stood: waving the palm, the myrtle, the willow, and the lemony *etrog* in the seven directions of the world.

Seven? Surely only six: east, west, north, south, up, down! The seventh is within ourselves; for with each waving of the four we bring them close to our hearts as well as reaching them out into the world.

These four forms of plant life, the Rabbis taught, remind us of the four letters of the Name of God, the YHWH, *[yud, heh, vav, heh]* that can only be pronounced by simply breathing as all life breathes together. The small *etrog* echoes the *Yud;* the myrtle and the willow, the two curving letters *Heh;* the tall, stiff palm branch, the *Vav.*

In the traditional posture for holding and waving these four, the *etrog,* the *Yud,* is held in the right hand. If one were reading as Hebrew is read, from left to right, the four would read "HWHY." It is only when I "read" the four that you are waving, and you read the four that I am waving, that the letters fall into place as the sacred Name. We can see God only when we look to see each other.

The sukkah not only invites our bodies to become physically vulnerable, but also invites our minds to become vulnerable to new ideas. To live in the sukkah for a week, as Jewish tradition teaches, would be to leave behind not only the rigid walls of our cities, but also our rigidified ideas, our assumptions, our habits, our accustomed lives. Sukkot is a time not only for individual reflection and change, but also for society-wide reflection. Indeed, the Torah proclaims that at the Sukkot just after the *shemitah* or sabbatical year (when the land and its farmers were to have a yearlong Sabbath, and those who had fallen into debt were to recover their economic equality), the whole people should assemble to hear the king and Priests read the Torah passages on the limited powers of a king and the responsibilities of the whole society to the poor.

Furthermore, the tradition teaches that Sukkot is the festival during which we open ourselves to what is foreign to us. When the rabbis wondered why the temple sacrifice for Sukkot was 70 bulls, they asserted that on Sukkot, alone among the festivals, we were seeking for prosperity and peace to pervade all "70 nations" of the world, not only the Jewish people. Traditionally, we invite holy guests into the sukkah—"guests" precisely because they are our higher selves, our unaccustomed selves.

In a world of vulnerable houses, we must reach out to heal and prosper each other. Only a world where all communities feel vulnerable, and therefore responsible to all other communities, can we prevent mass murder, unending war, and the poisoning of the planet.

What would it mean to apply these lessons today, throughout the world?

Could we not only pray for world prosperity but act to make it real through economic aid that goes directly to the grass roots of poverty-stricken communities, to people who are living in homes as fragile as the sukkah, rather than to giant dams and the "privatization" (really, the corporatization) of water supplies?

Could all of us teach all our children the Torah, the Prophets, the Song of Songs, the Talmud, the Gospels, the Quran, the Upanishads, the teachings of the Buddha and of King and Gandhi, as treasuries of wisdom—and sometimes of great danger—that are as crucial to the world as Plato and Darwin and Einstein?

Could we learn to see the dangers in "our own" as well as in "the other" teachings, and learn to strengthen those elements in all traditions that call for nonviolence, not bloody crusades and jihads and holy wars for holy lands?

The choice we face is broader than politics, deeper than charity. It is whether we see the world chiefly as property to be controlled, defined by walls and fences that must be built ever higher, ever thicker, ever tougher; or made up chiefly of an open weave of compassion and connection, open sukkah next to open sukkah.

The Season of Our Rejoicing

by Miriyam Glazer

> After you gather in from your threshing floor and your winepress, you shall hold the Festival of Huts for seven days ... for the Lord your God will bless your crops and all your undertakings, and you shall have nothing but joy.
> —Deut. 16:13–15

> Lord Who saves ... cause an abundance of crops, trees, vegetation ... sweeten the luscious fruits ... bring the soaring clouds. ... Renew the face of the earth, planting trees in desolate lands ... invigorate with flowers ... rain on the sprouts, pour a stream of cool waters to elevate the thirsty earth....
>
> Answer those who ask bearing the four species, planted near water.
> —from the *Hoshanah Rabbah* liturgy

In the month of Tishrei—just about the time of the autumn equinox—after the grapes had been pressed, the figs dried in the sun, the grain threshed, and the crops gathered in, the people of ancient Israel were at last ready to take pleasure in their hard-earned leisure. For the farmers of Israel, like those of other religious communities in the ancient world—as Maimonides, quoting Aristotle, reminds us (*Guide of the Perplexed* 3:45)—the end of the harvest was marked by a joyous festival. "Each bearing his own gift" (Deut. 16:17), they set out on a pilgrimage to Jerusalem prepared both to celebrate the end of the agricultural year and to perform sacrifices to the LORD in the hope that the year to come would bring enough rain to keep the earth fertile. All of Jerusalem shared in the celebration, for the harvest festival of Sukkot, the "season of our rejoicing," was also the time of the Water Drawing at the Temple, an ecstatic event alive with dance, trumpet music, singing, and so many flaming candles that "every courtyard in Jerusalem was illuminated by the light of the Place of the Water Drawing" (B.Talmud, *Sukkah* 51a). So powerful was the experience, says the Mishnah, that anyone who never saw the celebration of the Water Drawing "never saw rejoicing in his life" (ibid).

Urbanites though we have become today, our earth is as thirsty for the nourishment of water as it was in the day of our ancestors; the crops of our farmers are as much in need of blessing as they were in ancient days. And, though the Temple long ago fell and centuries of Diaspora have infused Sukkot with symbolic and mystical associations, the rituals of the festival at the heart of our own celebration are as rooted in the ancient agricultural meanings as they were more than a 1,000 years ago.

We still gather palm fronds to roof over the temporary "huts" that we build and which give the festival its name. We still wave "the four species" before God—the palm frond, willow, myrtle of our *lulav*—along with the fragrant citron, or *etrog*, the "fruit of goodly trees." During the festival, on 21 Tishrei, the day of *Hoshanah Rabbah,* our *hakafot* resound with our ancestors' pleas to merit rainfall in the agricultural season to come; and the next day, Shemini Atzeret, we chant the year's first prayer for rain, culminating in praise and a plea:

> For You are YHVH our God
>
> *Who makes the wind blow and the rain descend*
> *For blessing and not for curse.*
>
> For life and not for death
>
> *For plenty and not for scarcity.*

For it is during Sukkot, the Talmud teaches us, that "the world is judged for water" (B. Talmud, *Rosh Hashanah* 16a).

Yet what connection is there between our hutsitting and our prayers for rain? And how are they both connected with the four species?

While it's tempting to think of those huts as recalling the little temporary shelters set up by the farm workers in their fields during the harvest season, upon further thought that explanation makes little sense. Why would a festival *at the end of the harvest season* entail setting up huts like the ones the weary farmers just left? Indeed, as Israeli botanist Nogah Hareuveni points out, the real clue to the significance of the huts is the *palm fronds* we use as roofs. For the date palm flourishes in desert oases. Just around Tishrei—the "seventh month" (Lev. 23:34)—when the wells and cisterns of the Sinai have dried up, shepherds today—just as in ancient times—lead their flocks to the oases, where the dates have just ripened and can be picked and dried in the sun, providing food for the year to come. Every part of the palm tree finds its use: the pits are ground into fodder for camels; the fronds' thin fibers are plaited into ropes, and the fronds themselves woven into baskets and … *shelters.*

Thus, just as Maimonides understood, the sukkot we sit in commemorate the wandering of the Israelites before they ever reached the Promised Land. When we eat, live, and sleep under a roof of palm fronds, we are meant to reenact the experience of our ancestors, "poor desert-dwellers," before they entered "the best and most fertile place on earth" (*Guide of the Perplexed* 3:43).[124]

But what, then, of the four species? Maimonides' explanation is suggestive. If the sukkot evoke the desert, the four species are icons, he says, of "the joy and gladness" of *leaving* the desert for a fertile land "in which there were fruit-bearing trees and rivers" (*Guide* 3:43)—*Eretz Yisra'el.* Each of the species has its part to play in the drama of homecoming. According to Hareuveni, the palm frond is a reminder of the nomadic past; the willow, which grows along the banks of the Jordan, recalls the river the Israelites crossed when they came into the land; the myrtle evokes the hillside forests where it is plentiful; and the fragrant citron symbolizes the peoples' success in cultivating fruit-bearing trees once they had settled the land.

Scholar Arthur Schaffer goes even further and helps us to understand the rich connectedness of the four species with the festival liturgy. For the four species are very *specific* markers of regions of *Eretz Yisra'el,* each symbolizing water in the country's very different ecological zones: "the desert wilderness, the mountains and the hills, the cultivated plains, and the river valleys." From this point of view, the *lulav*—an unopened date frond—recalls not life in the desert per se, but rather the presence of an oasis there—"an island of water in a sea of sand." The willows, "water-loving plants" that grow in habitats "too wet for other species to survive," serve as "advocates for an abundance of rain." The *etrog,* which flourish in the plains only if it is cultivated with human care and attention, is meant to evoke our own efforts to plant, nurture, irrigate. And, finally, the aromatic myrtle, which is plentiful in the river in thickets and on the slopes of stream banks in the hills and mountains of Israel, is the very epitome of the healing prophecy of Isaiah: "I, the God of Israel, will not forsake them. I will open upstreams on the bare hills and fountains amid the valleys" (41:17–20).[125]

Waving these four richly evocative species in six different directions, as if to every nation of the world and every corner of the universe, we thus pray that rainfall will not be withheld, that thirst will be satisfied, that the soil of our earth will be saved from curses, our crops from destruction, our flocks from disease, and our "souls from terror." Written thousands of years ago, how profoundly apt these words still are today.

Never-ending Joy

by Alan Abrams

What is joy? Is it the flash of exhilaration I feel when I buy a new gadget or shirt, or when a check comes in the mail? Is that how I find it—by acquiring things? How can I make joy stay? Why is it so fleeting?

Our sages dubbed Sukkot as *z'man simchateinu,* the time of our joy. *Simchah* is the Hebrew word for joy,. and the Torah itself[1] commands us to be joyful—to feel *simchah*—on this holiday. But Sukkot also commemorates the long years of wandering in the desert before entering the Land of Israel. What could be joyful about such wandering? And how is the joy of this holiday, this *simchah,* connected to the sukkot, these fragile structures that keep out neither wind nor rain, and that must, like the leaves of a tree, both let in light and create shade?

The Torah explains that we build the sukkah in order that "future generations may know that I made the Israelite people live in booths when I brought them out of the land of Egypt" (Lev. 23:43).

In the Talmud, Rabbi Yishmael says that these sukkot were not actual huts, but rather the clouds of God's glory that guided the people Israel through the desert.[2] The medieval Bible commentator Ramban explains: We build sukkot to remind us of this great miracle of sheltering protection that God wrought for them.

Thus, our holiday of *simchah* teaches us that true joy comes not from acquiring material things, but from having the faith to trust in God's eternal protection, just as God protected our ancestors in the desert.

Rabbi Akiva, however, disagrees. He says the biblical sukkot really were huts. Another medieval writer, the Rashbam, reminds us that Sukkot comes at a natural time of joy for people who make their living off the land—at harvest time. He explains that we leave our comfortable houses full of joy-giving, harvest-time produce in order to remind us of how much God has given us compared to our ancestors who had only huts to live in.

Thus, despite his differences with Rabbi Yishmael, Rabbi Akiva also teaches us that the true source of joy comes not from our power to acquire material things, but from acknowledging that God is the true source of the lasting things of joy.

The sukkah itself is a constant reminder of this lesson. We go to it for the same reasons some people leave their homes to go walking in the wilderness with only a pack on their backs—to be reminded of what truly matters to us and who it is who truly runs the world. In the sukkah, when it rains, the rain falls upon us. In the day, we see the sun filtered through vegetation. At night, we see the stars. When the wind blows, we feel it. And our joy is amplified by the food and friends who are with us there.

In the Land of Israel, this exposure to the elements is even more joy giving—if you feel rain in a sukkah there, it is very likely to be the first rain of the season after the long, hot, rainless summer of that land has left the earth barren and brown. It is the joy of the life-giving green that only the new rains of winter can bring.

Sukkot, then, is not just the end of one agricultural season, but it is also the start of the next one. End meets beginning, completing a great unending circle.

Circles, in fact, characterize much of Sukkot and the two holidays—Shemini Atzeret and Simchat Torah—that immediately follow it. On each day of Sukkot, during the *hoshanah* prayers, we circle around the synagogue calling on God to save us. On the last day of Sukkot—Hoshanah Rabbah—we do this procession seven separate times. And, tradition tells us, when pilgrims entered ancient Jerusalem on Sukkot, they would cry out the words of Psalm 125:2 "Jerusalem enfolds it, and the LORD enfolds His people, for now and forever!"

Sukkot was also called "ha-hag" by our sages, which means the holiday, or the pilgrimage. But the word *hag* can also mean "he went around in a circle." In the secular world, we use the phrase "going in circles" in the very negative sense of going nowhere. But, in Judaism, the cycle of constant return to the same place—of marking both ending and new beginning as we do on Sukkot—is the most joyful and perhaps even holy thing we can do.

During their long wandering in the desert, the people Israel may have gone in circles many times, but were they really going nowhere? Were they not, instead, constantly arriving? Arriving at the presence of God, who surrounded them everywhere in the clouds of glory and who provided for their every need with manna from the sky. They had both nothing and everything.

This is the promise we encounter when we enter the sukkah—that by having nothing around us we will in fact have everything. Our lives will be a joyous circle where every end will promise a beginning, like the rains following Sukkot promise new green.

The ultimate cyclical meeting of end and beginning in the Jewish tradition comes at the end of the Sukkot season, on Simchat Torah. On that day, we both complete the annual Torah portion cycle by reading the final words of the Torah and start the next cycle by reading the beginning of the Torah—the story of the Creation of our wondrous and infinitely complex universe out of *tohu va-vohu,* the vast, unformed void.

In our lives, we experience many endings and we are forced to say good-bye to many people and things. But the wisdom of our holidays of *simchah*—of joy—teaches us that the path to joy is to acknowledge that our Creator is the source of all, and to have the wisdom to see our world as it truly is—a circle where every ending is really a beginning and every good-bye is really a hello.

Sukkot
Alternative Meditations

Imagining Zaydeh's Sukkah[126]

by Harold Schulweis

It was incongruous to even in imagination. Though I never witnessed the actual construction with my own eyes, I did see it and everyone testified that Zaydeh ["grandfather"] had built it.

But how? On the tar-pitched roof of a two-story building on South Ninth Street in Brooklyn was a sukkah with three sides leaning against a brick wall. Incredible to think of that old man with gray-white beard and black derby hauling boards and palm branches up to the roof from the street. Where did he find the material, and who could imagine Reb Avraham pounding nails into the wood, he whose commitment to study led him to look down on working with one's hands? He could never understand my playing with the interior workings of an old clock. It was *bittul zeman,* a waste of time taken away from study of Torah. Who could imagine the wasted time Zaydeh has to have spent constructing the sukkah?

Zaydeh sitting in a hut, outside the home, eating at a table surrounded by the aroma of leaves and fruits, a sight as strange as imagining Zaydeh at a camping jamboree. There he was outdoors, sitting hunched up with his suit collar raised, eating and drinking while it rained through the thatched roof. In the sukkah, Bubbe never ran short of soup. The law, of course, exempted him from dwelling in the sukkah if it rained. "If one suffers discomfort in a sukkah, he is exempt from the obligation of dwelling in it" (B. Talmud, *Sukkah* 25b). If there is no joy, the mitzvah is suspended. But protected by his derby and his sense of mitzvah, Zaydeh felt no discomfort.

Jewish codes state that if guests are invited to the sukkah on the first night and rain begins to fall, one should wait until midnight to eat in the sukkah. Perhaps the rain will stop by that time. But if the invited guests are poor, one should not wait for the rain to stop. Being poor the guests have most likely not eaten anything all day. For them to wait is discomfort enough. Let them eat with you in the dining room and forgo the mitzvah of dwelling in the sukkah. So my Zaydeh taught.

The sukkah brought out an unsuspected side of Zaydeh even as the holiday revealed an unexpected side of Jewish piety. Sukkot is different, especially when contrasted with the days of Rosh Hashanah and Yom Kippur which precede it. Rosh Hashanah is cerebral, a matter of the head; Yom Kippur is affective, a matter of the heart. But Sukkot is physical, a mitzvah of the entire body with which one enters the sukkah, even in one's boots. As if to compensate for the fast and the solemnity of the Day of Atonement, Sukkot is insistent upon rejoicing the body and the spirit, celebrating the taste and aroma of nature and reading the almost not canonized biblical text of Ecclesiastes. The wisdom of Ecclesiastes doesn't quite fit the conventional view of piety. "In the morning sow thy seed, and in the evening withhold not thy hand ... truly the light is sweet, and it is a pleasant thing for the eyes to behold the sun ... rejoice, young man, in thy youth, and let thy heart cheer thee in the days of thy youth."

Even the stories told about Sukkot possess an eccentric, irreverent Jewish charm. There is the one told about the rebbe whom the villagers entrusted with money to buy an etrog. He prepared to travel to the nearest city to select a choice citron-like fruit, one fresh, firm, with a fine aroma, and wrinkled. Why wrinkled? Because the etrog symbolizes the heart, and which heart that feels the anguish of the world can be smooth? A smooth-skinned etrog is a symbol of a callous heart.

On the way to the city the rebbe came upon a wagoner crying beside his horse who had fallen dead. Without a horse, a wagon is as useless as a man without *mazal* ["good fortune"], the wagoner explained. Without a horse, he and his family would starve. The rebbe asked no questions, handed over to the wagoner the bag of money allocated by the villagers for the purchase of an etrog, and returned home.

He explained what had happened to the distraught villagers, who cried aloud, "What will we do when Sukkot comes?" The rebbe consoled them, "Do not be sad. The whole world will recite the benedictions over an etrog, but we here will recite them over a dead horse." Irreverent but true to the spirit of Sukkot. For if the meaning of the festival of joy is gratitude, what greater rejoicing can there be than to lift up the lot of the fallen and thereby to rejoice God as well? If on Yom Kippur the way to expiate sins is through fasting and repenting before the King who dwells on high, on Sukkot one turns away from transgression by means of laughter and rejoicing. Along these lines Zaydeh taught us that there are two different ways to turn, to do *teshuvah* ["repentance"]. One way is through fear, remembering that God transcends the world and is enthroned on High. That is the way of the solemn Day of Atonement.

The other way to turn is through love, remembering that God dwells in the midst of the sukkah. One way is the way of self-judgment, the other the way of self-forgiveness. Both are needed, and that is why there are so many feasts and fasts in our tradition. So Zaydeh taught.

That Tzaddik's Etrog[127]

by S. Y. Agnon

You heard the story from whomever you may have heard it, whereas I heard it from a Hasid son of a Hasid who heard it from his teacher Reb Shlomo the Tzaddik of Zhivel, the direct seventh-generation descendent of Reb Mikheleh the Holy Preacher of Zloczow. And there is no question that the way I heard it from that Hasid who heard from his Rebbe, is exactly the way it happened, since that righteous Reb Shlomo of Zhivel had it from his fathers and in the very language of his fathers he told it, not adding a word except for the clarification. So whatever he added was of the very stuff of the original.

Reb Mikheleh the Holy Preacher of Zloczow started out a pauper in a house devoid of material goods. Often he had nothing except the slice he had stashed away in the hat on his head for a beggar, so that in case a beggar should happen along he would not leave humiliated, for so devoted was that righteous man to his

Maker that he neglected his own needs, paying attention only to the needs of the Shekhinah ["God's presence"]—that is Torah prayer and good deeds.

Doesn't Solomon tell us in his Proverbs that the righteous man understands the soul of his beast? Well, so too the wife of that righteous man understood the soul of her righteous husband. She did all she could to keep aggravation away from him and to protect him against all distractions from his holy work, unlike most women who, when the cupboard is bare, come muttering and nattering.

One year it was already hours before Sukkot and the rabbi's wife did not have a morsel in the house for celebrating the holiday. She thought, I will go tell my husband—he will hear and know my distress. She went to his solitude room, stood in the doorway, and said, "Sukkot eve is upon us and I still have no festival provisions."

That righteous man lifted himself from his chair, poked his head out from under his tallit, put his hand on his tefillin, and said to her, "You are worried about meat and fish, and I am worried about not yet having an etrog."

She kissed the mezuzah on the doorpost of his room and left dejectedly.

That righteous man stood up and went all over the house looking for something to sell and use the money to buy an etrog. He looked and looked but did not find a single thing worth an etrog.

He fondled his tefillin and mused, The nine festival days are approaching, and during the festival tefillin aren't worn, and my tefillin were written by a holy man of God, who writes each and every letter in holiness and purity, investing the most sublime and most awesome intents and purposes in the writing of each and every character. Tefillin of his make are much sought after and command a high price. I will sell them, and with the proceeds I will get an etrog.

Reb Mikheleh removed his tefillin and took them and went to his Beit Midrash and asked, "Who would like to buy my tefillin?" A certain man stood up and said, "I will buy them." He took out a gold dinar and gave it to the righteous man, and the righteous man handed him his tefillin.

The righteous man took the dinar and ran to the etrog seller to get an etrog. He saw a beautiful etrog and judged it to be kosher and perfectly formed. Now a truly pious man, when he buys an object for performing a divine precept, doesn't bargain. All the more so when it comes to an etrog, about which it is written, "And on the first day [of Sukkot] you shall take a fruit of the beautiful tree ... and rejoice before the LORD your God" (Lev. 23:40).

Reb Mikheleh returned home happy that he had come by a beautiful etrog possessing all the qualities that are lauded in an etrog. He went in to his sukkah to fix something and returned to his solitude.

He sat down in his chair and placed the etrog before him and ruminated on its precept that God had given the Jewish people to observe during these holy days of Sukkot, a holiday adorned with a multitude of precepts to observe.

His wife the rebbetzin heard that her husband had been to market. She went in his room.

She saw the glow in his face and the ecstasy emanating from his entire being. The rebbetzin thought that he had brought home all the festive victuals. She said to him, "I see that you are happy. You must have brought us the festival provisions. Give them to me and I will prepare them, for it is nearly time."

The righteous man rose from his chair and put his hand on his eyes and said, "Praised be the blessed and sublime Name for bestowing His grace on me and fulfilling my every need."

The rebbetzin stood there waiting for her husband to deliver. He sat back down in his chair and told her that he had been privileged to acquire a kosher etrog.

She asked him, "How did you have money to get an etrog?" He said to her, "I sold my tefillin for a gold dinar and bought an etrog." She said to him, "In that case, give me the change." He said to her, "They didn't give me any change. All the money they gave me for my tefillin, I gave for my etrog." He started to enumerate with steadily mounting enthusiasm all the virtues of the etrog.

The rebbetzin swallowed her tears and said, "I want to see this great find of yours." The righteous man took out the etrog and unwrapped it. It radiated its beauty and emitted its fragrance, a feast for the eyes and truly fit for the benediction.

The woman said, "Give it to me so I can have a good look at it." She reached out and picked up the etrog.

She thought of the pitiful state of her house and the distress of her children who had nothing to eat, and how the festival of Sukkot was nearly here and she had nothing with which to make it festive. Grief drove the strength from her hands, and the etrog slipped and fell. And having fallen, its stem broke. And the stem having broken, the etrog was no longer fit for ritual use.

The righteous man saw that his etrog was no longer fit for the benediction. He stretched out his two holy hands in despair and said, "Tefillin I have not and etrog I have not; all I have left is anger. But I will not be angry, but I will not be angry."

Now that Hasid who told me this story said to me: I asked my rebbe, "Is that really how it happened?" And my rebbe told me, "That is how it happened, exactly as I told it to you." And my rebbe said to me, "This story—the daughter-in-law of the Holy Preacher, wife of Yosef of Yampol, told it to the father of her son-in-law, Rabbi Baruch of Mezbizh. On the very day that his incident occurred she had been in the Holy Preacher's home and had seen it with her own eyes. And when she told it to Rabbi Baruch the Tzaddik of Mezbizh, Rabbi Baruch, father of her son-in-law, said to her, 'Mother of my daughter-in-law, tell me the story again from the beginning to the end. This is a story worth hearing twice.'"

New Rituals for Simchat Torah[128]

by Jill Hammer

I have on rare occasions stayed in bed during Yom Kippur because of the flu, but I have never in my adult life missed the festival of Simchat Torah. I have danced with the Torah in student chapels, in formal synagogues, in seminaries, on streets in New York and Boston and Jerusalem. To join a dance circle, I have leaned out over balconies, run down stairs, crept through crowds, and scrambled around parked cars. Simchat Torah is the holiday I look forward to all year—not only because of its celebration of joy, motion, and music, but because its celebration of God is a change-maker.

Simchat Torah celebrates the moment when Jews complete the reading of the Torah and begin it again. As a Jew seeking to make Judaism more inclusive of previously silenced voices, for me Simchat Torah celebrates the possibility of rereading the Torah in a new way. Simchat Torah allows us to literally start over, moving in a circle from the farewell of Moses the lawgiver to the beginning of a new creation. Though the words of the Torah are always the same, Simchat Torah reminds us that as we change, our interpretations too may change. Our new commentaries become part of our people's long-standing conversation with God. Each new person added to the circle makes the Torah grow.

"Turn it and turn it," says *Pirkei Avot,* "for everything is in it." Many of us struggle to maintain the faith that if we keep looking in the Torah, we will find truths that speak to us in spite of the pain the text may sometimes cause us. Simchat Torah is a time to strengthen ourselves in that endeavor and remind ourselves of our continuing commitment. In my own understanding, Simchat Torah is a time when God makes the Torah new for all the old and new souls who will meet Torah that year.

Here is a prayer to be recited by an individual or community at the time that the Torah is lifted, or before one's own personal *aliyah:*

> *Makor ha-chayim, b'khol shanah v'shanah attah noteh banu etz chayim chadash. Y'hi ratzon milfanekha she-ha-shanah midrasheinu yifr'chu chesed v'lo achzarut, chokhmah v'lo k'silut, t'vunah v'lo kalut rosh. Lamdeinu Torat chesed she-ta'achilenu ba-yamim ha-ba'im u-v'khol sha'ah. Amen.*
>
> Source of Life, every year you plant within us a new tree of life. May it be your will that this year our interpretations will blossom forth kindness and not cruelty, wisdom and not foolishness, awareness and not thoughtlessness. May you teach us a Torah of love that will nourish us in the coming days at every hour. Amen.

Or try this: During the *hakafot,* ask to dance with a Torah. Let your dance be a reflection of the new wisdom you want to receive in the coming year.

Simchat Torah is also a symbolic move from death to life—the death of Moses and of the old year, the birth of the new year and the newly created plants, animals, and humans. It is the rebirth of the Torah. That makes Simchat Torah a good time to celebrate all renewals and transformations. If you have experienced a major change during the year, such as the loss of a loved one or a relationship, a wedding, conversion, coming out, or birth of a child, you can recite the following prayer as the Torah scroll used for Deuteronomy is exchanged for the Torah scroll used for Genesis (or as the Torah scroll is rolled from one place to another).

K'shem she-ha-Torah niglelet mi-makom l'makom b'simcha u-v'shalom, ken eglol mi-makom l'makom b'rachamim u-v'ratzon.

Just as the Torah is rolled from place to place amid joy and peace, so too may I roll from place to place surrounded by compassion and good will.

PART 6

Guidance along the Way

Revelation is but a beginning, our deeds must continue, our lives must complete it. . . . The will of God is eternal, transcending all moments, all events, including acts of revelation. The significance of time depends upon what is done in time in relation to His will. The moment at Sinai depends for its fulfillment upon the present moment, upon all moments.

—Abraham Joshua Heschel

Is It Law or Custom?

JUDAISM IS LIKE A GRAND MURAL composed of a multitude of colors and patterns. Within it are the most awe-inspiring, humbling, and beautiful parts of personal and communal life. Certainly, its design includes elements representing God, Torah, Israel, morality, *halakhah* (Jewish law), and *minhag* (Jewish custom), all woven together in harmony. Part of the beauty and complexity of Judaism, however, lies in how difficult it is to distinguish when one element ends and another begins. How can one separate Torah from God, its most important protagonist? Despite the fact that many try, how can one completely separate *halakhah* from morality, given the fact that the behavioral prescriptions of *halakhah* are undifferentiated from our moral prescriptions? And how can one totally separate *halakhah* from *minhag*?

In fact, these two have always intersected. Together, they have played an enormous role in the lives of Jews—throughout history to the present time. They provide the framework for the observance and practices of life-cycle events, such as birth, marriage, and death, as well as our holiday celebrations. In addition, *halakhah* and *minhag* combined together help people express their moral values and spiritual identities as Jews. The importance of this combination is evident in the myriad volumes on Jewish practice; not one deals with Jewish law devoid of Jewish custom.

The practices of *halakhah* (the word is often translated as "the way," stemming from the root meaning "to go") and *minhag* are actually often derived from the same origin. When the Rabbinic sages of the Talmud were unsure of a practice or law, they would commonly say *puk chazi mai amma devar,* "go out and see why this is the way it is," referring to the established customs of the people.[1] Today, observing the development of Judaism over the centuries, we can see that law guides the customs, but customs also guide the law. One can even argue that it is the customs of the people that truly dictate Jewish law; that is, if the legal basis for a practice was never defined or has been lost, the rabbis and scholars look to customs as a way to define and preserve the practice. Thus, in the end, no Jew abides by either *halakhah* or *minhagim* alone, for they overlap in too many ways.[2]

Exploring Traditional Sources

Many primary sources, halakhists, and thinkers have directly and indirectly informed Jewish practice—both *halakhah* and *minhag*. Some of the sources described here comprise stories and lore, while others are codes of law. Any of these codes may claim to be the total authority in a particular area, despite differing from and even contradicting other works. Most of the discrepancies are likely due to influences on Jewish practice that were drawn from the culture of time and place. Accordingly, for people living then and there, these practices were probably the authoritative norms. This point, however, highlights a problem that can develop with codes of law in Judaism. The arguably rigid nature of such works seems antithetical to the nature of custom, which arises and functions in an organic manner, signifying the evolving relationships that people have with their communities. Nonetheless, such musings should not diminish our perception of the highly valuable scholarship of any of these authors, nor the significance of these books for Jews worldwide. They help us maintain communal standards of practice and commitment that are informed and enriched by the brilliance of our ancestors.

Abarbanel, Don Yitzchak

(b. 1437–d. 1508, Portugal, Spain, and Italy) One of the great Bible commentators and philosophers. A very influential political leader, Abarbanel served as treasurer for Alfonso V of Portugal and later as minister of finance for Ferdinand and Isabella of Spain. Despite his strong influence upon the monarchy, he could not prevent the onset of the Spanish Inquisition and the expulsion of Jews in 1492. He fled to Italy, where he continued to write commentaries on *Avot*, the Passover *haggadah*, and Maimonides' *Guide of the Perplexed.* His work helped strengthen the spirits of the exiled Jews.

Aboab, Isaac

(lived circa 1300, Spain) The talmudic scholar and author of *Menorat Ha-Me'or.* His popular book of Jewish morality was translated into colloquial languages such as Yiddish and Ladino. Aboab was part of a family of scholars whose work spanned several centuries and nations.

Apocrypha

(literally, "Hidden Writings" in Greek) A collection of books that is part of Jerome's Vulgate translation of the Christian Bible, but not part of the Hebrew Bible (TANAKH). All 15 books are now canonized except for Prayer of Manasseh and I and

2 Esdras, which are a part of the Christian Bible appendix. The Apocrypha was a part of the Greek Bible used by Jews in Egypt, and scholars today question why these books did not become part of the TANAKH. Most scholars say that they were written too late and that 2 Maccabees and Wisdom of Solomon were composed in Greek. Among the titles included in the Apocrypha are I Maccabees, Ben Sira, Tobit, Judith, Baruch, Susanna, and Bel and the Dragon.

Arukh Ha-Shulchan

(literally, "Laying the table") A comprehensive code of Jewish law compiled by Rabbi Yechiel Michel Ha-Levi Epstein (b. 1835–d. 1905, Russia). This code attempts to update the Shulchan Arukh (literally, "Set Table") by Joseph Karo and claims to be the final authority on many customs.

Bible *See* TANAKH.

Chaye Adam

A commentary written by Rabbi Avraham Danzig (b. 1748–d. 1820, Poland) on *Orach Chayyim* (matters of daily Jewish life) of the Shulchan Arukh. Danzig is also famous for his commentary on the laws of kashrut from *Yoreh De'ah* of the Shulchan Arukh, called *Chokhmat Adam.*

Chaye Avraham

A book of miscellaneous rituals and customs of *Orach Chayyim* in the Shuchan Arukh, focusing on prayer, Shabbat, and holidays. Written by Rabbi Avraham ben Raphael Halfon (b. unknown–d. 1803, Tripoli).

Cohen, Hermann

(b. 1842–d. 1918, Germany) One of the great Jewish philosophers. Cohen's ideas blended Immanuel Kant's conception of ethics with that of Jewish faith. His thoughts and writings have influenced many other important Jewish philosophers to this day. His posthumously published exposition of classical Judaism can be found in English under the title *Religion of Reason Out of the Sources of Judaism,* translated by Simon Kaplan.

Enoch

A book in the Pseudepigrapha. The title character is Enoch, or "Chanokh," from Genesis 5:18–24. Canonized in the Coptic (Egyptian-Ethiopian) Christian Bible, the book is a composite work from the 1st through 3rd centuries. The work in its entirety existed only in Ethiopic; but parts have been found in Greek, Latin, and—in the Dead Sea Scrolls—in Aramaic. The book contributes an explanation of the odd account of the "divine beings" in Genesis 6:1–8 and of the term "Azazel." The bulk of the work, however, describes Enoch's ascent to heaven, where he is permitted to view the throne of God and the highest realms of the angels, and where he is given a vision of the final apocalypse.

Gemara

Usually referred to as the Talmud, even though this description is technically erroneous. Written in Aramaic, the Gemara (literally, "Learning") is the discussion of and commentary on the laws of the Mishnah by the Rabbinic sages of the 2nd through 5th centuries, who are known as *amoraim.* In their explanation and elucidation of the Mishnah, the *amoraim* draw from other sources including the Midrash, the Tosefta, and postbiblical works (e.g., Ben Sira, aka Ecclesiasticus). Two 5th-century Babylonian sages, Ravina and Rav Ashi, have traditionally been given credit for finalizing the Gemara; modern scholars believe that it did not reach its present form until the end of the 7th century.

Guide of the Perplexed *See* Maimonides.

Hirsch, Samson Raphael

(b. 1808–d. 1888, Germany) The founder of contemporary Orthodox Judaism and one of the preeminent rabbis, preachers, and philosophers in Jewish history. His writings often reflect his strong opposition to the current of Reform Judaism and modernization that swept through Western Europe during his time, especially in Germany.

Ibn Ezra, Avraham

(b. 1089–d. 1164, Spain) A poet, grammarian, and astronomer, known best for his commentary on most of the TANAKH. His commentary is unique in its grammatical analysis and independent ideas. After his son converted to Islam in 1140, Ibn Ezra went into self-chosen exile, traveling through North Africa and Europe.

Isserles, Moses See Shulchan Arukh.

Jerusalem Talmud See Talmud.

Jubilees

A book in the postbiblical Jewish literature known as the Pseudepigrapha. It retells and expands upon much of Genesis and Exodus and falsely claims to be the hidden revelation of Moses. (However, the ancient community at Qumran, where the Dead Sea Scrolls were found, considered it to be authoritative.) The book is called "Jubilees" because of its concern with cycles of time.

Karo, Joseph See Shulchan Arukh.

Kethuvim

(literally, "Writings") The third of the three sections of the TANAKH. It was the last to be canonized and consists of Psalms, Proverbs, Job, the Song of Songs, Ruth, Lamentations, Ecclesiastes, Esther, Daniel, Ezra, Nehemiah, 1 Chronicles and 2 Chronicles. It is also known by its Greek rendering, "Hagiographa."

Kitzur Shulchan Arukh

An abridgement *(kitzur)* of Joseph Karo's Shulchan Arukh by Solomon Ganzfried (b. 1804–d. 1886, Hungary). Ganzfried was a firm traditionalist who fought to preserve traditional observance amidst the rapid changes of modernity. In this abridgement, Ganzfried tended to select the most stringent views and eliminate minority or alternative opinions on Jewish law.

Klein, Isaac

(b. 1905–d.1979, Hungary and United States) Author of *A Guide to Jewish Religious Practice* (1979, reprinted 1992; Jewish Theological Seminary). This is one of the most popular and expansive books of customs and observances written in English. Rabbi Klein's work is considered authoritative by the Modern Orthodox, Conservative, and Reform streams of Judaism.

Levush

A collection of laws and customs, including elements of *Tur* and Shulchan Arukh, by Rabbi Mordecai ben Avraham Jaffe or Baal Ha-Levush (b. circa 1535–d. 1612; Prague). This work can be found in the back of many traditional volumes of the *Tur.*

Luria, Isaac Ashkenazi

(b. 1534–d. 1572, Safed, Israel) Renowned teacher of Kabbalah and *halakhah.* Born in

Jerusalem, he grew up in Egypt and later settled in Tzfat, northern Israel. His teachings inspired a school of thought; and although Luria himself really did not write much, his followers produced volumes of material representing his teachings. Lurianic Kabbalah basically teaches that the purpose of Creation is to have the community and each individual heal the world (*tikun olam,* literally, "fixing the world"), thus gradually reuniting and perfecting the divine realms (see *Sefirot*), as well as humanity.

Luzzatto, Moses Chaim

(b. 1707–d. 1747, Italy, Holland, and Israel) A leading mystic and kabbalist who headed a secret messianic order. Known by the acronym, Ramchal, Luzzatto authored several kabbalistic writings including popular volumes such as *Mesillat Yesharim, Migdal Oz,* and *Derech Hashem.* He was a leading supporter of Shabbetai Tzvi (the most famous false Messiah) and was, therefore, exiled by the Italian rabbinical court. Luzzatto and his family all died of the plague in Acre.

Magen Avraham

A popular commentary to the *Orach Chayyim* section of the Shulchan Arukh, which seeks to harmonize differences between Moses Isserles and Joseph Karo, as well as uphold the authority of the Shulchan Arukh over the *Tur.* It was written by Rabbi Avraham Abele Gombiner (b. circa 1637–d. circa 1683, Poland).

Maggid of Mezritch

The commonly used name for Rabbi Dov Baer of Mezritch (b. circa 1704–d. 1772, Poland and Ukraine), who posthumously became one of the most powerful of the Hasidic leaders. He was a very influential teacher and his disciples included Elimelech of Lizensk, Shneur Zalman of Liady (founder of Chabad), and Levi Yitzchak of Berditchev, who published the Maggid's teachings. The term "maggid" refers to a popular preacher, especially in Hasidic circles.

Maharil

(b. circa 1360–d. 1427, Austria) Rabbi Jacob Ha-Levi of Moelin, sometimes referred to as the "Father of Ashkenazic Customs." He wrote his compendium on the yearly customs of Ashkenazic Jewry, called *Minhagei Maharil.* He is widely quoted by many Ashkenazic codifiers, including Moses Issereles. Maharil is an acronym for "Our teacher, the Rabbi, Israel, Levi." (The patriarch Jacob was known by the name Israel).

Maimonides

(b. 1135–d. 1204, Spain and Egypt) Rabbi Moses ben Maimon, a physician and possibly the greatest Jewish thinker of all time. He wrote many important works, including legal codes and philosophic expositions. Among them are the *Mishneh Torah,* the first written Jewish legal code, which is written in remarkably clear Hebrew, and the *Guide of the Perplexed (Moreh Nevuchim),* a work showing a tremendous Aristotelian influence, which interprets the Torah with the objective of eliminating apparent contradictions with philosophy. Maimonides is also known by the acronymn Rambam.

Me'am Lo'ez

An encyclopedic commentary on the Bible, written in Ladino (Judeo-Spanish) by Rabbi Yaakov Culi (b. 1685–d. 1732, Turkey). With *Me'am Lo'ez,* Culi intended to make much of the Jewish tradition available to Sephardic Jewry in the colloquial language. He drew from many sources including the Talmud, Midrash, and Zohar. Culi died before the work was finished, but left groundwork and notes for his successors, Yitzchak Magriso and Yitzchak Perachyah, who completed it.

Mei Ha-Shiloach

A commentary and kabbalistic exposition on the Bible; also the commonly used name of its author, Rabbi Mordechai Yosef Leiner of Isbitza (b. 1800–d. 1854, Poland). Rabbi Leiner was part of a Hasidic dynasty; his son and grandson succeeded him as its leaders. Study of *Mei Ha-Shiloach* recently gained popularity through Rabbi Shlomo Carlebach and through Carlebach's student, Betsalel Philip Edwards, who made an English translation called *Living Waters.*

Midrash

(literally, "Elucidation" or "Exposition") A body of work that combines the theological, homiletical, and ethical lore of the Rabbis in the Land of Israel from the 3rd through 10th centuries C.E. The word "midrash" is derived from the verb root *darash,* which denotes searching out and discovering other meanings and information from Scripture.

Midrash Rabbah

An important series of books that expounds upon and further illustrates each book of the Torah as well as the *megillot* (five historical tales that are part of the biblical book called The Writings): the Song of Songs, Ruth, Esther, Ecclesiastes, and

Lamentations. Each volume is identified by the name of the corresponding book from the Bible, followed by the word *Rabbah* ("great"), for example, *Exodus Rabbah* and *Song of Songs Rabbah.* As a series, these works were edited and redacted between the 5th and 10th centuries C.E. Final touches to *Numbers Rabbah* and *Esther Rabbah* were made as late as the 13th century. *Genesis Rabbah,* the oldest (425 C.E.) of the series, includes material from the Apocrypha, Philo, and Josephus.

Mishnah

(literally, "Teaching") The first compilation of the Oral Law and the foundational text for the Talmud and for the Rabbinic tradition. Most scholars attribute it to Rabbi Yehudah Ha-Nasi (Rabbi Judah the Patriarch, who lived in Judea under control of the Roman Empire) and date its final editing to circa 200 C.E. There are six "orders," or volumes, of the Mishnah, categorized by different areas of Jewish law: *Zera'im* (laws governing agriculture and farm products); *Mo'ed* (laws relating to seasons and holidays); *Nashim* (laws relating to women and family life, marriage and divorce); *Nezikin* (summaries of Jewish civil and criminal law); *Kodashim* (laws relating to holiness in matters of sacrifices and ritual slaughter); and *Toharot* (laws about purity). The word "Mishnah" is derived from the verb root "repetition," indicating the primary method for learning and oral study at that time.

Mishnah Berurah

One of the most authoritative commentaries on the part of the Shulchan Arukh that is devoted to everyday Jewish life, *Orach Chayyim.* It was written by Rabbi Yisrael Meir Ha-Kohen (b. 1838–d. 1933, Poland), who is known by the name of his first book, *Chofetz Chaim* (which primarily deals with the laws of *lashon ha-ra* or guarding one's speech).

Mishneh Torah See Maimonides.

Moses ben Jacob of Coucy

(lived circa first half of 13th century, France and Spain) One of the tosafists, medieval rabbis who created critical and explanatory glosses on the Talmud. He is most well known for his *Sefer Mitzvot Gadol,* often abbreviated as *SeMaG* (as opposed to *Sefer Mitzvot Katan,* or *SeMaK,* by Isaac of Corbeil). *SeMaG* is a delineation and explanation of Judaism's 613 commandments (mitzvot)—365 prohibitions and 248 positive prescriptions. Unlike Maimonides' delineation of the 613 mitzvot,

Moses ben Jacob's includes sources. He is also known for a concise commentary on the tractate of the Talmud about Yom Kippur, called *Tosafot Yeshanim.*

Nachmanides/Ramban

(b. 1194–d. 1270, Spain and Israel) Rabbi Moses ben Nachman, a physician and one of the most important scholars in Jewish history. He is most well known for his commentary on the Torah, but he was also an important halakhist, kabbalist, and poet. Between 1263 and 1265, he represented Spanish Jewry in an official debate between Christians and Jews about religious truths. Victorious in his aggressive refutations of Christianity, he recorded the points of the debate in *Sefer Ha-Vikkuach,* a publication that led to a papal warrant for his arrest; he escaped to Israel.

Nevi'im

(literally, "Prophets") The second of the three parts of the TANAKH. It is often further divided into its first set of books, Nevi'im Rishonim (Former Prophets), which are primarily historical in nature, and its second set, Nevi'im Acharonim (Latter Prophets), which are the speeches of the prophets whose names they bear. One or two chapters from Nevi'im are read each Sabbath and on most holidays. Called *haftarot* (pl. of haftarah), they each have particular relevance to the Torah reading for that day.

Or Ha-Chaim

(b. 1696–d. 1743, Morocco and Israel) Rabbi Chaim ben Attar, who was known by the name of his best known work, *Or Ha-Chaim* (literally, "The Light of Life"), a very popular commentary on the Torah. He became quite renowned in the Hasidic world and is often referred to as "The Holy" because many believed he could perform miracles.

Pesikta de-Rav Kahana and *Pesikta Rabbati*

Two versions of Palestinian midrashim written about parts of the TANAKH: the Five Books of Moses and the Prophets. (*Pesikta* means "section" in Aramaic.) *Pesikta de-Rav Kahana* was probably completed by the 5th century C.E., while the *Pesikta Rabbati*—a later version that draws upon the former—was completed after the 9th century and includes glosses from the 13th century. A critical edition of the work was translated into English by William G. Braude in 1968.[3]

Pirke de-Rebbe Eliezer

Narrative midrash, or exposition, on biblical stories, falsely attributed to the 2nd-century sage Eliezer ben Hyrcanus. Modern scholars claim that this work was probably written in the Land of Israel in the 8th century. The work has furthered Rabbinic thought and is the basis for many customs. (See Pseudepigrapha.)

Prophets, The See Nevi'im.

Pseudepigrapha

A postbiblical (circa 200 B.C.E.–200 C.E.) collection of works, literally named "False (from *pseudo*) Writings (from *graph*)." These books were falsely attributed to ancient heroes to gain in authenticity and authority and possibly to coerce biblical canonization. Nonetheless, these works are highly significant for Jews and Christians. Examples of the Pseudepigrapha include Jubilees, 1 Enoch, 2 Enoch, Life of Adam and Eve, and Joseph and Asenath.

Ran

(b. circa 1315–d. 1375, Spain) Hebrew acronym for Rabbi Nissim ben Reuven Gerondi, a great talmudist, *rosh yeshivah* (head of a Jewish school of higher learning), and court physician. He is best known for his discourse on Judaism called *Derashot* (loosely, "Interpretations") and for his commentary on the Rif's *Sefer Ha-Halakhot.* (The Book of Laws).

Rashi

(b. 1040–d. 1105, France) Hebrew acronym for Rabbi Shlomo ben Yitzchak, generally regarded as the greatest commentator on both the Torah and the Talmud. Without his explanations, both would be much more difficult to understand. His commentary on the Torah was the first book to be printed in Hebrew; the semicursive typeface, which the printer created to distinguish the explanations from the biblical text, is called "Rashi script" and is still used today.

Rif

Hebrew acronymn for Rabbi Yitzchak Alfasi (b. 1013–d. 1103, Morocco), one of the most influential authorities on Jewish law. His work *Sefer Ha-Halakhot* (The Book of Laws) is generally included in the back of traditional volumes of the Talmud and served as a primary source for other notable codifiers of *halakhah,* such as Maimonides, Jacob ben Asher, and Joseph Karo.

Rosh

Hebrew acronymn for Rabbi Asher ben Yechiel (b. circa 1250–d. 1327, Germany and Spain), the leading student of Rabbi Meir of Rothenburg and the father of Jacob ben Asher (author of the *Tur*). He is recognized as one of the top halakhic authorities, and his work *Piskei Ha-Rosh* was one of the primary sources for the *Tur* and for the Shulchan Arukh. His explanations on the Talmud were collected and appear in the back of most traditional volumes of the Talmud.

Sa'adia Ga'on

Sa'adia ben Yosef Al-Fayumi (b. 882–d. 942, Egypt, Israel, and Babylonia), head ("Ga'on") of the Academy of Sura in Babylonia and one of the greatest contributors to the Jewish tradition in *halakhah,* liturgy, and philosophic discourse. His *siddur* (prayer book), is the first known attempt to transcribe the weekly ritual of Jewish prayers for weekdays, the Sabbath, and festivals. The text also contains liturgical poetry by Sa'adia, as well as Arabic-language commentary. His *Emunot ve-De'ot* (The Book of Beliefs and Opinions), was the first medieval classic on Jewish philosophy and is considered his greatest contribution. Influenced by Aristotle and Plato, Sa'adia argues that faith in Judaism and Jewish practice do not contradict reason.

Sefat Emet

A five-volume work (The Language of Truth) that contains some of the most creative and enriching commentaries on the Torah and holidays. Written by Rabbi Yehuda Aryeh Leib Alter of Ger (b. 1847–d. 1904, Poland), it is still widely studied. In 1998, parts of it were published in English, translated by Arthur Green.[4]

Sefer Abudraham

A comprehensive commentary on synagogue ritual and prayers, composed by Rabbi David ben Joseph Abudraham (b. and d. 1300s, Spain). Abudraham culled from many sources to explain the differences between local customs and the calendar.

Sefer Ha-Hinnukh

(literally, "The Book of Education") An anonymous work from the 13th century, intended to be a simple guide to Jewish belief and practice. A 16th century author attributed it to the talmudist Aaron ben Joseph Ha-Levi (b. 1235–d. 1300, Spain), and this attribution has been generally been accepted. *Sefer Ha-Hinnukh* is an enumeration of the 613 mitzvot, arranged according to the order of the Torah portions *(parshiyot)*, which includes their halakhic and ethical aspects.

Sefer Ha-Manhig

(literally, "The Guide Book") One of the earliest books on Jewish customs. Written by Rabbi Abraham ben Nathan of Lunel (b. 1155–d. 1215, France), this particular work describes the customs of various Jewish communities as well as the rationale for their practice.

Sefer Ha-Minhagim

A highly popular work in its time, it was created by Rabbi Isaac of Tyrnau (b. end of 14th century–d. 15th century, Hungary). The book *(sefer)* describes the customs *(minhagim)* of different Ashkenazic communities. Moses Isserles, the Ashkenazic authority on *halakhah,* often refers to Tyrnau's work in his additions and comments in the Shulchan Arukh.

Sefer Ha-Toda'ah

A popular 1962 work by Rabbi Abraham Eliyahu Ki Tov (b. 1912–d. 1976, U.S.A.) that concentrates on the holidays and seasons and includes halakhic and folkloric material. Published in English as *The Book of Our Heritage: The Jewish Year and Its Days of Significance.*[5]

Sefer Mordechai

A work that discusses halakhic teachings and many customs of Ashkenazic Jewry, written by Rabbi Mordechai ben Hillel (b. circa 1250–d. 1298, Germany). It records many doctrines of the author's principal teacher, Rabbi Meir ben Baruch of Rothenburg, as well as those of the Rif. Many subsequent codes quote this work, and it appears in the back of the traditional Talmud.

Sforno, Ovadiah ben Yaakov

(b. 1475–d. 1550, Italy) One of the great Bible commentators and medieval Jewish philosophers, a physician by trade. Sforno's commentary is usually on the plain meaning *(peshat)* of the biblical text and grammar. He also authored a commentary on

Pirkei Avot (literally, "Chapters of the Sages"; commonly known as Ethics of the Fathers) and a philosophic treatise called *Or Ammim* (literally, "Light of Nations").

Shulchan Arukh

(literally, "Set Table") The standard code of Jewish law, first published in 1565. It was compiled by Rabbi Joseph Karo (b. 1488–d. 1575, Spain, Turkey, and Israel). Karo, clearly one of the greatest legal authorities and mystics in Jewish history, followed the style of Jacob ben Asher's *Tur.* He devised the Shulchan Arukh as a key for and synopsis of his own magnificent commentary and elucidation of the *Tur,* known as *Beit Yosef.* The Shulchan Arukh includes the gloss of Rabbi Moses Isserles, also known as Rema or Rama, (b. circa 1525–d. 1572, Poland), which is titled the *Mapa* (literally, "Tablecloth"). The Shulchan Arukh emphasizes Sephardic customs and practices, while the *Mapa* treats those of the Ashkenazim.

Sifra

(literally, "Book" in Aramaic) Also known as *Torat Kohanim.* A midrash that focuses on the halakhic aspects of the Book of Leviticus. The material comes primarily from the *tannaim* (the Rabbis quoted in the Mishnah). Most scholars believe the final redactor of the work to be a student of Yehudah Ha-Nasi, either Abba Aricha (known as "Rav")[6] or Rabbi Chiya.

Ta'amei Ha-Minhagim

Written in 1896 by Rabbi Abraham Isaac Sperling (b. 1850–d. 1920, Ukraine). In 1968, Rabbi Abraham Matts translated the work into English as *Reasons for Jewish Customs and Traditions.*[7] This compendium contains nearly 600 questions and answers that discuss many aspects of Jewish life, including prayer, life-cycle events, and holidays.

Talmud

The central and most important body of Rabbinic literature. Combining the Mishnah and Gemara, the Talmud contains material from the Rabbinic academies that dates from sometime before the 2nd century C.E. through the 6th century. It includes halakhic and midrashic expositions, wisdom, personal stories, and arguments. There are two versions: the Jerusalem *(Yerushalmi)*, or Palestinian, Talmud and the Babylonian *(Bavli)* Talmud. When people speak of the Talmud generically, they are referring to the *Bavli,* as it is more extensive and widely used. There are 63 areas of study that make up the Talmud, called tractates *(masechtot)*. The Talmud serves as the primary source for all later codes of Jewish law.

TANAKH

An acronym for the three books that make up the cornerstone of Jewish belief comprising Torah (the Five Books of Moses); Nevi'im (The Prophets); and Kethuvim (The Writings). When Jews speak of the Bible, they are referring to the TANAKH.

Tanchuma or *Tanchuma Yelamednu*

A collection of midrashic literature, including large sections from *Midrash Rabbah* and *Pesikta Rabbati,* based on the triennial cycle of Torah readings. Much of it is attributed to the 4th-century Palestinian sage Tanchuma ben Abba, hence the name *Tanchuma.* It is distinguished by the repetition of an opening phrase, *yelamednu rabbenu,* "Let our master teach us." Scholars are unsure of the date for the final version of *Tanchuma;* the first printed edition appeared in approximately 1521. This work is sometimes confused with a different collection of midrashic material called *Tanchuma Buber* published in 1875 by scholar Solomon Buber (b. 1827–d. 1906, Ukraine).

Tanna de-be Eliyahu

An aggadic midrash narrated in the name of the prophet Eliyahu (Elijah). It comprises teachings on the rationale for mitzvot and morality. Scholars put its start date in the 3rd century C.E., with final redaction in the 10th century. The identity of the author is unknown, although his location has been attributed to Jerusalem, Babylon, or Italy. The work has two sections: *Seder Eliyahu Rabbah* and *Seder Eliyahu Zuta.*

Tosafot

(literally, "Additions") Additions to and continuations of Rashi's talmudic commentary and the talmudic process in general. They were written between the 12th and 14th centuries in France and Germany by many scholars, including Rashi's grandchildren, for example, Rashbam. An indispensable part of Talmud study, the Tosafot are printed in the margins of each page of Talmud, opposite Rashi's commentary.

Tosefta

(literally, "Supplement") A collection of additional teachings and statements by the Rabbinic sages organized in the same arrangement as the Mishnah. Scholars debate whether the Tosefta comprises solely *tannaitic* material (circa 2nd century C.E.) or if it includes material of a later date. Either way, Tosefta is considered authoritative, and much of it is quoted in the Gemara. The Tosefta can usually be found in the back of traditional volumes of the Talmud.

Tur

A book also known as *Arba'ah Turim* (literally, "Four Columns"). It was created by Rabbi Jacob ben Asher (b. circa 1270–d. circa 1340, Germany and Spain), who was known also as the Baal Ha-Turim ("Master of the Columns"). This ambitious work attempts to bridge the gulf between Ashkenazic and Sephardic laws and opinions in force at the time. The legal decisions of great Rabbis are divided into four main topics, called columns, or *turim.* The Baal Ha-Turim emphasizes the work and thought of Maimonides and even more so of the Rosh (an acronym for the name of his own father, Rabbenu Asher). Joseph Karo's Shulchan Arukh, the fundamental code of Jewish law, follows the basic structure of the *Tur.*

Turei Zahav

(literally, "Columns of Gold") Also known by the acronymn *Taz.* One of the standard commentaries on the Shulchan Arukh. It was written by Rabbi David ben Shmuel Ha-Levi (b. 1586–d. 1667, Poland), known also as the Taz, after the name of his most prominent work. Conversely, the work is also referred to as *Magen David,* after the author's first name. Ha-Levi was the student of and successor to Rabbi Joel Sirkes, author of *Bayit Chadash,* or *Bach,* one of the standard commentaries that accompany the *Tur.*

Writings, The

See Kethuvim.

Yalkut Shimoni

An anthology of midrashim on all portions of the TANAKH. Rabbi Shimon Ha-Darshan of Frankfurt compiled it in the 13th century as a handbook on religious beliefs for Jews throughout the Diaspora. With midrashim culled from 50 different sources, it is very useful for critical analysis.

Yehuda Ha-Levi

An important and influential Jewish poet and philosopher (b. 1075–d. 1141, Spain) who was a physician by profession. His poetry, tending toward the mystical, has been placed in the liturgy (including the *Yamim Noraim*); but his most famous work is the *Kuzari,* written in Arabic and given a structure similar to a Platonic dialogue. The *Kuzari* describes the conversion of the king of the Khazars (a seminomadic people from Central Asia). Ha-Levi uses the dialogue to argue three things: faith is not inconsistent with reason; revelation is superior to reason; and both of the preceding ideas are proven by looking at Jewish history.

Zohar

(literally, "Illumination") A book of mystical commentaries on the TANAKH that mixes together theology, psychology, myth, ancient Gnosticism, and superstition. The objective is to uncover the deepest mysteries of the world, namely why God created the universe, how God is manifest in the world, and what the forces of life are. Although some accept the claim that the Zohar was authored by Rabbinic sage Shimon bar Yochai (b. and d. 2nd century C.E., Israel) and his saintly contemporaries, most scholars believe it to have been largely written by Moshe de Leon (b. 1240–d. 1305, Spain).

Endnotes

Part 1: Heart, Mind, and Celebration

1 B. Talmud, *Shabbat* 127a.

2 Maimonides, Mishneh Torah, *Hilkhot Yesodei Ha-Torah,* 1:1.

3 B. Talmud, *Sukkah* 37b.

4 *Sefer Ha-Minhagim,* 32; Isaac Klein, *A Guide to Religious Jewish Practice* (New York: *Jewish Theological Seminary,* 1979), 179.

5 Shulchan Arukh, *Orach Chayyim* 583:2; *Darkei Moshe* 583:1. In fact, the word for nut in Hebrew, *egoz,* is only equal to 17 while "sin," *het* is 18, yet the custom stuck. It is also worth mentioning that 18 is the equivalent for life and generally accepted as a "lucky" number.

6 B. Talmud, *Sanhedrin* 21a. See I Kings 11, which recounts Solomon's trangressions and divine punishment. His heavy taxation, many political marriages (700 wives and 300 concubines), and idolatry led to the dissolution of the united monarchy after his death.

7 B. Talmud, *Rosh Hashanah* 25b.

Part 2: Origins of the Jewish Calendar

1 Georges Roux, *Ancient Iraq* (London: Penguin, 1964) 42–43, 66–67.

2 B. Talmud, *Rosh Hashanah* 22b.

3 Ibid.

4 Ibid., 19b; Maimonides, Mishneh Torah, *Hilkhot Kiddush Ha-Chodesh* 5:7. Two-day festivals and new months are still observed today in the Diaspora. According to the Rabbis, there was a harmony in the universe between the sun, moon, and earth when a new month occurred. They understood that the waning globe of the moon from the old month birthed *(molad)* the glimmer of the new moon's crescent. With the moon's rotation in concert with the earth, this birthing happened on either the 30th or 31st day after the prior new moon.

5 This is Hillel Ha-Nasi (the Patriarch), son of Rabbi Yehudah Ha-Nasi. Shlomo Yosef Zevin, *The Festivals in Halakhah,* vol. 1 (New York: Mesorah Publications, 1999), 81. Zevin cites Nachmanides' *(Ramban) Sefer Ha-Zechut* on chapter 4 of B. Talmud, *Gittin,* as the source of the date (359 C.E.). He also notes other rabbis, namely Isaac Ha-Levi (author of *Dorot Ha-Rishonim*), emphasize that Hillel II only innovated the permanence of the months and leap years, but the methods and structure of the calendar were previously established by the Sanhedrin.

6 Until the abolishment of the Rabbinic patriarchate, about 425 C.E.

7 Nathan Bushwick, *Understanding the Jewish Calendar* (New York: Moznaim Publishing Corporation, 1989).

8 Adar was chosen because it is the last month of the Babylonian year as well as the biblical year; Nisan was the first biblical month.

9 Rosh Hashanah is two days because it is the only holiday that begins a month; it is both the New Year (Rosh Hashanah) and the new month (Rosh Hodesh) of Tishrei. *See* note 8.

10 Rosh Hodesh is considered a partial holiday. It is observed for two days when the preceding month has 30 days—the last day of the old month and the first of the new. If the preceding month has only 29 days, Rosh Hodesh is only on the first day of the new month.

11 A Committee on Jewish Laws and Standards passed a responsum stating that *yom tov sheini* in the Diaspora is a *minhag* (literally, custom) and does not have to be observed (*Teshuvot* by Rabbis Philip Sigal and Abraham Ehrlich, as well as by Rabbi Aaron Blumenthal, 1969). *See also* Mark Washofsky, *Jewish Living: A Guide to Contemporary Reform Practice* (New York: Union of American Hebrew Congregations, 2001), 93–96.

12 It is also very important to note that medieval authorities debated whether Rosh Hashanah should be one or two days in Israel. Ultimately, Rosh Hashanah is celebrated for two days in Israel because of the claim that the Sanhedrin legislated the two days to be considered one sanctity, or *yoma arikhta,* meaning one long day. Strictly speaking, Yom Kippur should also be observed for two days, but the Rabbis disapproved owing to the harmful effect of fasting for two days.

13 Starting the year in the spring was a natural choice because of the seasonal rebirth of nature. So too one of the four Jewish new years is the first of Nisan, which falls around late March, congruent with the start of spring.

Part 3: Rosh Hashanah

1 Mishnah, *Rosh Hashanah* 1:1–2.

2 B. Talmud, *Rosh Hashanah* 8a.

3 Ibid., 18a.

4 Exod. 34:22.

5 Exod. 12:2.

6 Nachmanides' commentary on Exod. 12:2.

7 Rabbi Moses ben Nachman of Gerondi (b. 1194–d. about 1270) lived in Spain. He was commonly known as Nachmanides or Ramban. He was a kabbalist, physician, and biblical commentator.

8 Exod. 12:2.

9 Esther 3:7.

10 B. Talmud, *Rosh Hashanah* 10b-11a, and *Genesis Rabbah* 22:4.

11 First appearance of this expression is in J. Talmud, *Rosh Hashanah* 1:3. See also *Pesikta Rabbati,* 40. This time period is also known as the Ten Days of Pentitence. The word penitence implies a sad and humble state of regret for one's misdeeds. However, I am translating the Hebrew word *teshuvah* in the way many people do, as "repentance," which means the resolve of a person in such a state to change.

12 James H. Charlesworth, ed., translation from *The Old Testament Pseudepigrapha,* vol. 2 (New York: Doubleday, 1985), 81.

13 *See also* Num. 29:1–6 and Ps. 81:4–5.

14 Born Moshe ben Maimon, Maimonides is also known by the acronym Rambam.

15 Mishneh Torah, *Hilkhot Shofar v'Sukkah v'Lulav* 1:1.

16 *Etz Hayim: Torah and Commentary* (Philadelphia: The Jewish Publication Society, 2001), 112–13.

17 According to Jewish law, which is called *halakhah,* Jews are not permitted to carry objects on Shabbat and transfer them to different domains. This rule is one of the many that are related to refraining from work and enjoying the day. Therefore, to prevent people from carrying things and violating the laws of Shabbat, the Rabbis eliminated the sounding of the shofar on Saturday.

18 Satan is an important figure in Jewish folklore and custom and even in the Bible and Rabbinic thought. Satan's stance in Judaism is by no means uniform. Generally speaking, Satan is the adversary against humanity who works to influence God to distrust human beings and not offer them mercy.

19 *Sefer Ha-Minhagim* 32, 39. This source offers the same reason for why we do not announce the start of the new month (Tishrei) on the preceding Shabbat, unlike the pattern for the start of every other month.

20 *Pirke de-Rebbe Eliezer,* 46; *Tur, Orach Chayyim* 581.

21 *Sefer Ha-Toda'ah,* 2:434.

22 *Tanna de-be Eliyahu,* chap. 23; *Tur*/Shulchan Arukh, *Orach Chayyim* 581:1.

23 Shulchan Arukh, *Orach Chayyim* 581:1.

24 *Arukh Ha-Shulchan* 581:3.

25 *Baer Heitev* comment 5 on Shulchan Arukh, *Orach Chayyim* 581:1. *See also* Abraham Chill, *The Minhagim* (New York: Sepher-Hermon Press, 1979), 179. Chill cites *Minhage Yeshurun,* 185, a Yiddish work by Rabbi Avraham Ever Hirshowitz (b. circa 1914; Pittsburgh, Pa.).

26 One commentary says that this is to distinguish the voluntary blowing of the shofar

during Elul and the mandatory blowing of the shofar on Rosh Hashanah. See *Turei Zahav* 581:4.

27 *Magen Avraham* on Shulchan Arukh, *Orach Chayyim* 581:3.

28 Isaac Klein, *A Guide to Religious Jewish Practice* (New York: Jewish Theological Society, 1979), 180.

29 B. Talmud, *Rosh Hashanah* 16b.

30 B. Talmud, *Rosh Hashanah* 21b.

31 Shlomo Yosef Zevin, *The Festivals in Halakhah,* vol. I (New York: Mesorah Publications, 1999), 82–83.

32 *Tur, Orach Chayyim* 600; see there *Beit Yosef* 2–3; Kitzur Shulchan Arukh 129.

33 Shulchan Arukh, *Orach Chayyim* 583.

34 B. Talmud, *Kritut* 6a; Tur, *Orach Chayyim* 583.

35 *Tur, Orach Chayyim* 583.

36 Arukh Ha-Shulchan 583:3.

37 *Sefer Abudraham,* 143.

38 Abraham Chill, *The Minhagim* (NewYork: Sepher-Hermon Press: 1999). 185, citing *Massa Bavel,* 222.

39 The practice of identifying the numerical value of words and associating the words to other words of equal numerical value is longstanding in Judaism and carries weight in many customs originating in the medieval period. It should also be noted that *egoz (alef.gimel.vav.zayin)* is equal to 17, whereas *het (cheit.tet.alef)* is equal to 18. Those who follow this line of reasoning say that one is added to *egoz* for the word itself.

40 Gen. 22.

41 Chill, 186.

42 *Chaye Avraham,* 46b.

43 Klein, 201.

44 *Tanchuma, Va-Yeira* 22

45 Klein, 201; Chill, 196 citing *Minhage Yeshurun,* 192.

46 This translation is by H. Freedman and Maurice Simon (London: Soncino, 1939–51).

47 *See* interpretation in David Hartman, *A Living Covenant* (Vermont: Jewish Lights Publishing, 1997), 56–57.

48 My translation is guided by the Silverman machzor. See *High Holiday Prayer Book,* compiled and arranged by Rabbi Morris Silverman (Bridgeport, Conn.: Prayer Book Press, 1951), 148. The last line is variously translated in different *machzorim.* The variation is caused by the problem of translating the words *ro'a ha-gezeirah* (literally, "evil of the decree"). I maintain the literal connection in my translation, while including

"severity" in brackets, as that is how it appears in many popular *machzorim.*

49 Jacob is associated with the attribute of harmony *(tiferet)* in the *sefirot* of Kabbalah.

50 Translation from *The Zohar,* vol. 2, trans. Daniel C. Matt (Stanford, Calif.: Stanford University Press, 2004), 172.

51 *Sefer Mitzvot Ha-Gadol,* Introduction to Positive Commandments. Translation from Silverman Machzor, 443.

52 Translation by Rabbi Chaim Feuer in *Light of Life: A Compendium of the Writings of Rabbi Chaim ben Attar* (North Hollywood, Calif.: Newcastle, 1986), 44–45. This translation of the Or Ha-Chaim's comment seems to be more of a paraphrase than a literal translation, but it stays well within the spirit and meaning of the original Hebrew.

53 From *Tiferet Yosef,* which was written by the grandson of Mei Ha-Shiloach, Mordechai Yosef Elazar of Radzin. This translation of the *Mei Ha-Shiloach* is from *Living Waters,* trans. and ed. Betsalel Philip Edwards (Northvale, New Jersey: Jason Aronson, 2001), 391–92.

54 Yiddish for rabbi.

55 From *piyyut* (liturgical poem) by Eleazar Kalir in repetition of morning *Amidah,* beginning with phrase *Atah hu eloheinu.* Actual Hebrew is *sitro yosher, atzamato emunah, pe'ulato emet. See* Silverman machzor, 79.

56 Louis I. Newman, *The Hasidic Anthology* (Northvale, New Jersey: Jason Aronson, 1963), 207.

57 Literally, "great" and "teacher." The Hebrew word used in Israel and in some traditional congregations to refer to the rabbi.

58 Abraham Isaac Kook, *The Lights of Return,* trans. Alter B. Z. Metzger (New York: Yeshiva University, 1978), 30.

59 Arthur Green, *Seek My Face, Speak My Name: A Contemporary Jewish Theology* (Northvale, New Jersey: Jason Aronson, 1994), 173–74.

60 Rif 3a. *See* Ran *d"h b'Rosh Hashanah.*

61 B. Talmud, *Rosh Hashanah* 11a. *See* Rashi *d"h nifkedah Sarah.*

62 Gen. 40:14,23 and 41:9.

63 This idea was inspired by my rabbi and teacher Bradley Shavit Artson, who said something similar in his address at the 2005 Ziegler School rabbinic ordination.

64 *Sefer Abudraham* 269.

65 Mishneh Torah, *Hilkhot Teshuvah* 3:4.

66 *Sefat Emet* 5:138. See also *The Language of Truth: The Torah Commentary of the Sefat Emet, Rabbi Yehudah Leib Alter of Ger.* Translated and interpreted by Arthur Green (Philadelphia: The Jewish Publication Society, 1998).

67 Maimonides, Mishneh Torah, *Hilkhot Teshuvah* 3:1; *SeMaG, Asin* 77.

68 See *Rosh Hashanah* 16b, *d"h v'nechtamin l'altar l'chayim.*

69 My translation.

70 *Pardes Rimmonim* 5:4, 25d.

71 *Zimrat Yah: Prayers and Songs for Shabbat and Festivals* (New York: Congregation B'nai Jeshurun, 2002), 91.

72 This meditation was originally published in its entirety in *New Menorah,* the journal of ALEPH: The Alliance for Jewish Renewal.

73 Gail Twersky Reimer and Judith A. Kates, eds., *Beginning Anew* (New York: Touchtsone, 1997), 32–34.

Part 4: Yom Kippur

1 Nahum. N. Glatzer, *Franz Rosenzweig: His Life and Thought* (New York: Schocken, 1953).

2 Ibid., 25.

3 *Genesis Rabbah* 3:10; See also *Genesis Rabbah* 2:3, *Pesikta Rabbati* 23:1, and Maimonides, *Guide of the Perplexed* 3:43.

4 Mishnah, *Yoma* 8:9. See also *Kli Yakar* on Lev. 16:30.

5 Lev. 23:27–28.

6 Num. 29:7–11.

7 Mishnah, *Yoma* 8:1. Jewish law mandates that those who are ill, pregnant, or nursing should certainly follow doctors' orders to eat, drink, and take medicine. *See* B. Talmud, *Yoma* 83a.

8 Num. 29:7.

9 Lev. 16:30 expresses this concept most clearly: "For on this day atonement shall be made for you to cleanse you of all your sins; you shall be clean before the LORD."

10 B. Talmud, *Yoma* 53a. It teaches that death would occur if a person entered the *Kodesh Ha-Kodashim* on a day other than Yom Kippur and would occur even on Yom Kippur if the person was not the *Kohen Gadol.* It should also be noted that after Israel's 1967 war, when Jews became the proprietors over the Temple Mount, a discussion occurred about the possibility of building a Third Temple. This unique discussion crossed over the bounds of *halakhah* and politics. Ultimately the Orthodox rabbinate ruled that only the Messiah may build the Third Temple, and we can do nothing but wait and pray. This view is based on the Rashi and Tosefot positions that derive from the biblical verse "The sanctuary, O Lord, which Your hands established" (Exod. 15:17). Moreover, given that Jews are in a state of ritual impurity in the absence of the "red heifer" (required for the ritual that expunges impurity caused by contact with dead bodies), the rabbinate ruled that Jews are forbidden to enter the area where the Temple was located. Punishment for being in the *Kodesh Ha-Kodashim* while ritually impure is excommunication *(karet).* In the

absence of precise data about the location of this "Holy of Holies," a blanket ban was imposed on Jewish access to the entire Temple Mount. Proponents of this school of thought included Chief Rabbis Abraham Isaac Kook, Ovadiah Yosef, Isser Unterman, Itzhak Nissim, Avraham Shapiro, Eliahu Bakshi-Doron, and Israel Lau. In 2005, in the face of a popular movement to build the Third Temple, the rabbinate reiterated the ruling. Some non-Orthodox authorities continue to question that ruling. They claim that since the Temple no longer exists and a red heifer has not been found, the Jewish laws regarding the Third Temple no longer applies. These authorities also argue that God's presence is truly everywhere and in heaven, not one place on earth. This view is based upon Deuteronomy 26:15, which states, "Look down from Your holy abode, from heaven...," implying that the Temple is not the exclusive place where God dwells.

11 The biblical procedure in chapter 16 of Leviticus now serves as the basis for the traditional *avodah* service found in the Yom Kippur repetition of the *Musaf Amidah.*

12 *See* Mishnah, *Yoma* 1–7. In *The Complete Artscroll Machzor: Yom Kippur* (New York: Mesorah Publications, 1991), see chart of the steps on pg. 232.

13 There is a precise order to the ritual. If the *Kohen Gadol* does not follow the correct sequence, the ritual will not work; and he must start again from where he broke order. See Mishnah, *Yoma* 5:7.

14 *Genesis Rabbah* 65:10 says that the pair of identical goats was intended to remind us of Jacob and Esau, who were identical twins. Esau, being a man of the wilderness and deemed sinful by the Rabbis, is representative of the goat for Azazel; and Jacob, being a man of God, is representative of the goat for the purity offering.

15 Mishnah, *Yoma* 6:2.

16 Baruch Levine, *The JPS Torah Commentary: Leviticus* (Philadelphia: The Jewish Publication Scoiety, 1989), 102, 250–53.

17 The word "scapegoat" first appeared in the 1530 English translation of the Bible by William Tyndale.

18 B. Talmud, *Yoma* 67b.

19 Ibid. Rashi comments on *Yoma* 67b that Uza and Aza'el are demonic angels who descended to earth at the time of Naamah, the sister of Tubal-cain mentioned in Gen. 4:22. It is interesting to note that according to the Torah, Tubal-cain is the first human who forges the elements of protoweaponry, namely copper and iron. The legend cited in notes 16 and 17 tells of these demonic angels teaching humans the art of weaponry.

20 *See* Ramban and Ibn Ezra on Lev. 16:8.

21 Lev. 17:7.

22 The legend expands upon the strange story of Genesis 6:1–8. This curious section in

Genesis tells of "the Nephilim" appearing on earth and "the divine beings" cohabiting and impregnating women. For Jewish midrashim that include this legend, see *Yalkut Shimoni, Bereishit* 44, and *Emet Ha-Melech* by Naftali Hirsch ben Elchanan (Amsterdam, 1653). Both are translated into English and retold by Howard Schwartz, *Miriam's Tambourine* (New York: Oxford University Press, 1986), 79–90.

23 James H. Charlesworth, ed., "The Book of Enoch," in *The Old Testament Pseudepigrapha*, vol. I (New York: Doubleday, 1983). *See* I Enoch 1–14:7, p. 13–20.

24 *Pirke de-Rebbe Eliezer*, 46. It is noteworthy that in ancient Babylonian ritual, a goat carrying the sins of the community is substituted for a human being and offered to Ereshkigal, goddess of the Deep (a version of hell).

25 Rashi on Exod. 2:14.

26 B. Talmud, *Yoma* 39b. See also Tosefta, *Yoma* 2:2; Mishneh Torah, *Hilkhot Yom Ha-Kippurim* 2:6.

27 Ibid.

28 According to Jewish law, writing the name of God in Hebrew is permissible, but erasing it is forbidden. A *genizah* (literally, "hidden away") is a place for documents and religious articles with God's name to be stored indefinitely or until they can be buried. These items should be properly interred rather than destroyed by trashing or burning. This tradition has existed since ancient times.

29 Technically the holidays themselves are included in the count of 10.

30 B. Talmud, *Rosh Hashanah* 16b.

31 J. Talmud, *Rosh Hashanah* 1:3; *Pesikta Rabbati* 40.

32 B. Talmud, *Kiddushin*, 40a–b.

33 B. Talmud, *Berachot* 12b.

34 Shulchan Arukh, *Orach Chayyim* 602 in the *Mapa.*

35 Mishneh Torah, *Hilkhot Teshuvah* 3:4; *Tur*/Shulchan Arukh, *Orach Chayyim* 602.

36 *Tur, Orach Chayyim* 602; see also Levush, *Orach Chayyim* 602:2.

37 2 Kings 25:22–26; Jeremiah 40:7–41:3; B. Talmud, *Rosh Hashanah* 18b.

38 B. Talmud, *Yoma* 81b. *See* Rashi *d"h kol ha-okhel ve-shoteh.*

39 Shulchan Arukh, *Orach Chayyim* 604:2 in the *Mapa.*

40 Shulchan Arukh, *Orach Chayyim* 205 in the *Mapa;* Kitzur Shulchan Arukh 130:1.

41 Rosh on *Yoma* 8:23; *Sefer Mordechai* on *Yoma* 723; *Tur, Orach Chayyim* 605.

42 Tur, *Orach Chayyim* 605 in *Beit Yosef.* The *Beit Yosef* cites the Ramban's prohibition of *kaparot* because of pagan connotations. In addition, Karo seems to say personally that the custom is foolish. Despite Karo's objection to *kaparot,* Jews (including the Sephardim) kept it because Isaac Luria (the great 16th-century kabbalist) passionately

supported it (as noted by *Magen Avraham* 605:1).

43 *Mishnah Berurah* 605:2, *Chayei Adam* 144:4. These sources (along with *Arukh Ha-Shulchan, Orach Chayyim* 605:3) are primarily concerned with the *shochet,* the one slaughtering the chickens. He may run into problems, such as nicks in the knives caused by having to slaughter so many chickens at once, which would render the fowl unkosher. Therefore, two books on Jewish law, the *Mishnah Berurah* (literally, "Clarified Teaching") by the Chofetz Chaim and *Chayei Adam* (literally, "The Life of Man") by Rabbi Avraham Danzig permit the substitution of money for chickens, to alleviate the burden on the *shochet.* Rabbi Ovadia Yosef (*Teshuvot Yechaveh Da'at* 2:71), on the other hand, does not permit money; he solves the problem by permitting *kaparot* on any day of the *Aseret Yemei Teshuvah. Chayei Adam* goes even further in this discussion to cite a comment of Rashi's on the B. Talmud, *Yoma* 81b, which claims that the original *kaparot* ceremony was not done on chickens, but rather on plants grown by the household children. Thus *Chayei Adam* states that money is actually preferable to a chicken.

44 *Arukh Ha-Shulchan* 605:4.

45 *Tur, Orach Chayyim* 605.

46 *Sefer Ha-Toda'ah,* 2:40.

47 Ibid.

48 *Tur, Orakh Chayim* 606.

49 B. Talmud, *Yoma* 87b.

50 Mishneh Torah, *Hilkhot Teshuvah* 2:7.

51 *Tur, Orach Chayyim* 604, and *Arukh Ha-Shulchan* 604:4.

52 *Sefer Mordechai* on *Yoma* 723; *Tur, Orach Chayyim* 606:4; Shulchan Arukh, *Orach Chayyim* 606:4. This paragraph also mentions the ancient custom of flogging oneself on Erev Yom Kippur as a purification rite, which is no longer practiced.

53 Kitzur Shulchan Arukh 131:16, *Chayei Adam* 144:19.

54 Shulchan Arukh, *Orakh Chayim* 610:4 in the *Mapa.* See also *Mishnah Berurah* there, paragraph 16.

55 *Sefer Mordechai* on *Yoma* 723; *Darkei Moshe* on *Tur, Orakh Chayim* 610:4.

56 *Sefer Ha-Toda'ah,* 1:48. The *kitel* is a white garment, primarily part of Ashkenazic custom, in which the dead are buried. It is also worn on certain special occasions and holidays: Rosh Hashanah, Yom Kippur, *Musaf* of the eighth day of Pesach (for *Tefillat Tal*), *Musaf* of the eighth day of Sukkot (for *Tefillat Geshem*), and on one's wedding day. Some men wear a *kitel* every Shabbat.

57 Shulchan Arukh, *Orach Chayyim* 610:1–3. *Sefer Mordechai,* on *Yoma* 723, mentions a custom of having everyone in the household lighting their own candle as a symbol of their

individual Yom Kippur experience and spiritual assessment.

58 Exod. 34. *See* B. Talmud, *Ta'anit* 28b; *Lamentations Rabbah* 33; Maimonides, *Guide* 3:43; Tanna de-be Eliayhu, *Eliyahu Zuta* 4.

59 *Sefer Ha-Minhagim,* 48.

60 Shulchan Arukh, *Orach Chayyim* 610:4 in the *Mapa.* See also *Mishnah Berurah* there, paragraph 12.

61 *Sefer Ha-Minhagim,* 48.

62 Romans 6–8, especially 7:14–29; Galatians 5:16–24; I Corinthians 7:2–38.

63 Most notable are Maimonides, *Guide* 3:33, and Philo—*see* Hans Lewy, Alexander Altman, and Isaak Heinemann, eds., *Three Jewish Philosophers* (Philadelphia: The Jewish Publication Society, 1960), 71–75. *See also* Robert Seltzer, *Jewish People, Jewish Thought* (Englewood Cliffs, N.J.: Prentice-Hall, 1980), 386–418.

64 Elliot N. Dorff, *Matters of Life and Death* (Philadelphia: The Jewish Publication Society, 1998), 20–24.

65 B. Talmud, *Sanhedrin* 91b.

66 Mishnah, *Yoma* 8:1.

67 *Sefer Ha-Toda'ah,* I:72.

68 *Ta'amei Ha-Minhagim* 331.

69 *See* Gen. 3:17: "To Adam He said, "Because you did as your wife said
and ate of the tree about which I commanded you, 'You shall not eat of it,'
Cursed be the ground because of you;
By toil shall you eat of it
All the days of your life...."

70 *Mishneh Torah,* Laws of Repentance 1:3, 2:1,9,10. *Maimonides' Mishneh Torah,* ed. and trans. Philip Birnbaum (New York: Hebrew Publishing Co., 1967), 36–37.

71 B. Talmud, *Yoma* 53b.

72 This translation is by Louis Jacobs in *Jewish Mystical Testimonies* (New York: Schocken Press, 1976), 105.

73 *The Kuzari,* Book IIII, "Religious Life," par. 5. *See* Ha-Levi, Judah, *Kitab Al Khazari,* trans. Hartwig Hirshfeld (New York: Bernard G. Richards Co., 1927), 140–41.

74 This is a paraphrase of many of the significant laws from the noted chapter of the Kitzur Shulchan Arukh as it appears in Philip Goodman, *The Yom Kippur Anthology* (Philadelphia: The Jewish Publication Society, 1992), 46–47.

75 A preacher, often meaning an itinerant preacher.

76 *Hasidic Tales,* trans. and annotated by Rami Shapiro (Woodstock, Vt.: Skylight Paths Publishing, 2004), 147.

77 This story appears in S. Y. Agnon, *Days of Awe* (New York: Schocken Press, 1965). This is the version retold and found in Abraham J. Twerski, *Living Each Day* (New York: Mesorah Publications, 1988), 342.

78 Nahum N. Glatzer, *Franz Rosenzweig: His Life and Thought* (New York: Schocken Press, 1953), 328–29. This piece can also be found in Goodman, *Yom Kippur Anthology*, 134–35.

79 Dov Peretz Elkins, ed., *Moments of Transcendence: Inspirational Readings for Yom Kippur* (Northvale, N.J.: Jason Aronson, 1994), 103.

80 Erich Fromm, *The Art of Loving* (New York: Harper & Brothers, 1956), 25–26.

81 Rabban is a title given only to patriarchs and presidents of the Sanhedrin (Jewish supreme court). Rabban Gamliel was the first person to be given this title, and he alone ruled over the Sanhedrin, making him sole master.

82 B. Talmud, *Ta'anit* 31a, says that unmarried men would also participate.

83 *See* Rashi there, *d"h she'ulin.*

84 B. Talmud, *Ta'anit* 30b-31a.

85 B. Talmud, *Ta'anit* 28b. See also *Lamentations Rabbah* 33; Maimonides, *Guide* 3:43; and Tanna de-be Eliyahu, *Eliyahu Zuta* 4.

86 *Leviticus Rabbah* 30:7; *Pesikta Rabbati* 40:5, 45:2.

87 *See* B. Talmud, *Ta'anit* 31a, at the very end, for a description of God in the Garden of Eden, being circled (like a bride and groom) by the righteous people who then point and extend their fingers for their marriage rings. Furthermore, every day when wrapping tefillin around their hands, Jews recite the verse from Hosea (2:22), stating that they are betrothed to God, *v'arstikh li le-olam v'yadat et adonai.*

88 B. Talmud, *Yoma* 87b.

89 *Ecclesiastes Rabbah* 7:2.

90 Mishnah, *Yoma* 8:9.

91 Norman Bentwich, *Solomon Schechter: A Biography* (New York: Burning Bush Press, 1964), 238.

92 *See also* Num. 14:18 and Ps. 86:15.

93 The JPS TANAKH renders the word *emet* here as "faithfulness." *Emet* in its most literal sense means "truth," which explains why it is placed in brackets. *Emet,* however, is etymologically connected to the word *emunah* meaning "trust" or "faith"; hence the presumed choice to translate it as "faithfulness." After all, one's "truth" is in effect one's "faith."

94 *See also* Num. 14:18 and Ps. 86:15.

95 The exact same phrasing is used in Joel 2:13, and nearly exact in Ps. 103:8 and Ps. 145:8 *(Ashrei).*

96 The Torah portion beginning in Exod. 30:11. *Ki Tissa* is translated as "When you take a census...."

97 *See* B. Talmud, *Rosh Hashanah* 17b, and Rabbenu Tam in Tosafot there; *Tomer Devorah* by Moshe Cordovero, chap. 1. For an English translation of *Tomer Devorah, see* Moses Cordovero, *The Palm Tree of Devorah,* trans. Moshe Miller (Southfield, Mich.: Targum Press, 1993, 2–47.)

98 *Yalkut Shimoni, Yonah* 1.

99 *Abarbanel, Yonah.*

100 J. Talmud, *Ta'anit* 2:1, cites Rabbi Yochanan's claim that the Ninevites only partially repented, because they did not return all of what they stole. B. Talmud, *Ta'anit* 16a, cites Shmuel saying that the Ninevites went to great lengths to return everything they had stolen. This discrepancy reflects a greater discussion among commentators as to the perception of non-Jews. Some emphasize Jonah's anger toward non-Jews, claiming the text is elitist; while others claim that the anger is specifically aimed toward the Ninevites, not non-Jews in general. The obvious problem with the elitist reading of Jonah is that Jonah never criticizes the Ninevites because they are non-Jews. See *The Jewish Study Bible* (New York: Oxford Univeristy Press, 2004), 1203.

101 Newman, *Hasidic Anthology,* 207–8, cites, "The Koretzer Rebbe said, 'The actions of men send forth either direct or reflected rays. The first are compassion and mercy, the second justice. He who lends money sends forth the positive rays; he who repays a loan, merely reflected rays. A father, in his mercy and compassion toward his children sends direct rays; the son who aids his father, merely reflected rays. This is why it says in the Book of Proverbs, *One father can support ten sons, but ten sons cannot support one father.* The reflected rays are many times weaker than the direct rays, just as justice is many times weaker than mercy and compassion.'"

102 Sa'adia Ga'on, *Emunot ve-De'ot,* chap. 5.

103 From *U-neteneh Tokef* prayer, High Holiday Machzor.

104 English translation of *U-netaneh Tokef* from *Mahzor Hadash* (Bridgeport, Conn.: Prayer Book Press, 1998), 285.

105 First published in Austria in 1946. This English translation was first published by Beacon Press in 1959.

106 Ellen Frankel, *The Five Books of Miriam* (New York, HarperSanFrancisco, 1996), 172–73.

107 Gail Twersky Reimer and Judith A. Kates, eds., *Beginning Anew* (New York: Touchtsone Press, 1997), 325–31.

108 Avraham Finkel, *The Essence of the Holy Days* (Northvale, N.J.: Jason Aronson, 1993). Finkel attributes this saying to Rabbi Yitzchak Luria; and he also cites Rabbi Simcha Bunim, a Hasidic leader in 17th- and 18th-century Poland, who explains that the affliction of Purim is greater than that demanded of us on Yom Kippur, since the

commandment to drink *ad shelo yada* afflicts our reason and judgment, the loss of which is the greatest possible catastrophe (130–31). I am indebted to Chaim Seidler-Feller for calling this citation to my attention.

109 My [Adler] translation.

110 Paul Ricoeur, "The Hermeneutical Function of Distanciation," in *Hermeneutics and the Human Sciences,* ed., trans. John B. Thompson (Cambridge Univeristy Press: 1981), 139.

111 Michael Lerner, *Jewish Renewal* (New York: G. P. Putnam Sons, 1994). Lerner sees liberation from the repetition of compulsion to abuse as the central ethical theme of Judaism.

112 Rabbi Jules Harlow, ed., *Mahzor for Rosh Hashanah and Yom Kippur,* 2nd ed. (New York: Rabbinical Assembly, 1978), many locations, but *see* p. 715. These words are based on *Kohelet* (Ecclesiastes) 2:15–23.

113 My [Adler] more literal translation of this sentence in the prayer referenced above in note 5. This verse is taken from *Kohelet* (Ecclesiastes) 3:19.

114 Although I will generally use the JPS TANAKH for biblical quotes in this essay, this passage has been quoted from the *Schocken Bible, vol. 1 The Five Books of Moses,* trans., commentary, and notes by Everett Fox (New York: Schocken Press, 1995). I [Adler] have quoted Fox's translation because I wanted to convey the features of the Hebrew upon which later interpretation would rest.

115 Both "clearing" and "he will surely not clear" are accounted for by the Rabbinic exegesis in B. Talmud, *Yoma* 86a: God will clear the guilty who do *teshuvah,* but not the unrepentant sinner. This provides a liturgical justification for ending the verse with "clearing" (the guilty), since prayer is part of the penitential process. B. Talmud, *Rosh Hashanah* 17b refers to the liturgical use of this passage.

116 The foundational work on this theme is Mikhail Bakhtin, *Rabelais and His World,* trans. Helene Iswolsky (Bloomington: Indiana University Press, 1984).

117 Some of the material in the following paragraphs has been adapted and expanded from Rachel Adler, *Engendering Judaism: Inclusive Theology and Egalitarian Ethics for the Twenty-First Century* (Philadelphia: The Jewish Publication Society, 1997).

118 Ismar Elbogen, *Jewish Liturgy: A Comprehensive History,* trans. Raymond Scheindlin (Philadelphia and Jerusalem: The Jewish Publication Society and Jewish Theological Seminary, 1993). Elbogen notes that this is the only prophetic reading for an afternoon service that can be proven to exist from the time of the Talmud.

119 Arnold Band, "Swallowing Jonah: The Eclipse of Parody," *Prooftexts* 10 (May 1990), 177–95.

120 Alder echoing Fox's Translation of Exod. 34:7 in the *Schocken Bible.* The final phrase is my translation.

Part 5: Sukkot

1 My translation, guided by the translation in *Siddur Sim Shalom for Shabbat and Festivals* (New York: The Rabbinical Assembly, 1998).

2 Exod. 23:14–17.

3 Deut. 16:16.

4 This is interpreted by the Rabbis to be the end of the agricultural year. *See* Ibn Ezra on Exod. 23:16; and Nahum M. Sarna, *The JPS Torah Commentary: Exodus* (Philadelphia: The Jewish Publication Society, 1991), 146.

5 Some scholars assert Lev. 23:39–43 (the commandments regarding booths and the four species) to be an insertion by a later bibilical redactor. *See* Richard Elliot Friedman, *The Bible with Sources Revealed* (New York: HarperSanFrancisco, 2003), 228–29.

6 Shulchan Arukh, *Orach Chayyim* 661–63; Levush, *Orach Chayyim* 663:1.

7 James H. Charlesworth, ed., *The Old Testament Pseudepigrapha,* vol 2. (New York: Doubleday, 1985), 88–89.

8 Several places in Rabbinic literature describe Sukkot as the culmination of the process of *teshuvah* and judgment in Rosh Hashanah and Yom Kippur. *See* midrash on Ps. 17:5: Zohar 31b-32a, *Pesikta Rabbati* 51:8. This book in the Pseudepigrapha may be one of the earliest textual associations; R. H. Charles dated Jubilees to the second half of the 2nd century B.C.E.

9 C. G. Jung, *Man and His Symbols* (New York: Dell Publishing, 1964); Peter Gay, ed., *The Freud Reader* (London: Norton, 1989); Joseph Campbell, *The Power of Myth* (New York: Anchor Books, 1988). This is a central principle for each of these thinkers and is found in many of their works.

10 Mishnah, *Sukkah* 1:1–2. For a thorough discussion of all regulations concerning the sukkah, *see* Maimonides, Mishneh Torah, *Hilkhot Shofar, Sukkah, v'Lulav* chap. 4–6.

11 B. Talmud, *Beitzah* 30b.

12 Mishnah, *Sukkah* 2:6; B. Talmud, *Sukkah* 26a, 27a, 29a.

13 Lev. 23:43.

14 B. Talmud, *Sukkah* 11b.

15 *Tur, Orach Chayyim* 625. Presumably, this refers to the same cloud described in Exodus 13:21.

16 Culi's anthology is called Me'am Lo'ez.

17 Tosefta, *Sotah* 4:3; *Numbers Rabbah* 1:2; *Me'am Lo'ez, Emor* 13.

18 In the Torah clouds signify God's direct presence: "Moses could not enter the Tent of Meeting, because the cloud had settled upon it and the Presence of the LORD filled the Tabernacle" (Exod. 40:35).

19 Rabbi Michael Strassfeld illustrates this point well in *The Jewish Holidays* (New York: Harper & Row, 1985), 143–44.

20 B. Talmud, *Sanhedrin* 110b. Rabbi Akiva cites Num. 14:33–35 as his prooftext. It describes God promising that those who join together against Him will surely die in the desert.

21 The views of both Rabbis Eliezer and Akiva, as I explicated them, have found support throughout the tradition. Notable supporters of the more pietistic view of Rabbi Eliezer are the Shulchan Arukh, *Orach Chayyim* 625:1; Zohar (3:255b-256a); Ramban (comment on Lev. 23:43); and Isaac Aboab (*Menorat Ha-Me'or* 3, 6:1). Maimonides supports and elucidates Rabbi Akiva's view (*Guide of the Perplexed* 3:43,47). *See also* Mordecai Kaplan, *The Meaning of God in Modern Jewish Religion* (New York: Wayne State University Press, 1937; repr., 1994), 202–11.

22 This expression is used frequently throughout Rabbinic literature. A wonderful example of its use can be found in B. Talmud, *Eruvin* 13b.

23 *Mapa* and *Darkhei Moshe, Orach Chayyim* 624. Isserles credits the Maharil with this maxim.

24 Mishnah, *Sukkah* 1:2; *Tur*/Shulchan Arukh, *Orach Chayyim* 626.

25 B. Talmud, *Sukkah* 22b–23a; *Tur*/Shulchan Arukh, *Orach Chayyim* 628:2–3.

26 Mishnah, *Sukkah* 1:4. The Talmud (B. *Sukkah* 23a) tells the amusing story of Rabbi Akiva and Rabban Gamliel erecting a sukkah on a ship. The wind of the sea tore the sukkah away. From this story we learn that "temporariness" is defined by the fact that the structure can take a normal land wind but not a normal sea wind. See also *Tur*/Shulchan Arukh, *Orach Chayyim* 628:2–3.

27 *Tur*/Shulchan Arukh, *Orach Chayyim* 630:1.

28 Mishnah, *Sukkah* 1:1,9; *Tur*/Shulchan Arukh, *Orach Chayyim* 633–34.

29 *Tur*/Shulchan Arukh, *Orach Chayyim* 631:1.

30 Ibid., 631:3.

31 *Tur*/Shulchan Arukh, *Orach Chayyim* 626:3. In constructing the sukkah, one should not violate the principle *ta'aseh ve-lo min ha-asuyi*, "you shall make [anew] but not use something already made."

32 Although women are technically exempt from most Jewish laws that are bound to a time, such as praying at three specific times a day, they should be encouraged to take on other *mitzvot*, such as sleeping and spending time in the sukkah. Not only are they permitted to do so, they have much to gain spiritually and communally from adhering to these *mitzvot*.

33 B. Talmud, *Sukkah* 27a; *Tur*/Shulchan Arukh, *Orach Chayyim* 639. Classic Jewish law claims that women are in the category of slaves and minors, and are exempt from the

customs and laws of the sukkah; see *Tur*/Shulchan Arukh, *Orach Chayyim* 640. Although women are technically exempt from most Jewish laws that are bound to a time (women are obligated for taking the *lulav* and eating *matzah,* which are both time bound), they should be encouraged to take on such mitzvot; not only are they permitted, but they also have much to gain spiritually and communally from adhering to them.

34 Ibid. *See also* Maimonides, Mishneh Torah, *Hilkhot Shofar, Sukkah, v'Lulav* 6:9–10.

35 *Leviticus Rabbah* chap. 30; Mishnah, *Sukkah* chap. 3.

36 *Leviticus Rabbah* 30:12.

37 Ibid., 30:14.

38 *Sefer Abudraham,* 159, based on *Tanchuma; Sefer Ha-Toda'ah,* 157.

39 Produced as the film *Ushpizin* in 2005.

40 *Genesis Rabbah* 15:8.

41 After the seventh day, Hoshanah Rabbah.

42 Mei Ha-Shilo'ach, *Parshat Yitro,* on Exod. 19:5. For more on these fertility folk customs and rites see Chava Weissler, *Voices of the Matriarchs* (Boston: Beacon Press, 1999) and Michele Klein, *A Time to Be Born* (Philadelphia: The Jewish Publication Society, 1998).

43 B. Talmud, *Menachot* 27a.

44 Mishnah, *Sukkah* 3:1,2,3,7; Maimonides, Mishneh Torah, *Hilkhot Shofar, Sukkah, v'Lulav* 7:1–8; Shulkhan Arukh, *Orach Chayyim* 645–48.

45 Tur/Shulchan Arukh, *Orach Chayyim* 658:7. *See* B. Talmud, *Bava Batra* 137b, for a discussion of the law of an *etrog* owned in partnership. See also the story of Rabbis Elazar ben Azaryah and Joshua sharing *lulav* in B. Talmud *Sukkah* 41b; also Tosafot there.

47 According to Sephardic practice, a left-handed individual should take the *etrog* in his left hand and the other three species in his right hand. According to Ashkenazic practice, a left-handed person should take the *etrog* in his right hand and the other three species in his left hand. *See* Shulchan Arukh, *Orach Chayyim* 651:3. Also some Sephardic practices include reciting the blessing of *Shehecheyanu* and then picking up the *lulav* and *etrog. See* Beit Yosef, *Orach Chayyim* 551; Shulchan Arukh, *Orach Chayyim* 651:4; and *Mishnah Berurah* there, *se'if* 25.

48 If the *pittam* falls off later, during or after harvesting, the *etrog* is not kosher and thus not sold for ritual use.

49 *Tur*/Shulchan Arukh, *Orach Chayyim* 651:9–10. *Sefer Abudraham* (p. 158) reports an opinion arguing that east, north, west, and south were sufficient (*see* Rosh on *Sukkah* 3:26), but another authority claims that by only doing those four directions, we appear to be making the sign of the cross.

50 *Tur*/Shulchan Arukh, *Orach Chayyim* 652:1.

51 *Arukh Ha-Shulchan* 651:21.

52 *Sefer Abudraham,* 158; *see also* Midrash *Tehillim* 17:5.

53 According to Kabbalah, these seven of the ten *sefirot* are the ones that are comprehensible to human beings and combine to form what we understand as Creation (seven is the number symbolic of Creation, seven days). *See* Gershom Scholem, *Origins of Kabbalah,* trans. Allan Arkush (Princeton: Princeton University Press: 1962, 1987), 82. The Shulchan Arukh, *Orach Chayyim* 651:12, says that the seven parts of the *arba minim* are to remind us of Creation.

54 Sefat Emet, *D'rash Le-Sukkot* 5:181. For this in English *see* Arthur Green, *The Language of Truth* (Philadelphia: The Jewish Publication Society, 1998), 358–59.

55 Quoted in Michael Strassfeld, *The Jewish Holidays* (New York: Harper & Row, 1985), 132, margin note.

56 Shulchan Arukh, *Orach Chayyim* 641. On the first night, the blessing for the sukkah *(leshev ba-sukkah)* precedes the *Shehecheyanu;* but the order is reversed on the second night.

57 Zohar, *Emor,* 103b–104a. The Zohar teaches that the hosts should set out actual places for the *ushpizin* to eat and allow the poor to come and sit in those places for a meal.

58 There are two basic traditions for the order of the *ushpizin.* The prevalent Sephardic custom follows Rabbi Yitzchak Luria, who placed Moses and Aaron ahead of Joseph. The other tradition which is presented here, uses a chronological order.

59 *Sefer Ha-Toda'ah,* 1:82–83.

60 *Siddur Sim Shalom,* 330–33.

61 Sarah's story can be found in Gen. 12–23; Miriam's in Exodus (particularly Exod. 15:20) through Num. 20:1; Deborah's in Judges 4–5; Hannah's in 1 Samuel 1–2; Abigail in 2 Samuel 25; Haldah's in Kings 22; and Esther's in the Book of Esther.

62 The Talmud specifically identifies these seven as prophetesses; *see* B. Talmud, *Megillah* 14a-b. *See* www.ritualwell.org, the Web site of Ma'yan: The Jewish Women's Project of the JCC of Manhattan, which provides an *"Ushpizot Guide."* It claims that the source for these *ushpizot* is the kabbalist Menachem Azariah. Other guides about *ushpizot* simply link the *ushpizin* to their respective wives from the tradition: Abraham with Sarah; Isaac with Rebecca; Jacob with Leah and Rachel; Joseph with Osnat; Moses with Tzippora; Aaron with Elisheva; and David with Michal, Abigail, and Bathsheba.

63 Mishnah, *Sukkah* 5:1–4.

64 Ps. 120 to 135, the "Psalms of Ascent." The Rabbis (Mishnah, *Middot* 2:5; B. Talmud, *Sukkah* 51b) associate these 15 psalms wth the 15 steps of the Temple upon which the Levites stood when they sang. Other scholars see them as the psalms sung by pilgrims.

65 B. Talmud, *Sukkah* 53a.

66 Ibid.

67 *Sefer Ha-Manhig, Hilkhot Etrog* 38.

68 B. Talmud, *Sukkah* 47b-48a. The rites associated with Yom Kippur (or any other rites centered around the Temple cult) developed and expanded after the destruction of the Second Temple. Presumably the same situation occurred with Sukkot and Hoshanah Rabbah. The spiritual gap left by the absence of Temple ritual needed to be filled with other rites and observances—ones that Jews could perform and keep elsewhere. *See* Reuven Hammer, *Entering the High Holidays* (Philadelphia: The Jewish Publication Society, 1998), 17–18. In the medieval period, religious leaders expanded upon the work of the Rabbis of the 1st–3rd centuries. In some cases, this expansion process continues today (e.g., adding to the list of heavenly sukkah visitors, the *ushpizin*).

69 There are also Jewish folk beliefs of "magic rings" that have the power to ward off evil spirits. The power of magic circles can also be seen in the famous story of *Honi Ha-Ma'agal,* Honi the Circle Maker, in Mishnah, *Ta'anit* 3:8, and B. Talmud, *Ta'anit* 23a. Through a ritual of prayer and drawing circles, Honi is able to mysteriously influence God to provide the needed amount of rain.

70 The custom among some people is to shake the willow branch before beating it.

71 Mishnah, *Sukkah* 4:5–6.

72 The worldview of the ancient Near East, as we understand it from ancient myths such as the *Epic of Gilgamesh* and the *Enuma Elish,* included two beliefs about water. One is that beneath the earth lies an enormous ocean, the existence of which would explain springs. The second is that above the sky is a great ocean, which would explain rain. Sukkot and the harvest begin the season of rain, and this beating of the willows may have been a way of "waking" the waters so that there would be enough during the winter.

73 B. Talmud, *Yoma* 21b.

74 Zohar, *Tzav* 31b.

75 Ibid.

76 Strassfeld, *Jewish Holidays,* 135–36.

77 For a discussion on the meaning of Hoshanah Rabbah rites *see* "Beat It! The Ritual of Havatat Aravot" by Bradley Shavit Artson in *Conservative Judaism,* (Summer) 48:26–33.

78 Theodor Herzl Gaster, *Festivals of the Jewish Year* (New York: Morrow Quill, 1952), 95.

79 This point is supported by the following Hasidic teaching by the Medizbozer Rebbe: The Jew serves God with his brain on Rosh Hashanah, his heart on Yom Kippur, his hands on Sukkot, and his feet on Simchat Torah.

80 *Sefer Ha-Toda'ah Vol. 1,* 195–96.

81 Lev. 23:36 and Num. 29:15.

82 *See* Rashi on Leviticus 23:36, *d"h Atzeret hee.*

83 Mishnah, *Ta'anit* 1:1.

84 B. Talmud, *Sukkah* 48a.

85 Ibid., 55a–b.

86 *See* David Lieber, ed., *Etz Hayim: Torah and Commentary* (New York: The Rabbinical Assembly, 2001), 729.

87 *Sefer Mordechai* 772; *Tur*/Shulchan Arukh, *Orach Chayyim* 668:1.

88 *Levush* 668:2. See also *Mishnah Berurah* 668:2, *se'if katan* 15.

89 Ibid.

90 Deut. 31:9–13.

91 Mishnah, *Sotah* 7:8.

92 Mishnah, *Megillah* 3:4–6, *Ta'anit* 4:2–3.

93 B. Talmud, *Megillah* 29b.

94 "Torah Reading" by Lionel Moses in *Etz Hayim* 1483. *See also* "The Haftarot of Etz Hayim: Exploring the Historical Interplay of Customs, Humashim, and Halakhah," by David E. S. Stein, in *Conservative Judaism* 54 (Spring 2002).

95 *Proceedings of the Committee on Jewish Law and Standards of the Conservative Movement 1986–1990* (New York: The Rabbinic Assembly, 2001), 327ff. All three papers by Rabbis Elliot Dorff, Lionel Moses, and Richard Eisenberg are significant.

96 *Tur, Orach Chayyim* 669; Mapa, *Orach Chayyim* 669.

97 Ibid. Note that Jacob's blessing is Gen. 48:15–16.

98 Mishnah, *Eduyot* 5:3; B. Talmud, *Shabbat* 30b.

99 For an example *see* Deut. 11:13–21.

100 Adele Berlin and Marc Zvi Brettler, eds., *The Jewish Study Bible* (New York: Oxford University Press, 2004), 1621. There Rashbam, Rabbi Shmuel ben Meir, (b. 1080–d. 1160, France) is cited as one of the scholars who argues that these verses are editorial glosses.

101 Eccles. 11:9–10.

102 Strassfeld, *Jewish Holidays,* 134. Consequently, the other four *megillot* from the Writings in the Bible were already assigned because they had obvious associations. They are as follows: Esther to Purim; The Song of Songs to Passover; Ruth to Shavuot; and Lamentations to Tisha b'Av.

103 Translation from Phillip Goodman, ed., *The Sukkot/Simchat Torah Anthology* (Philadelphia: The Jewish Publication Society, 1988), 24–26. Goodman retained this translation from William G. Braude, trans., *Pesikta Rabbati: Discourses for Feasts, Fasts and Special Sabbaths* (New Haven: Yale University Press, 1968), 2:867–68.

104 Translation from H. Freedman and Maurice Simon, eds., *Songs of Songs Rabbah* (London: Soncino Press, 1939). B. Talmud, *Sukkah* 55b, and Rashi on Lev. 23:36, *d"h Atzeret hee,*

both tell of similar stories wherein a king wishes to linger with all his children one extra day, that day being Shemini Atzeret—the eighth day of Sukkot.

105 Mapa, *Orach Chayyim* 663:2, quoting the Maharil.

106 *(Levush), Orach Chayyim* 663:2.

107 These first few words of this verse are not according to JPS TANAKH. Rashi is basing his comment on a more literal translation, especially touching upon the word *yafeh,* meaning "beautiful," whereas JPS translated it as "precisely."

108 The first part of this verse is not translated according to the JPS TANAKH. Rashi is basing his comment on a more literal translation, especially touching upon the word *yafeh,* meaning "beautiful," whereas JPS translates it as "precisely."

109 Translation by Rabbis Avrohom Davis and Yaakov Y. H. Pupko in *The Metsudah Five Megillos* (with *Rashi*) (New York: Metsudah Publications, 2001), 228–29.

110 This translation is by Louis Jacobs in *Jewish Mystical Testimonies* (New York: Schocken Press, 1976), 233–34. For a further discussion of the Zohar and its concern for the poor *see* Lawrence Fine, *Physician of the Soul, Healer of the Cosmos* (Stanford: Stanford University Press, 2003), 187–219, esp. 205–6.

111 Translation by Aryeh Newman, ed., *The Festival: Pesach, Rosh Hashanah, Sukkot* (Jerusalem: Department for Torah Education and Culture in the Diaspora, World Zionist Organization, 1956), 97. Also found in *Sukkot/Simchat Torah Anthology,* 51.

112 Ramchal, *Derech Ha-Shem, Ba-Avodat Borainu* 8:2.

113 Howard Schwartz, *Gabriel's Palace: Jewish Mystical Tales* (New York: Oxford University Press, 1993), 265–66.

114 Samson Raphael Hirsch, *Judaism Eternal,* trans. Isidor Grunfeld (London: Soncino Press, 1956), 1:12–13. This is also quoted in *Sukkot/Simchat Torah Anthology,* 107–8.

115 Originally found in *One Man's Prayer* by Elie Weisel in Joseph Lookstein Memorial Volume (New Jersey: KTAV Publishing House, 1980), this piece was quoted in *Or Hadash* by Reuven Hammer (New York: The Rabbinical Assembly, 2003), 125.

116 The recitation of the first part (*mashiv ha-ru'ach,* "the one who causes the wind to blow") is said voluntarily, as it is not obligatory; *see* B. Talmud, *Ta'anit* 3a. The prevalence of the custom is attributed to Rashi's comment on 3b, where he says that the wind's drying effect after rainfall is almost as beneficial as the rain itself. A voluntary custom prevalent among Sephardim and less so among Ashkenazim is to also recite the line *morid ha-tal,* "the one who causes the dew to fall," which is said from Passover through Sukkot. *See* Tosafot on 3a, *d"h betal u'v'ruchot.*

117 The *Amidah (Shemoneh Esrei)* was expanded from 18 to 19 blessings in the 2nd century C.E., under the leadership of Rabbi Gamliel the Elder.

118 Each verse begins with a letter of the Hebrew alphabet, taken in order.

119 People in Israel begin including this request at a time specifically suited to the climate and season there, rather than the date used in the Diaspora. The date in Israel is the 7th of Heshvan, which falls 15 days after Shemini Atzeret (the 22nd of Tishrei).

120 Isaac Klein, *A Guide to Religious Jewish Practice* (New York: Jewish Theological Seminary, 1979) 170. *See also* Maimonides, Mishneh Torah, *Hilkhot Tefilah* 16; *Tur*/Shulchan Arukh, *Orach Chayyim* 117:1.

121 1 cubit = 22.08 inches.

122 1 handbreadth = 3.65 inches.

123 Theoretically, two complete sides and half of a third fulfill the minimum requirements.

124 *See* Nogah Hareuveni, *Nature in Our Biblical Heritage* (Israel: Neot Kedumim, 1980).

125 In Martin Yaffe, *Judaism and Environmental Ethics: A Reader* (Lanham, Md.: Rowman and Littlefield, 2001), 112–24.

126 Harold M. Schulweis, *In God's Mirror* (New Jersey: KTVA Publishing, 2003), 260–62.

127 Alan Mintz and Anne Golomb Hoffman, eds., S. Y. Agnon, *The Book that was Lost* (New York: Schocken Press, 1995), 184–87.

128 Jill Hammer, "New Rituals for Simhat Torah" from http://www.ritual.well.org.

Part 6: Guidance along the Way

1 *See also* J. Talmud, *Pe'ah* 7:6, 20c where it says, "When there is no clearly established law on any matter before the court and you do not know what its true nature is, go and ascertain the custom of the people and act accordingly."

2 For an excellent discussion on the relationship between Jewish customs and laws see Elliot N. Dorff and Arthur Rosett, *A Living Tree: The Roots and Growth of Jewish Law* (New York: State University of New York Press, 1988), 421ff.

3 *Pesikta Rabbati: Homiletical Discourses for Festal Days and Special Sabbaths 1 & 2*. Yale University Press, as part of the Yale Judaica Series.

4 *The Language of Truth: The Torah Commentary of the Sefat Emet.* The Jewish Publication Society.

5 Translated by Nachman Bulman. Revised and adapted by Dovid Landesman and Joyce Bennett. (Jerusalem and New York: Feldheim Publishers, 1997).

6 The Talmud refers to the work as *Sifra de-be Rav.*

7 Bloch Publishing Company, New York.

Glossary

aggadah
The nonlegal portions of Rabbinic literature, including moral lessons, prayers, legends, and folklore. Their analysis and explication of the Bible are primarily homiletic.

Akedah (literally, "Binding")
The story of the Binding of Isaac by his father Abraham in Genesis, chapter 22. It is the designated Torah reading for the second day of Rosh Hashanah.

Al Het (literally, "Regarding the Sin")
A confessional recited on Yom Kippur.

aliyah (literally, "ascension"); pl. ***aliyot***
A division within a given Torah reading. The number of *aliyot* varies by day: a minimum of three *aliyot* at a weekday Torah reading, four on Rosh Hodesh, five on a festival day, six on Yom Kippur, and seven on Shabbat. *Aliyah* is also the term for the honor of reciting the blessings before and after the reading.

All Vows See *Kol Nidre.*

Amidah (literally, "Standing")
The central Jewish prayer that is said silently while standing. It is also referred to as *Ha-Tefilah* (The Prayer) and as the *Shemoneh Esrei* (Eighteen Blessings).

Aramaic
An ancient Semitic language closely related to Hebrew. Jews are understood to have adopted Aramaic during the Babylonian exile, thus leading to the use of Aramaic in parts of the TANAKH (e.g., Daniel), the Talmud, and the Zohar. The *Kol Nidre* prayer on the evening of Yom Kippur and the *Kaddish* are in Aramaic.

aravah (literally, "willow"); pl. ***aravot***
One of the four species. See *arba minim.*

arba minim (literally, "four species")
A group of plants used in Sukkot rituals: *lulav, etrog, hadas,* and *aravah.* They symbolize joy for life and dedication to God.

Aseret Yemei Teshuvah (literally, "Ten Days of Penitence/Repentance")
A name for the 10 days at the beginning of the Hebrew month of Tishrei. The period opens with Rosh Hashanah and concludes with Yom Kippur.

Ashkenazim
Jews with long-ago ancestors from Germany or France. Throughout the medieval period of persecution, many Ashkenazim migrated to other parts of Europe, especially Poland and Russia.

Avinu Malkeinu (literally, "Our Father, Our King")
A prayer of request for God's mercy and compassion. It is recited throughout the *Yamim Noraim.*

beinoni (literally, "in between")
One of the three talmudic categories of people in the world; the other two are the good and the wicked. The period of the High Holidays is an opportunity for the *beinoni* to gain God's favor and mercy, and to be inscribed for life along with the good people.

bimah (literally, "stage" or "pulpit")
The platform in the synagogue from which the services are conducted and the Torah is read.

Hatan Bereishit (literally, "Bridegroom of Genesis")
Designation of honor for the person who is called up to the very first *aliyah* of the Book of Genesis on the morning of Simchat Torah.

Hatan Torah (literally, "Bridegroom of the Torah")
Designation of honor for the person who is called up to the very last *aliyah* of the Book of Deuteronomy on the morning of Simchat Torah.

Days of Awe See *Yamim Noraim.*

Day of Atonement *See* Yom Kippur.

derash (literally, "inquiry")
An interpretation of a text as opposed to *peshat,* which is the plain meaning of a text.

Ecclesiastes See Kohelet.

Elul
The sixth Hebrew month. It immediately precedes Rosh Hashanah and holds special significance in the Jewish calendar. During this month that leads to the High Holy Days, there are special observances and customs.

etrog (literally, "citron")
One of the four species. See *arba minim.*

Feast of Booths or **Tabernacles** *See* Sukkot.

four species See *arba minim.*

gemar chatimah tovah (literally, "a good finishing seal [in the Book of Life]")
The traditional greeting in the days after Rosh Hashanah and before Yom Kippur.

gematria
The system that creates parallels between the Hebrew alphabet and numbers, i.e., each Hebrew letter is equal to a number. The Jewish tradition has long sought meaning in numbers through their word equivalence and in words through their numerical equivalence.

Geshem (literally, "Rain")
Additional prayer for rain read on Shemini Atzeret in the fall, introduced in the poetic form of an alphabetic acrostic, which is said until the beginning of Passover in the spring.

hadas (literally, "myrtle"); pl. ***hadasim***
One of the four species. See *arba minim.*

haftarah; pl. ***haftarot***
A selected portion from the Bible's prophetic books that is read following the Torah reading *(parashah)* on Shabbat and most holidays.

hag (literally, "celebration" or "holiday"); pl. ***hagim***
A holiday for which there are traditional observances and customs. Also refers to the principal days of the festivals of Passover and Sukkot. See also *hol ha-moed.*

hakafah (literally, "circuit"); pl. ***hakafot***
A celebratory processional inside the synagogue on Hoshanah Rabbah and Simchat Torah. On Hoshanah Rabbah, when all the Torah scrolls are taken from the Holy Ark, the members of the congregation, holding their *arba minim,* parade around the scrolls. On Simchat Torah, people carry the Torah scrolls themselves in multiple circuits around the perimeter of the sanctuary.

halakhah (literally, "the way"); pl. ***halakhot***
Jewish law originating in the Torah and organized by the Rabbis in the Mishnah and Talmud.

Hallel (literally, "Praise")
Psalms 113 to 118, recited on festivals and Rosh Hodesh as a display of joy and gratitude.

hatarat nedarim (literally, "annulment of vows")
On the eve of Rosh Hashanah, a ritual of confessing and annulling certain vows made to oneself or to God.

hazkarat neshamot (literally, "remembrance of the souls") See *Yizkor.*

High Holy Days See *Yamim Noraim.*

hol ha-moed (literally, "the mundane of the festival")
The intermediary days between falling the most sacred days *(hagim)* of the festivals of Passover and Sukkot. In the Diaspora, these are the third through sixth days; in Israel, they are observed as "half holidays," with fewer restrictions than during the *hagim.*

Hoshanah Rabbah (literally, "the Great Call for Help")
The seventh day of Sukkot during which *hakafot* are made and *Hoshanot* are recited. According to one tradition, it is the very last day for God to seal a judgment.

Hoshanot
The prayers for salvation that are chanted on Hoshanah Rabbah while holding the *arba minim.* At the end of the *hakafot,* each congregant takes a bundle of willow twigs (two from the *arba minim* and one extra), and strikes it on the ground for symbolic purposes. Each prayer begins with the word *hoshanah,* which means, "Save, I pray."

Kabbalah (literally, "Reception")
The tradition of Jewish mysticism, which maintains that there are hidden truths within the Torah. The primary resource for Kabbalah is the Zohar. Hasidism bases many of its teachings upon Kabbalah.

kaparot
A ritual performed on the eve of Yom Kippur. It traditionally involves chanting while holding a live fowl overhead. Then later the animal is slaughtered. A symbolic gesture of atonement, its practice is less prevalent than in the past.

kashrut (literally, "fit" or "proper")
The body of Jewish dietary laws dealing with foods, combinations of foods, and how these foods are to be prepared and eaten. The term in English is "kosher," which is also used to describe objects that are made in accordance with Jewish law and are fit for ritual use.

ke'arot (literally, "plates")
Plates traditionally used in the synagogue the day before Yom Kippur for collecting funds for *tzedakah.*

Kiddush (literally, "Sanctification")
The blessing recited over wine. It is said every Sabbath, on Jewish holidays, and before celebratory meals to sanctify these occasions.

kitel (literally, "a gown")
A man's white robe, usually of linen. It is part of the clothing in which the dead are buried. It is also worn on certain special occasions and holidays: Rosh Hashanah, Yom Kippur, *musaf* of the eighth day of Pesach (for *Tefilat Tal*), *musaf* of the eighth day of Sukkot (for *Tefilat Geshem*), and on one's wedding day. The wearing of a kitel is primarily an Ashkenazic custom.

Kohelet
The Book of Ecclesiastes, a collection of wisdom, traditionally attributed to King Solomon, It is one of the five *megillot* from the part of the Bible called the Writings and is read on the intermediary Shabbat of Sukkot.

Kohen; pl. ***Kohanim***
A member of the Jewish priesthood. Priestly status is inherited, as all *Kohanim* are to be descendants of the patriarch Aaron, the first Priest, who was a member of the tribe Levi. The *Kohanim* performed the sacred rituals during the era of the Temple in Jerusalem.

Kohen Gadol (literally, "Great Priest")
The leader of all the *kohanim* (priests), whose sacred duties included the ritual offering of sacrifices and the burning of incense.

Kol Nidrei (literally, "All Vows")
The beginning of a formula in Aramaic for releasing us from vows. This formula is chanted at the start of the Yom Kippur evening service, which is itself usually referred to as *Kol Nidrei.*

Lag ba-Omer
A spring holiday that falls 33 days from the second day of Passover, during the counting of the Omer. Its origins are obscure; today people celebrate with dancing, singing, bonfires, and picnics. The Hebrew calendar date is the 18th of Iyar. See Omer

lulav (literally, "palm branch")
One of the four species. It is also the name given to the general bundle of willow, myrtle, and palm branches. See *arba minim.*

machzor; pl. ***machzorim***
A specialized prayer book for the holidays and festivals. The most prevalent *machzor* is the one for the High Holy Days.

Malchuyot (literally, "Kingship")
A part of the High Holy Day liturgy recited within the *Amidah* that includes 10 verses from the TANAKH. These verses express a hope for God's kingship to be accepted.

megillot (literally, "scrolls")
Refers to a series of five books in Kethuvim Writings, the last part of the TANAKH. Each book is read on a different holiday: the Song of Songs on Passover; Ruth on Shavuot; Lamentations on Tisha b'Av; Ecclesiastes on Sukkot; and Esther on Purim.

mikveh; pl. ***mikvaot***
The ritual bath for purification. The most traditional use of the *mikveh* involves women and the laws of family purity. Immersion in the *mikveh* can also be part of the ceremony for conversion to Judaism. Men may purify themselves in the *mikveh* before Shabbat, Yom Kippur, on their wedding day, or on other occasions.

minhag (literally, "custom"); pl. ***minhagim***
A custom observed and transmitted by the Jewish people. *Minhagim* often reflect the time and place of the Jews who first kept them. For many people, adherence to Jewish customs can be as strictly maintained as adherence to Jewish law *(halakhah)*.

mishkan
The Tabernacle, a portable sanctuary built by the ancient Israelites after the Exodus, for use while wandering in the wilderness. It was their center for performance of ritual and sacrifice. Once the Jews were no longer wandering, the *mishkan* evolved into the Temple in Jerusalem.

mitzvah (literally, "commandment"); pl. ***mitzvot***
One of the religious obligations detailed in the Torah, the majority of which fall into the positive category of religious, ethical, or moral obligations. The Torah also contains negative mitzvot, which are prohibitions.

Musaf (literally, "Additional")
The additional *Amidah* prayer recited on Shabbat, Rosh Hodesh, and holidays. It commemorates the additional temple sacrifice that was given on such days.

myrtle See *hadas.*

na'anuim (literally, "movements")
The gentle shakings of the four species in each of six directions (east, north, west, south, up, and down) that are made upon the blessing of "taking the *lulav.*" This ceremony is performed twice during the Sukkot morning service.

Ne'ilah (literally, "Shutting" or "Locking")
The final ceremony near the conclusion to Yom Kippur, during which prayers are said with particular attention and intensity before the "gates of redemption and prayer" are closed.

New Month or **New Moon** *See* Rosh Hodesh.

New Year *See* Rosh Hashanah.

Omer (literally, "Sheaf")
A grain offering that was made at the Temple in Jerusalem on the second day of Passover. It signaled the start of the harvest season. Today, in lieu of the offering, Jews "count the Omer" by saying a blessing on each of the 50 days from the second day of Passover until the start of the holiday of Shavuot.

parashah (literally, "portion"); pl. ***parshiyot***
The weekly Torah portion, also called *sidrah.* The Torah is divided into 54 of these portions—one section for each week of a leap year on the Hebrew lunar calendar. In nonleap years some of the portions are combined to create double *parshiyot* that compensate for the reduced number of weeks.

Passover
The spring pilgrimage festival commemorating the Israelites' Exodus from Egypt. It is also known as the Feast of Freedom or the Feast of Matzot. The Hebrew name

is Pesach. Its Hebrew calendar date is the 15th of Nisan, which corresponds to late March or early April.

peshat (literally, "simple")
The plain meaning of a text in context as opposed to *derash,* which is the homiletical meaning.

pittam (literally, "protuberance")
The bulging tip at the blossom end of the *etrog.* If it falls off natually, the etrog is considered to be kosher. If it has been knocked off, the fruit is considered to have a blemish and thus be unfit for ritual use as one of the *arba minim.*

piyyut, pl. ***piyyutim***
A liturgical poem that is recited on Rosh Hashanah or Yom Kippur.

Purim (literally, "Lots")
A holiday recorded in the biblical Book of Esther that commemorates the Persian Jews' deliverance from an attempted extermination. It is celebrated on the 14th of Adar, which corresponds to late February or mid-March.

Rabbinic era
The time of greatest Rabbinic development, when Rabbinic Judaism evolved to become normative Judaism. The first division of this era was that of the sages. They were called *tannaim,* a word that comes from the Aramaic word for "repeat," for which the Aramaic root "t.n.h." is equivalent to the Hebrew root "s.n.h." That Hebrew root is also the basis for the word "Mishnah" (Oral Law); thus the *tannaim* were "Mishnah teachers" who repeated and passed down the Oral Torah. Most of the *tannaim* lived in the period between the destruction of the Second Temple (70 C.E.) and the Bar Kochba Revolt (135 C.E.). The second division of the Rabbinic era is that of the *amoraim,* a word that comes from the Aramaic word for "speaker." The *amoraim* continued to interpret and transmit Jewish law, thought, and practice, expanding upon the foundations laid by the *tannaim.* This work occurred at academies in Palestine (Tiberias, Caesarea, and Tzippori) and in Babylonia (Nehardea, Pumpeditha, and Sura). The Talmud, which was primarily compiled about 400 C.E. in Palestine and about 500 C.E. in Babylonia, provides the fullest expression of the *amoraim.*

ram's horn *See* shofar.

Rosh Hodesh (literally, "Head of the Month")
The new moon and the beginning of each Hebrew month. While it is marked today as a special occasion with distinctive liturgy, in biblical times Rosh Hodesh was celebrated more elaborately, as an outright festival. During the early Diaspora, when long-distance communication became more difficult, two days of Rosh Hodesh celebration became customary for some months in certain years, as the custom remains today.

Rosh Hashanah (literally, "Head of the Year")
The Jewish New Year. It falls on the first and second days of Tishrei, the seventh Hebrew month (in September or October). Rosh Hashanah always falls on the Rosh Hodesh (new moon) that is closest to the autumn equinox.

sages
A descriptive term to indicate those rabbis who contributed the greatest insights and developments in Jewish thought and practice. Most references in this book are to Rabbis of the Rabbinic era, but there are several rabbis from the medieval period (for example, Nachmanides) for whom the term is also used.

Sanhedrin
The highest court of the Land of Israel from mid-2nd century B.C.E. to 425 C.E. At its height, the Sanhedrin did more than make judicial rulings on civil, criminal, and ritual matters; it also functioned to a large extent as a legislature, involved in the major communal issues of the day. The name comes from the Greek term for "Council of Elders" *(Synedrion).*

sefirah (literally, "portion"); pl. ***sefirot***
One of the 10 emanations, or varying aspects, of God in the universe. The *sefirot* play a central role throughout kabbalistic doctrine and teachings. Each *sefirah* embodies a divine quality and, according to Kabbalah, the *sefirot* are the underlying forces in the world and in the Torah.

Selichot (literally, "Forgiveness")
Prayers of penitence recited either from the week before Rosh Hashanah through

Yom Kippur (Askenazic tradition) or for the entire month of Elul (Sephardic tradition). They are often recited in the very early morning.

Sephardim

Jews who trace their ancestry back to Spain before the expulsion in 1492. (*Sepharad* is the Hebrew name for Spain.) Sephardic holiday customs, cuisine, liturgy, and even Hebrew differ in some ways from those of the Ashkenazim, the name of the group of Jews who trace their family history back to France and Germany. (*Ashkenaz* is the Hebrew name for Germany.)

Se'udah Ha-Mafseket (literally, "The Dividing Meal")

The large and nourishing meal eaten before beginning the fast of Yom Kippur.

Shabbat; pl. ***Shabbatot***

The Sabbath, or day of rest. It begins at sunset on Friday night and ends about 25 hours later, after sunset on Saturday night. (The extra hour ensures that the full 24-hour period is observed.)

Shabbat Shuvah (literally, "Sabbath of Return")

The Shabbat that falls between Rosh Hashanah and Yom Kippur. It is named for the season of return and repentance, as well as for the haftarah portion read on that Shabbat that begins with the words "Return, O Israel...." (Hosea 14:2).

Shalosh Regalim (literally, "Three Pilgrimages")

The three major festivals of Passover, Shavuot, and Sukkot. On these occasions during biblical times Jews went on pilgrimages to Jerusalem to make special offerings at the Temple.

Shavuot (literally, "Weeks")

One of the three pilgrimage festivals. Also known as the Feast of Weeks and as the Harvest Festival, it commemorates the giving of the Torah at Mount Sinai and celebrates the first harvest of the fruits of spring. The seven-week period that falls between Shavuot and Passover is called the Omer. The Hebrew calendar date for Shavuot, which usually falls in May or June, is the 6th of Sivan.

Shekhinah (literally, "Dwelling")
One of the names for God, and explicitly the presence of God, commonly described as a light or radiance that illuminates the world. The word *Shekhinah* has the same root as the word *shochen,* meaning "to dwell." It is often associated with the *mishkan* and the Temple.

Shem Ha-Meforash (literally, "The Ineffable or Inexpressible Name")
A reference to the actual name of God that was pronounced by the *Kohen Gadol* on Yom Kippur.

Shemini Atzeret
The eighth day of Sukkot, which holds special significance as its own holiday. Jews thank God for the harvest and ask for winter rain to prepare the ground for spring planting.

shevarim (literally, "broken")
One of the three sounds of the shofar, consisting of three broken, short notes.

shofar; pl. *shofarot*
The ram's horn that is sounded during the month of Elul, on Rosh Hashanah, and at the end of Yom Kippur. It is mentioned numerous times in the Bible, in reference to its ceremonial use in the Temple and to its function as a signal-horn of war.

Shofarot
A part of the High Holy Day liturgy within the *Amidah* that includes 10 verses from the Bible referring to the shofar. It expresses a hope that the dispersed exiles will be ingathered to Israel.

simchah (literally, "joy" or "happiness"); pl. ***simchot***
A joyous celebration, such as a wedding or bar mitzvah.

Simchat Torah (literally, "Rejoicing in the Torah")
The holiday that celebrates both the end and renewal of the annual cycle of reading the Torah. Typically, the congregation takes the Torah scrolls from the ark and parades with them in circles *(hakafot)* around the perimeter of the sanctuary.

Simchat Torah is generally the ninth day of Sukkot in most American synagogues. In Israel and in some synagogues in the United States, it is combined with Shemini Atzeret on the eighth day. The calendar date is the 23rd of Tishrei, which corresponds to late September or early-to mid-October.

s'khakh (literally, "covering")
The roofing of the sukkah, which is made from natural materials such as bamboo or palm branches.

sukkah, (literally, "hut" or "booth"); pl. *sukkot*
A temporary structure that a Jew builds and ideally dwells within at the holiday of Sukkot. Its purpose is to commemorate the Israelites' Exodus from Egypt and to make a symbolic gesture that acknowledges humankind's reliance upon God. The construction of a sukkah follows a set of specific regulations.

Sukkot (literally, "Booths")
One of the three pilgrimage festivals, it occurs on the 15th of Tishrei in late September or early October. Sukkot marks the fall harvest and commemorates the Exodus from Egypt. The Torah says that the Israelites dwelt in *sukkot* (temporary huts or booths) during their desert journey.

Tashlikh (literally, "Cast Away")
A ceremony observed on the afternoon of the first day of Rosh Hashanah, in which sins are symbolically cast away into a natural body of water. The term and custom are derived from a verse in the Book of Micah (7:19).

tekiah (literally, "blowing")
One of the three sounds of the shofar, consisting of one long, deep note.

tekiah gedolah (literally, "big *tekiah*")
An extremely long blast of the shofar that concludes a series of soundings of the shofar.

teruah (literally, "sound")
One of the three sounds of the shofar, consisting of nine staccato notes.

teshuvah (literally, "return")
Referring to the "return to God," *teshuvah* is often translated as "repentance." It is one of the most significant themes and spiritual components to the High Holy Days.

Tisha b'Av (literally, "the 9th of Av")
A day of mourning and fasting that marks the dates of destruction of both the First and Second Temples.

Tishrei
The seventh Hebrew month, during which Rosh Hashanah, Yom Kippur, and Sukkot all occur.

Tu b'Av (literally, "the 15th of Av")
A joyous and romantic holiday celebrated during the summer in Israel. In ancient times, it marked the beginning of the wine harvest.

Tu b'Shevat (literally, "the 15th of Shevat")
A holiday designated by the Talmud as the new year of the trees. It is celebrated when the almond trees are in bloom in Israel, a time in the calendar that corresponds to January or February.

Tzom Gedalyah (literally, "The Fast of Gedalyah")
A fast held on the day after Rosh Hashanah, which is the 3rd of Tishrei on the Hebrew calendar. (If that date falls on Shabbat, the fast will occur the following day, the 4th of Tishrei.). After the Babylonian King Nebuchadnezzar destroyed the First Temple in Jerusalem, most of the nation of Israel was exiled to Babylon. Nebuchadnezzar appointed Gedalyah ben Achikam, a righteous Jew, as governor over those who remained; but Gedalyah was murdered by another Jew, who had been provoked into jealousy by a neighboring king. Gedalyah's assassination destroyed any hope for Jewish self-government and caused the remaining Jews to flee. We commemorate this day with a minor fast, which goes from sunrise to sunset (rather than sunset to sunset). Also known as Tzom Shevi'i.

ushpizin (literally, "guests")
The supernal guests that the Zohar teaches are to be invited into the sukkah (along with the poor) during each night of Sukkot. Traditionally these seven guests are

Abraham, Isaac, Jacob, Joseph, Moses, Aaron, and David. Today, many people add the names of women *(ushpizot)* to the list.

Vidui (literally, "Confession")
Special confessional prayer where one beats one's breast for each infraction mentioned. These confessionals recur throughout the Yom Kippur liturgy.

Yamim Noraim (literally, "Days of Awe")
Term that refers to the 10 days from Rosh Hashanah through Yom Kippur. It was coined by the Maharil.

Yizkor (literally, "May (God) Remember")
In the Ashkenazic tradition, the memorial service recited four times a year, including on Yom Kippur and Shemini Atzeret. The other two occasions occur during Passover and Shavuot. It is also known as *Hazkarat Neshamot* ("Remembrance of the Souls").

Yom Ha-Atzmaut (literally, "Day of Independence")
Israel Independence Day, which commemorates the founding of the State of Israel on May 14, 1948. Its Hebrew calendar date is the 5th of Iyar, the day after Yom Ha-Zikaron (the Day of Remembrance).

Yom Ha-Din (literally, "Day of Judgment")
One of the names for Rosh Hashanah, the Jewish New Year, which falls on the 1st day and 2nd days of the Hebrew month of Tishrei, usually in late September or early October.

Yom Ha-Shoah (literally, "Day of the Holocaust")
Holocaust Remembrance Day. The day set aside by the Israeli Knesset for remembering the six million Jews murdered by the Nazis. It corresponds to the day in 1943 when the Jews began an uprising in the Warsaw Ghetto. The Hebrew calendar date is the 27th of Nisan, a week after the seventh day of Passover.

Yom Ha-Zikaron (literally, "Day of Remembrance")
(1) A solemn Israeli holiday that honors the memory of soldiers and others killed defending the State of Israel. Its Hebrew calendar date is the 4th of Iyar, which

usually falls in September. (2) One of the alternate names for the holiday of Rosh Hashanah.

Yom Kippur (literally, "Day of Atonement")
The most holy and solemn day of the Jewish calendar, filled with pleas for forgiveness and acts of self-denial, including fasting. It falls on the 10th day of the Hebrew month of Tishrei, which is usually late September or early October.

Yom Teruah (literally, "Day of the Sounding")
One of the names used for Rosh Hashanah, the Jewish New Year, a holiday when the shofar (ram's horn) is sounded. The name is found in the Torah (Num. 29:1).

Zikhron Teruah (literally, "Remembrance of the Sounding")
One of the names used for Rosh Hashanah, the Jewish New Year, a holiday when the shofar (ram's horn) is sounded. The name is found in the Torah (Lev. 23:24).

Zikhronot (literally, "Remembrances")
A part of the High Holy Day liturgy within the *Amidah* that includes 10 verses from the Bible that refer to how God continually remembers His covenant with Israel.

z'man simchateinu (literally, "the time of our rejoicing")
An expression often used when referring to the days of Sukkot.

Contributing Authors

Alan Abrams is a teacher and chaplain at Reading Hospital and Medical Center in Reading, Pennsylvania. He was ordained by the American Jewish University and holds master's degrees in Talmud from the Jewish Theological Seminary and in public policy from Columbia University.

Rachel Adler is on the faculties of the School of Religion, University of Southern California, and the Rabbinical School of the Hebrew Union College-Jewish Institute of Religion. At both institutions, she holds the title Associate Professor of Modern Jewish Thought and Judaism and Gender. Dr. Adler was one of the first theologians to integrate feminist perspectives and concerns into the interpretation of Jewish texts and the renewal of Jewish law and ethics. Her writings have appeared in collections such as *A Companion to Feminist Philosophy, Beginning Anew: A Woman's Companion to the High Holy Days,* and *On Being a Jewish Feminist.* Her book *Engendering Judaism: A New Theology and Ethics* was published by The Jewish Publication Society. In 1999, she was awarded the National Jewish Book Award for Jewish Thought by the Jewish Book Council and, in 2000, received the Tuttleman Foundation Book Award of Gratz College.

S. Y. Agnon, one of the central figures in modern Hebrew literature, was born in Buczacz, Poland, in 1888 and emigrated to Palestine in 1907. His original name was Shmuel Yosef Halevi Czaczkes. His first short story, "Agunot" (Forsaken Wives), was published under the pen name Agnon, which bears a resemblance to the title of the story and became his official family name thereafter. Agnon was corecipient of the Nobel Prize for Literature in 1966, the first Hebrew writer to receive this award. His novels include *The Day Before Yesterday, The Bridal Canopy, A Guest for the Night,* and *A Simple Story.* He died in 1970.

Bradley Shavit Artson is vice-president of the American Jewish University and dean of its Ziegler School of Rabbinic Studies. A doctoral candidate in contemporary Jewish theology at Hebrew Union College-Jewish Institute of Religion, Rabbi Artson is the author of *The Bedside Torah: Wisdom, Dreams, & Visions.*

Will Berkovitz is the executive director of Hillel UW at the University of Washington. Before his ordination, Rabbi Berkovitz worked as a journalist in Seattle, where he wrote for and edited regional and national magazines focusing on back-country camping, mountain climbing, and cultural arts.

Rosellen Brown is the author of several novels, including *Before and After,* which was on *The New York Times* bestseller list; *Tender Mercies;* and *Civil Wars.* She has also written a collection of short stories and three books of poetry. Brown teaches in the master's degree program at the School of the Art Institute of Chicago.

Miriam Burg was ordained at the Hebrew Union College-Jewish Institute of Religion, where she also earned master of arts degrees in Jewish Education and Hebrew Letters. Rabbi Burg served as school rabbi and director of Judaic studies at the Stephen S. Wise Temple Elementary School in Los Angeles. She currently teaches and mentors Nadiv fellows at the Jewish Council on Urban Affairs.

Shlomo Carlebach was born in Berlin in 1925, the descendant of a rabbinic dynasty. His family fled from the Nazis to Austria in 1933 and six years later to America, where his father became the rabbi of a small synagogue in New York City. In the 1960s, Rabbi Shlomo Carlebach became a renowned writer and singer of religious music and a pioneer in his approach to the modern *baal teshuvah* (literally, "returnee") movement, encouraging Jews to reembrace their heritage and follow more observant religious practices. His influence persists through his teachings and the so-called Carlebach-style services that include much singing and dancing. He died in 1994.

Elliot N. Dorff directs the rabbinic and master's degree programs at the American Jewish University, where he is rector, cochair of the bioethics department, and Sol and Anne Dorff Distinguished Service Professor in Philosophy. Rabbi Dorff has written more than 150 articles on Jewish thought, law, and ethics, and is the author of more than 12 books including The Jewish Publication Society titles: *To Do the Right and the Good: A Jewish Approach to Modern Social Ethics; Love Your Neighbor as Yourself: A Jewish Approach to Modern Personal Ethics;* and *Matters of Life and Death: A Jewish Approach to Modern Medical Ethics.*

Ellen Frankel is chief executive officer and editor-in-chief of The Jewish Publication Society. Dr. Frankel, who received her Ph.D. in comparative literature from Princeton University, is an acclaimed storyteller, writer, and lecturer. She is the author of numerous books, including *The Five Books of Miriam: A Woman's Commentary on the Torah; The Classic Tales: Four Thousand Years of Jewish Lore;* and *The Illustrated Hebrew Bible.*

Miriyam Glazer is chair of the department of literature and communications at the American Jewish University. Rabbi Glazer has written numerous essays on literature, gender, and spirituality. Her books include *Dancing on the Edge of the World: Jewish Stories of Faith, Inspiration, and Love; Dreaming the Actual: Contemporary Fiction and Poetry by Israeli Women Writers;* and, with her sister, Phyllis Glazer, *The Essential Book of Jewish Festival Cooking: 200 Seasonal Holiday Recipes and Their Traditions.*

Shefa Gold received her ordination from both the Reconstructionist Rabbinical College and from Rabbi Zalman Schachter-Shalomi. She is the director of C-DEEP: The Center for Devotional, Energy and Ecstatic Practice and on the faculty of the Institute for Jewish Spirituality. Rabbi Gold composes and performs spiritual music and has produced 10 albums and CDs. She is the author of *Torah Journeys: The Inner Path to the Promised Land.*

Jill Hammer was ordained by the Jewish Theological Seminary and holds a doctorate in social psychology from the University of Connecticut. Rabbi Hammer is the director of Tel Shemesh, a Web resource and sponsor of community rituals for people who wish to integrate Jewish faith and practice with earth-based beliefs and ways of living. She is the author of two Jewish Publication Society titles, *Sisters at Sinai: New Tales of Biblical Women* and *The Jewish Book of Days: A Companion for All Seasons.*

Reuven Hammer served as president of the International Rabbinical Assembly from 2002–2004 and was the first Israeli to be elected to that position. He received his rabbinic ordination and doctorate in theology from the Jewish Theological Seminary and a doctorate in special education from Northwestern University. He is the editor of *The Jerusalem Anthology: A Literary Guide;* and the author of *Entering the High Holidays: A Complete Guide to the History, Prayers and Themes,* winner of the National Jewish Book Award. Both books were published by The Jewish Publication Society.

Cheryl Peretz is the associate dean of the Ziegler School of Rabbinic Studies at the American Jewish University in Los Angeles, California, and writes columns about the weekly Torah portion for a number of Jewish periodicals. Rabbi Peretz received degrees from the Jewish Theological Seminary and Columbia University, as well as Baruch College, where she earned a master's degree in business administration.

Joel Roth is the Louis Finkelstein Professor of Talmud and Jewish Law at the Jewish Theological Seminary and past chairman of the Committee on Jewish Law and Standards of the Rabbinical Assembly. He is the author of *The Halakhic Process: A Systemic Analysis* and *Sefer Ha-Mordecai: Tractate Kiddushin.*

Judith Sarah Schmidt, a clinical psychologist and writer, is cofounder of the Center for Intentional Living (CIL), an experiential learning community. CIL offers workshops, courses, and programs throughout the United States and Europe to healthcare professionals, clergy, and individuals interested in psychological growth and transformation.

Harold M. Shulweis, is the longtime spiritual leader of Congregation Valley Beth Shalom in Encino, California. He holds a masters degree in philosophy from New York University and was ordained at the Jewish Theological Seminary. Rabbi Schulweis has authored several books, including *For Those Who Can't Believe, Approach to the Philosophy of Religion; Evil and the Morality of God;* and *In God's Mirror.*

Arthur Waskow is a political activist and religious leader associated with the Jewish Renewal movement. Rabbi Waskow is director of The Shalom Center, which brings Jewish and other spiritual thought processes and practices to bear on seeking peace, pursuing justice, healing the earth, and celebrating community. He is the author of *Seasons of Our Joy, Godwrestling—Round 2: Ancient Wisdom, Future Paths;* coauthor, with Phyllis Berman, of *A Time for Every Purpose Under Heaven: The Jewish Life-Spiral As a Spiritual Path* and *Tales of Tikkun: New Jewish Stories to Heal the Wounded World;* and coeditor of *Trees, Earth, and Torah: A Tu B'Shvat Anthology* and *Torah of the Earth: Exploring 4,000 Years of Ecology in Jewish Thought.*

Simkha Y. Weintraub is a rabbi, social worker, and couples-and-family therapist, who serves as rabbinic director of the Jewish Board of Family and Children's Services in New York City and its Jewish healing programs. Rabbi Weintraub draws upon Jewish spiritual resources to help Jews deal with illness, bereavement, and life transition issues.

Index

17th of Tammuz, 89

A

Aaron. *see also* High Priest
- biblical description of, 66, 94, 98
- *ushpizin,* 128, 129

Aaron ben Joseph Halevi, 191
Abarbanel, Don Yitzchak, 182
Abba Aricha, 192
Aboab, Isaac, 182
Abraham
- building sukkah, 119
- and theme of Rosh Hashanah, 24, 25, 32, 45, 46, 49, 61–62
- and theme of Sukkot, 119, 132
- *ushpizin,* 129, 144

Abraham ben Nathan, R., 191
Abrams, Alan, 168–170
ad shelo yada, 109
Adam
- creation of, 33
- eating *etrog,* 125
- and theme of Yom Kippur, 76, 99

Adar Sheini, 15
Adler, Rachel, 108–114
Adonai, 70, 82
afterlife. see *olam ha-ba*
Agnon, S. Y., 83, 172–175
akedah. see Isaac
Akiva ben Joseph, R., 120–122
Akiva, R., 77, 168
Al Het, 90–91.
- *see also* confessions and confessionals

Aleinu, 85
aliyah, 137
Alter, R. Yehuda Aryeh Leib, 191
Amidah, 71, 84, 102, 152–153
Amnon of Mainz, R., 102
amoraim, 47, 184
annulling of vows, 28
Apocrypha, 183
apologizing, 66, 69, 77, 78
aravah, 9, 124–126, 128, 131, 132–133, 146, 158, 162, 163, 167
arba minim. see four species
Arba'ah Turim. see Tur
Aron Kodesh, 92
Artson, Bradley Shavit, 97–99
Arukh Ha-Shulchan, 27, 183
Aseret Yemei Teshuvah, 24, 49–50, 71–72. *see also* Ten Days of Repentance
Asher ben Yechiel, R., 191
Ashi, Rav, 184
atonement, 27, 39–40, 66–68, 72–73, 77–78, 80–81, 90–91, 94, 97–98
atzeret, 134, 156, 158, 160
Avinu Malkeinu, 71, 72
Avodah service, 96
Azazel, 67–69, 94–95, 107, 184

B

Baal Ha-Levush, 185
Baal Ha-Turim. *see* Jacob ben Asher
bein adam la-chaveiro, 77, 78, 91
bein adam la-Makom, 77, 78, 91
beinonim, 29, 42, 71
beit din, 28
Berkovitz, Will, 57–59
bittul zeman, 170
breathing, 5–6, 75, 163

Brown, Rosellen, 60–62
Burg, Miriam, 102–104

C

calendar
expression of spirit, 6
fixed, 14
Gregorian, 16
Julian, 16
lunar and solar, 14–15
candles, for Yom Kippur, 74
Carlebach, Shlomo, 59, 187
Chabad, 186
Chaim ben Attar, R., 37, 189
challah
for Rosh Hashanah, 23, 30
for Shabbat, 30
charity. *see tzedakah*
Chaye Adam, 183
Chaye Avraham, 183
cheshbon nefesh, 24, 58
chibbut aravah, 131, 132
children, 74, 110, 125, 137
Chiya, R., 192
Chofetz Chaim, 188
Chokhmat Adam, 183
circling, 131, 169–170
circumcision, 61
Cohen, Hermann, 183
confessions and confessionals, 50, 67, 73, 90–91, 97–99. *see also Al Het; Vidui*
Creation, 33, 44, 51–52, 53, 59
Culi, Yaakov, R., 121, 187

D

David (King), 128–129
David ben Joseph Abudraham, R., 191
David ben Shmuel Ha-Levi, R., 194–195
Day of Atonement. *see* Yom Kippur
days
names of, 16–17
Days of Awe. *see* Ten Days of Repentance
death
judgment at Rosh Hashanah, 28–29, 31, 42
decree at Yom Kippur, 102–104
knowing time of, 143–144
derash, definition, 42
Derashot, 190
Derekh Hashem, 146, 186
din, 35, 37
dor ha-midbar, 121
Dorff, Elliot, 53–55, 99–102
Dov Baer. *see* Maggid of Mezritch

E

Ecclesiastes. *see* Kohelet
Edwards, Betsalel Philip, 187
Eliezer ben Hyracanus, R., 44, 45, 56, 120–122, 189
Eliezer, R., 33, 152–153
Elimelech, R. *see* Lizensk, Rebbe of
Eliyahu Ki Tov, 76, 133, 192
Elul, 33, 105–106
preparation for Rosh Hashanah, 26–28
Elul (poem), 105–106
Emet, 70.
emotional intelligence, 6, 8–9
Emunot ve-De'ot, 191

Enoch, Book of, 68, 107, 184
environmentalism, 162–163
Epstein, R. Yechiel Michel Ha-Levi, 27, 183
erev Rosh Hashanah, 28
erev Yom Kippur, 72–74
etrog, 124–126, 128, 146, 147, 163, 167, 171–172, 172–175
etymologies
  alam-olam, 51
  neshamah-neshimah, 75
  universe, 50
Eve
  eating *etrog*, 125
  and theme of Yom Kippur, 99
evil impulse, 69
existentialism, 8
eyn sof, 127

F

faith
  conflicting with reason, 6–9
  of Abraham, 32
  theme on Rosh Hashanah, 38–40
  theme on Sukkot, 144–145, 168
false prophets, 93
Fast of Gedalyah. see *Tzom Gedalyah*
Fast of the Seventh Month. see *Tzom Shevi'i*
  on 17th of Tammuz, 89
  on Days of Awe, 72
  on Yom Kippur, 75, 101, 107–108
fish, 31–32
forgiveness. see also *Selichot*
  asking for, 78, 91, 93, 95, 99, 101
  impossibility of, 85
  of God, 83
four (number), 127–128
four species. *see also* Sukkot
  and Hasidism, 127–128
  as parts of body, 125
  biblical description, 118, 124
  mystical meaning of, 127–128
  representing types of Jews, 124–125
  symbol of blessing, 125
  symbolizing Israel, 167
  use during Hoshanah Rabbah, 131
  waving, 125–127, 163
Frankel, Ellen, 107
Frankl, Victor, 104
free will, 99–100
freedom
  moral, 99–102, 156
  spiritual, 39, 144, 159
Fromm, Erich, 86–87
futility, 110, 138–140, 151

G

Ga'on, 191
Ganzfried, Solomon, 185
Gaon of Vilna, 149
Gaster, Theodor, 132
Geihinnom, 43
Gemara, 47, 184
gematria
  four (number), 127
  nuts and sin, 7, 31
Gersonides, 7, 100
Geshem, 135, 152
gever, 73
gevurah, 128, 144
Gezer, Tel, 56
Glazer, Miriyam, 55–57, 165–168
God

coronation of, 48–49, 57–58
dwelling in heart, 45
existence of, 45
forgiving, 83
names of, 69–71, 82
nearness to, 84–85
primacy of, 51–52
relationship with individual, 89
relationship with Israel, 128–129
symbolized during Sukkot, 120–122
thirteen attributes of, 92–93, 110
Golden Calf, 89
Gold, Shefa 59–60
good impulse, 69
Green, Arthur, 40–41
Gregorian calendar, 16, 53
Guide of the Perplexed, 187

H

ha-yom harat olam, 53
hadar, 124
hadas, 124–126, 128, 146, 163, 167
haftarah, 150, 189
hag, 15, 117, 156, 169
Hagar, 25, 60–62
hakafot, 131, 137
halakhah, 181–182
Halfon, Avraham ben Raphael, 183
Hallel, 119, 126, 158
Hammer, Jill, 175–177
Hammer, Reuven, 48–50, 58
Hamnuna the Elder, R., 145
Hannah, 44–45, 47, 56
happiness
in performing mitzvot, 99–102
theme of Sukkot, 119–120, 145–146, 149, 151, 168–169, 171
Hareuveni, Nogah, 166, 167
Hasdai Crescas, 7
Ha-Shem, 70
Hasidism, 47, 88, 127–128
Hatan Bereishit, 137
Hatan Torah, 137
hatarat nedarim, 28
heart
dwelling place of God, 45
praying from, 47, 144
source of sin, 91, 171
heavenly guests, 128–130
Heschel, Abraham Joshua, 8, 85–86, 179
hesed, 35, 38, 128, 144
hevel, 110, 138
High Priest
duties on Rosh Hodesh, 13
duties on Yom Kippur, 66–67, 70, 79, 94–96
Hillel II, 14–15
Hirsch, Samson Raphael, 134, 147–148, 184
hod, 128
hodesh, 13
hol ha-mo'ed, 119
holidays
comical, 110
compared to holy days, 54
enjoying, 100–101
expression of spirituality, 5–6
second day of, 15–16
Holy of Holies, 66, 71, 79, 94
Hoshanah Rabbah, 131–134
hoshanot, 131–133, 158, 169

I

Ibn Ezra, Avraham, 184
Ibn Gabirol, Solomon, 75
Ineffable Name, pronouncing, 69–71, 84, 95–96
intellectualism, excessive, 133
intelligence, emotional, 8–9
Isaac
  and Ishmael, 62
  binding of, 25, 31, 32, 46, 49, 57
  birth of, 45, 62
  ushpizin 128, 129, 144
Isaac of Corbeil, 188
Isaac of Tyrnau, 191
Isaac, R., 79
Israel, Land of, description, 55–56
Isserles, Moses, 124, 185, 192, 193

J

Jacob
  ushpizin, 128
  voice of, 35
Jacob ben Asher, 71, 120, 194
Job, 139
Jonah, 86–87, 92–93, 111–113, 139
Joseph
  ushpizin, 128
  in prison, 45
Joshua ben Chananyah, R., 44, 45
Joshua ben Levi, R., 143, 160
Joshua of Siknin, R., 141
Joshua, R., 152–153
Jubilees, Book of, 24, 119, 185
Judah the Patriarch, R.
  see Yehudah Ha-Nasi, R.
Judah, R., 79
Julian calendar, 16
justice
  theme of Hoshanah Rabbah, 132
  theme of Purim, 110
  theme of Rosh Hashanah, 35, 37, 43, 49, 52, 141–142
  theme of Yom Kippur, 75, 86–87, 89, 101–102, 102, 141–142

K

Kabbalah, 35, 69, 70, 79, 127, 185–186.
  see also Zohar
Kalir, Eleazer, 97
Kamionka, rabbi of, 147
Kant, Immanuel, 183
kaparot, 72–73
karet, 66
Karo, Joseph, 71, 186, 192
kavanah, 46, 47, 77
Kethuvim, 185
keva, 47
ki hakol hevel, 110
Ki Tov, Eliyahu, 76, 133, 192
kiddush, in sukkah, 124
kitel, 74, 102, 109, 135
Kitzur Shulchan Arukh, 80–81, 185
Klein, R. Isaac, 185
Kodesh Ha-Kodashim. see Holy of Holies
Kohanim. see priests
Kohelet, 110, 138–140, 143–144, 151
Kol Ha-Ne'arim, 137
Kook, Abraham Isaac, 39–40
Kruspedai, R., 42, 43
Kuzari, 195

L

leap year, 15
Leibowitz, Yeshayahu, 52
Leiner, Mordechai Yosef, 38, 187
leshev ba-sukkah, 128
Levi Yitzchak of Berditchev, 186
Levi, R., 141
Levush, 186
life
 balance within, 151
 described in Kohelet, 138–140, 143–144
 futility of, 110
 making most of, 104
 transient nature of, 148
Lizensk, Rebbe of, 83, 186
loshon ha-ra, 188
love, essence of, 87
lulav. see also four species
 bringing good weather, 7
 description of, 124–126
 meaning of, 128, 146, 163, 167
Luria, Yitzchak, 186
Luzzatto, Chaim, 146, 186

M

machzor, 88, 90–91, 96–97
Magen Avraham, 186
Magen David, 195
Maggid of Mezritch, 81–83, 186
Magriso, Yitzchak, 187
Maharil. *see* Moelin, R. Jacob Ha-Levi
Maimonides. *see* Moses ben Maimon, R.
Makom, 70
malkhut, 128
Malkhuyot, 49, 54, 142
man
 animal-spiritual nature of, 36
 creation of, 33
Mani of Shaab, R., 141
Mapa, 193
mashiv ha-ruach. . ., 152
Me'am Lo'ez, 187
megillot, 138, 187
Mei Ha-Shiloach, 38, 187
Meir ben Baruch of Rothenburg, R., 97, 190, 192
memorial candles, 74
mercy
 theme during Elul, 26
 theme on Rosh Hashanah, 33, 35, 37, 39, 40
 theme on Yom Kippur, 73, 89, 92–93, 101
Meshullam ben Kalonymous, 97
Mesillat Yesharim, 186
midrash, 187–188
Midrash Rabbah, 188
Migdal Oz, 186
mikveh, 73–74
minhag, 181–182
Minhagei Maharil, 186
mishkan, 66, 71
Mishnah, 47, 88, 184, 188, 193
Mishnah Berurah, 188
Mishneh Torah, 189
mitzvot, reasons for observing, 7–9, 43, 46–47, 56–57, 100, 117, 120
Moelin, R. Jacob Ha-Levi, 24, 187
months
 biblical counting of, 23
 declaring new, 13, 29

full and deficient, 15
length of, 14
names of, 16, 18–19
origins of, 13
moon
and Rosh Hashanah, 48
and Sukkot, 157, 159–160
role in calendar, 13–15
Mordecai ben Avraham Jaffe, 71–72, 185
Mordechai ben Hillel, 192
Moreh Nevuchim, 187
Moses
ushpizin, 128
receiving 10 commandments, 26–27, 74, 92
reciting 13 attributes, 110
Moses ben Jacob of Coucy, R., 36, 189
Moses ben Maimon, R., 6, 7, 25, 46, 47, 58, 71, 73, 75, 77–78, 85, 165, 167, 187
Moses ben Nachman, R., 23, 168, 189
Moshe de Leon, 195
myrtle. see *hadas*

n

na'anuim, 126
Nachmanides. *see* Moses ben Nachman, R.
ner neshamah, 74
neshamah, 6, 74, 75
neshimah, 75
netzah, 128
Nevi'im, 189
nigunim, 47
Ninth of Av, 101
Nissim ben Reuven Gerondi, R., 44, 190
Nissin ben Reuven, R., 44
nisukh ha-mayim, 130
nuts, equated to sin, 7, 31

o

observance of mitzvot
purpose of, 5, 9, 43, 100, 117, 120
rationale for, 6–9, 46–47
olam, 51
olam ha-ba, 43, 121
Or Ammim, 192
Or Ha-Chaim, 37, 189
Orach Chayyim, 183, 186, 188

p

pakad, 44
parashah, parshiyot, 136
Passover, 6, 14–16, 155
Perachyah, Yitzchak, 187
Peretz, Cheryl, 94–97
peshat, definition, 42
Pesikta de-Rav Kahana, 190
Pesikta Rabbati, 190
Philo, 49, 75
philosophy, 7, 8–9, 139, 187, 191, 194
physical desire, holiness of, 75
Pirke de-Rebbe Eliezer, 190
pittam, 125–126
piyyutim, 88, 97, 102
poor, inviting to sukkah, 144–145, 171
prayer
communal nature of, 74, 153
components of, 47
priests, 66–67, 70, 130
Pseudepigrapha, 183, 185, 190
Purim
justice as theme of, 110
similar to Yom Kippur, 108

themes of, 109

R

Rabbenu Asher, 190
Rabbenu Nissim. *see* Nissim ben Reuven Gerondi, R.
rachamim, 37
Rachel, 44–45
rain
and sitting in sukkah, 120, 124, 152–153, 171
interpretations of, 55–57, 125, 151
prayer for, 131, 135, 152–153, 166–167
Rambam. *see* Moses ben Maimon, R.
Ramban. *see* Moses ben Nachman, R.
Ramchal. *see* Luzzatto, Chaim
Ran. *see* Nissim ben Reuven Gerondi, R.
Rashbam, 168, 194
Rashi. *see* Shlomo ben Yitzchak, R.
Ravina, 184
redemption, 150–151
relationships
components of, 86–87
with God, 89
Rema. *see* Isserles, Moses
repentance. see also *teshuvah*
collective, 97
on Days of Awe, 39–40
on Yom Kippur, 77–78, 97–98
responsibility, 101, 109
Rif. *see* Yitzchak Alfasi, R.
ritual bath, 73–74
rituals
limits of, 98
purpose of, 117
Rosenzweig, Franz, 65, 84–85
Rosh. *see* Asher ben Yechiel, R.
Rosh Hashanah. *see also* Elul
and Creation of world, 23–24, 28, 44, 55–56, 59
and God's coronation, 48–49, 57–58
biblical description, 24–26, 48
blowing shofar on, 35–36
challah for, 30
day before, 28
faith, theme for, 38–40
foods for, 30–31
greetings on, 28–29
historical origins, 48–49
judgment on, 33–36, 37, 42–43, 49, 52, 141–142
meanings of, 24, 25, 50, 54–55, 57
names for, 44, 49, 51, 52, 54
prayers for, 49, 54, 102–104
reciting *Shehechyanu,* 30
second day of, 15–16
sleeping during, 31
two days of, 29–30
wickedness, 28–29, 42
Rosh Hodesh
as holiday, 48
two days of, 14, 29
Roth, Joel, 156–158

S

s'khakh, 123, 148, 154–155, 166
Sa'adia Ga'on, 6, 46–47, 99, 191
Sa'adia ben Yosef Al-Fayumi. *see* Sa'adia Ga'on
Sabbath of Sabbaths. *see Shabbat Shabbaton*
Sabbatical year, 163
Sanhedrin, announcing new months, 13

Sarah
  and Hagar, 60–62
  infertility of, 44, 56, 119
Satan
  as accuser, 31, 35
  confused during Elul, 7, 26, 28
  delaying Abraham, 32
Saturnalia, 110
Schachter-Shalomi, Zalman, R., 127–128
Schaffer, Arthur, 167
Schechter, R. Solomon, 91
Schmidt, Judith Sarah, 105–106
Schulweis, Harold, 170–172
Seder Eliyahu Rabbah, 194
Seder Eliyahu Zuta, 194
Sefat Emet, 47
Sefat Emet al Ha-Torah, 191
Sefer Abudraham, 191–192
Sefer Ha-Halakhot, 190
Sefer Ha-Hinnukh, 145–146, 192
Sefer Ha-Manhig, 192
Sefer Ha-Minhagim, 192
Sefer Ha-Toda'ah, 192
Sefer Ha-Vikkuach, 189
Sefer Mitzvot Gadol, 188
Sefer Mitzvot Katan, 188
Sefer Mordechai, 192
sefirot, 79, 128, 144, 186
sei'r ha-mishtale'ach, 68
self-denial, 75–76, 94, 96
Selichot, 26–28, 72
SeMaG, 188
SeMaK, 188
seudah ha-mafseket, 73
Shabbat
  challah for, 30
  compared to Yom Kippur, 81, 101
  first full day of life, 27
Shabbat Shabbaton, 65, 84, 94.
  see also Yom Kippur
Shabbetai Tzvi, 186
Shalosh Regalim, 156
shana me'uberet, 15
Shavuot, second day of, 15–16
Shehechyanu, times for reciting, 30, 74, 126, 128
Shekhinah, 70, 145
Shem Ha-Meforash. see Ineffable Name,
  pronouncing
Shemini Atzeret, 134–135, 143, 152–153,
  160–161
Shemoneh Esrei, 71. see also *Amidah*
shevarim, 58–59
Shimon bar Yochai, R., 195
Shimon ben Gamliel, R., 88, 89
Shimon Ha-Darshan, R., 195
Shlomo ben Yitzchak, R., 70, 143–144,
  190, 194
shmitah, 163
Shneur Zalman of Liady, 186
shoes, not wearing on Yom Kippur, 76
shofar
  blowing during Elul, 26
  blowing on new moon, 13
  blowing on Rosh Hashanah, 35–36,
  48, 57–59
  fostering kavanah, 46–47
  hearing, 58–59
  not blowing on Rosh Hashanah, 7
  not blown *erev* Rosh Hashanah, 28
  sounds of, 46, 58
Shofarot, 49, 54

Shulchan Arukh, 71, 80–81, 183, 185, 186, 188, 190, 193
Sifra, 81, 193
simchat beit ha-sho'evah, 130, 158, 165
Simchat Torah
  description, 135–138
  new rituals for, 175–177
  timing of, 118
Solomon (King), 8, 119, 138, 151
soul. *see neshamah*
Sperling, Abraham Isaac, 193
spirit
  and Rosh Hashanah, 50
  and Yom Kippur, 75–76, 80
  definition of, 5–6
spirituality
  definition of, 6
  encompassing entire human being, 75
Steinberg, Paul, 50–52
Strelisk, Rebbe of, 38–39
Strelisker, Mordechai ben David, 39
sukkah. see also *s'khakh*
  as dwelling place, 119, 122, 124, 155, 159–160, 166–167
  exceptions for dwelling in, 120, 124, 152–153, 171
  inviting poor to, 144–145, 171
  meaning of, 120–122, 143, 146, 148, 153
  rules for building, 120, 123, 154
  time for building, 81, 122
Sukkot. *see also* four species
  agricultural meaning, 119, 157, 165–166
  and Hoshanah Rabbah, 131–134
  atmosphere of, 117–118
  biblical description of, 118–120, 156–157
  blessings for, 128
  cycles as theme of, 169–170
  environmentalism as theme of, 162–163
  faith as theme of, 144–145, 168
  freedom as theme of, 155
  historical meaning, 119, 157–158
  joy as theme of, 119–120, 145–146, 149, 151, 168–169, 171
  names for, 117, 118, 156, 157
  plenty as theme of, 159–160
  reading Kohelet on, 138–139
  reciting *Hallel* during, 119, 126
  redemption as theme of, 150–151
  second day of, 15–16
  social themes of, 163–164
  ushpizin, 128–130
  water ritual during, 130
symbols, meaning of, 120

T

ta'ammei ha-mitzvot. see mitzvot, reasons for observing
Ta'amei Ha-Minhagim, 193
Tabernacle. see *mishkan*
tal u'matar..., 153
Talmud, 42, 193–194
TANAKH, 194
Tanchuma, 194
Tanchuma Buber, 194
Tanna de-be Eliyahu, 194
tannaim, 47, 192
Tashlikh, 32
Taz, 194–195
tefillah, 41, 103

tekiah, teki'ot, 58–59
Ten Commandments, 66, 89, 92, 93
Ten Days of Repentance, 24, 29, 49–50, 71–72, 84–85, 101
teruah, 58–59
teshuvah, 24, 40, 81–82, 98, 103, 113. *see also* repentance
Tetragrammaton. *see* Ineffable Name, pronouncing
theodicy, 37, 42–43, 103
Thirteen Attributes of God, 92–93, 110
tiferet, 128
tikkun olam, 55, 186
tohu and *vohu,* 170
Torah
  reading cycles, 135–137, 170
  times for reading, 135
Torat Kohanim, 192
Tosafot Yeshanim, 188
Tosefot, 194
Tosefta, 195
triennial cycle, 135–136
truth
  achieving, 9, 36
  attribute of God, 92, 93
  in God's deeds, 39
Tu b'Av, 56, 88–89
Tu b'Shevat, 23
Tur, 185, 186, 190, 192, 195
Turei Zahav, 195
tzedakah, 41, 73, 81, 103, 144–145
tzelem elohim, 89
Tzom Gedalyah, 72
Tzom Shevi'i, 72

U

U-netaneh Tokef, 34–35, 102–104
ushpizin, 128–130, 144–145
ushpizot, 129–130

V

Vidui, 73. *see also* confessions and confessionals

W

Waskow, Arthur, 159–165
water. *see also* rain
  and Sukkot, 131, 132, 158, 167
  and *Tashlich,* 32
  and Yom Kippur, 77
  source of life, 132
water ritual, 130, 165
Weintraub, Simkha Y., 107–108
Wiesel, Elie, 149
willows. see *aravah; chibbut aravah*
wisdom, 100
women
  and *etrog,* 125
  infertility of, 44–45, 56, 119
  portrayal in Esther and Jonah, 111

Y

Yalkut Shimoni, 195
Yamim Noraim, 24, 39, 50, 65
years
  leap, 15
  length of, 14
  new, types of, 23, 49, 53
Yehuda Ha-Levi, R., 6, 79–80, 196
Yehudah Ha-Nasi, R., 47, 188

yesod, 128
yetzer ha-tov, ha-ra, 69
Yishmael, R., 168
Yisrael Meir Ha-Kohen, R., 188
Yitzchak Alfasi, R., 191, 192
Yizkor, 135
Yizkor candle, 74
Yochanan, R., 42, 43
Yom Ha-Din, 23, 52
Yom Ha-Zikaron, 51, 54
Yom Kippur
  after Temple period, 96–97
  atonement as theme of, 97–98
  Azazel ceremony, 68–69
  biblical description, 66, 67, 75, 94–95, 97
  candles for, 74
  cleansing spirit, 80
  clothes for, 74
  collective repentance on, 97
  commentary for, 188
  comparison with Purim, 108
  confessing on, 90–91
  date of giving Ten Commandments, 89
  deathdecree, 102–104
  description in Zohar, 79
  during Temple periods, 95–96
  evening of, 72–74
  exception to prohibitions on, 81
  fasting on, 75, 101, 107–108
  forgiveness as theme of, 78, 83, 85, 91, 93, 99, 101
  judgment as theme of, 75, 86–87, 89, 101–102, 102, 141–142
  love as theme of, 88–89
  names of, 65, 66, 84
  prayers during, 76, 90–91, 95–97, 102–104
  prohibitions on, 76, 80, 96
  pronouncing the Ineffable Name during, 69–71, 84, 95–96
  purpose of, 65–66, 71
  repentance during, 77–78
Yom Teruah, 52
yom tov, 54
yom tov sheini shel galuyot, 15
yoma arikhta, 30
Yoreh De'ah, 183

z'man simchateinu, 117
zachar, 44, 45
Zikhronot, 49, 50, 54
Zohar, 35–36, 38, 58, 79, 128, 132, 144–145, 196